Collectibly

MAD

The **MAD** and  Collectible...
by Grant Geissman

KITCHEN
SINK
PRESS ™

NORTHAMPTON, MASSACHUSETTS

INFORMATION AND CREDITS

Book design: **Jeff Hixson**, with **Barbara Mlawer** and **Grant Geissman**

Cover design: **Jeff Hixson** and **Karen Slayton**

Desktop production: **Barbara Mlawer** and **Grant Geissman**

Specialty photography by **Loni Specter; West Hills, California**

Editor: **Dave Schreiner**

Library of Congress Cataloging-in-Publication Data:

Geissman, Grant.
     Collectibly Mad: The Mad and EC Collectibles Guide/by Grant Geissman.
          p.   cm.
     Includes bibliographical references (p.) and index.
     ISBN 0-87816-202-X (softcover): $25.00 ($35.00 Canada)
     ISBN 0-87816-203-8 (hardcover): $40.00 ($56.00 Canada)
     ISBN 0-87816-343-3 (signed and numbered hardcover): $200.00 ($280.00 Canada)
     1. Mad (New York, NY:1958) 2. E.C. Publications Inc.
     3. Comic books, strips, etc. —Collectors and collecting. I. Title.
     PN6727.M22G45 1995
     741.5'0973—dc20   95-2612
                                      CIP

ISBN 0-87816-202-X (softcover) ISBN 0-87816-203-8 (hardcover)
ISBN 0-87816-343-3 (signed and numbered hardcover)

First Printing: April 1995

9 8 7 6 5 4 3 2 1

For a FREE catalog containing hundreds of comics, books, and related merchandise, write to the above address, or call 1-800-365-SINK (7465)

Printed in Canada.

SPECIAL THANKS TO:

Bill and Anne Gaines, Dorothy Crouch, Nick Meglin, Richard De Thuin, Denis Kitchen, Dave Schreiner, Jeff Hixson, Barbara Mlawer, Tamara Sibert, Chris Couch, Kevin Lison, Lisa Stone, Loni Specter (for all those extra hours behind the camera), Lloyd Moffitt and Karen Slayton, Ray Fehrenbach, Christi Scholl, Jesse Crumb, Frank Jacobs, Chris Gaines, Joe and Nadia Mannarino, Kell Stahl and Thomas Goransson of Svenska *Mad*, Herbert Feuerstein of German *Mad*, Russ Cochran, Chris Rock, Roger Hill, Rich Hauser, Jerry Weist, Michael Lerner (ace researcher), Ed Norris, Deron Wright, Louie Grubb (for finding me a *Mad* Straight Jacket), Bob Barrett, Jason Levine, Jim McClane, Mark Cohen, John Ficarra, Dick DeBartolo, Sergio Aragonés, Maple Communications, Jeff Boege, Gary Arlington, Dick Voll, George Moonoogian, Luca Biagini, Alexander Yudenitsch, Bob Sidebottom, Bill Bruegman, Les Christie, Mike Craig, Kelly Freas, Bhob Stewart, Steve Fiorilla, Jeff Keim, Dick Swan, Marie Severin, Lawrence Watt-Evans, Kent Melton, Paul Stilwell, Ted and Laura Cohen, Johnny Craig, Harvey Kurtzman, Al Feldstein, Maria Reidelbach, Lenny Brenner, Glenn Bray, Fred von Bernewitz, Bill Spicer, Jack Wohl, Wendy Gaines Bucci, Charlie Kochman, Dawn Evans, and Joe Orlando.
Without their help this volume would have been highly improbable.

EXTRA SPECIAL THANKS TO:

Lydia and Greer G., for putting up with this magnificent obsession.

We would like to know about material not listed, for use in future editions.
Also, if you have rare items for sale, like an EC charm bracelet or *Mad* jewelry,
contact me immediately at this address (I'm no fool!):

Grant Geissman
P.O. Box 56773
Sherman Oaks, CA 91413

ABOUT THE AUTHOR:

Grant Geissman has been collecting *Mad* material since 1961, and EC material since 1967. In his spare time, he is an internationally known jazz/pop guitarist with nine albums released under his own name, the latest being *Rustic Technology* (1993, Mesa/Bluemoon Recordings). His last three albums (including *Time Will Tell*, 1992, and *Flying Colors*, 1991) have risen to number one on the Contemporary Jazz airplay charts. He has recorded with such artists as David Benoit, Dan Hill, Chuck Mangione, Van Dyke Parks, Sheila E., Ce Ce Peniston, Dan Siegel, and Luis Miguel, and his playing has appeared on hundreds of commercial jingles. Geissman has written music for the Saturday morning cartoon shows *Slimer!*, *Camp Candy*, *The New Archies*, and *Alf Tales*. His compositions can occasionally be heard in supermarkets and elevators; in spite of this, most people think of him as a likable kind of guy.

TABLE OF CONTENTS

iNTRODUCTiON

I have been reading and collecting *Mad* magazine since 1961, when I was shown a few back issues by some neighborhood kids a few years older than me. I was astonished. Here was a publication that you could actually purchase at any drugstore (without a prescription) that blatantly stated you should not believe everything you read, that things are not always what they appear to be, that questioning authority might not be such a bad thing. I was hooked. My eight-year-old mind probably didn't catch all that was going on, but there was always that wonderful artwork to be admired (Wallace Wood was an early favorite, as were the cover paintings of Kelly Freas and Norman Mingo). "Where did you get these?" I asked the older kids, and from that moment I avidly collected anything I could get my hands on that had to do with *Mad* and Alfred E. Neuman. I wrote for back issues, frequented used book stores hunting for same, and sent away for the premiums that were offered in the magazine. I knew *Mad* was published by a William M. Gaines (the name was prominently printed on the masthead and on the covers of the paperback reprint books), I could identify the art styles of the "Usual Gang of Idiots," and because of the five *Mad* paperback reprint books published by Ballantine Books (*The Mad Reader, Mad Strikes Back, Inside Mad, Utterly Mad,* and *The Brothers Mad*), I knew that *Mad* had originally been a 10¢ comic book written by Harvey Kurtzman and published by EC Publications. In short, I was like millions of other kids of the time, except that, in spite of my mother's hopeful prediction that I would outgrow this youthful folly, I never did. I made it clear that I was saving my *Mad*s and that they were not to be thrown away during the periodic motherly raids on my closet, and miraculously, they never were.

I was introduced to EC Comics (ECs were originally published in the 1950s by a William M. Gaines, whose name should ring a bell) via the paperback reprints published by Ballantine Books (and there's *that* name again) in the mid-'60s. There were five in all: *Tales From the Crypt, The Vault of Horror, Tales of the Incredible*, and under Ray Bradbury's name, *Tomorrow Midnight* and *The Autumn People* (these were stories of Bradbury's that were adapted by EC "in the good old comics tradition"). I read and re-read these stories, admired the art ("Hey, it's the guys from *Mad*!"), and kept waiting for the next volume in the series. It never came, but the seeds were sown. In 1967 I fell through a door marked "comics fandom," and entered a larger world. I sent fifteen dollars to a guy in New York and got back a copy of *Mad* #1, which I still have. I sought out original copies of EC comics, most of which could be purchased at that time for two or three dollars apiece. These were halcyon days for second generation EC fans, and by extension, *Mad* fans. A few aficionados in Kansas were doing some first class detective work and self-publishing the results in a magazine entitled *Squa Tront*. A guy in Iowa named Russ Cochran offered a fine art poster of one of the EC horror comic's covers (*Haunt of Fear* #18) and a series of oversize portfolios of EC stories (shot from the original artwork), East Coast Comix began publishing a line of full color reprints of original EC issues, and on and on. As the years went by a phenomenal amount of EC material appeared, in addition to the material that appeared during EC's original incarnation. Meanwhile, EC's flagship title, *Mad*, continued its successful voyage on the seas of the publishing industry, leaving behind a staggering amount of flotsam and jetsam in the form of hardback books, record albums, games, clothing, jewelry, paperback books, foreign reprints, and so on. Which brings us to now. It has been 40 years since the last original EC comic book appeared, 28 years since the first issue of the fanzine *Squa Tront* was published, 20 years since the last issue of the short-lived East Coast Comix reprints, and 18 years since the last issue of Russ Cochran's EC Portfolios. *Mad* magazine celebrated its 40th year of continuous publication in 1992. Given this amount of time, many dealers of EC and *Mad* material have no idea that such items as the *Mad* Straight Jacket, *Mad* jewelry, and the original EC Fan-Addict Club Kit ever existed. On the bright side, both EC and *Mad* continue to be highly visible. Russ Cochran is now nearing completion of the massive EC Library, a reprinting of all the EC titles in slipcased hardcover editions, and he has introduced a new line of full color comic books reprinting (yet again) the EC comics. *Mad* continues on its merry way, producing new issues eight times a year (still selling just under a million copies per issue), annual *Mad Special* reprints, and paperback books. But what of the older material? Most of it is unavailable, and the fact is that most younger (and many older) fans don't even know it exists, let alone where to find it or how much it might cost on the collectors market.

This book, then, is an attempt to bring together for the first time all the various EC and *Mad* collectibles. Most of this material has never appeared in any guide or fan publication; I think the massive amount and variety of material represented here will surprise even the longtime fan, and delight readers who have even a casual interest in EC and *Mad* items.

—Grant Geissman

AN INTER
VIEW WITH
WILLIAM
M. GAINES

The interview took place the afternoon of July 17, 1990 in Bill Gaines's office at the *Mad* headquarters at 485 MADison Avenue, and was updated before publication. The suite of offices that make up *Mad* are truly Mecca for the EC and *Mad* fan; original framed *Mad* covers, posters, and other memorabilia line every square inch of the wall, and much of the floor space. In the inner sanctum of Gaines's office there are original oils and drawings by Al Feldstein, Johnny Craig, Jack Davis, Graham Ingels, and others. A glass and mahogany bookcase holds bound volumes of *Mad*, and everywhere one looks is a feast for the eyes of collectors. "The fans bow down every day at four o'clock," cracks *Mad* co-editor John Ficarra, and he's not far wrong, for out of this office, and several others like it, have poured some major cultural icons whose influence on the youth of the 1950s, '60s, '70s , '80s, and '90s cannot be measured.

Photo by Grant Geissman (1991)

GRANT GEISSMAN: *Bill, you've been quoted as saying you don't care for the merchandising items, so how do you explain that there have been so many items merchandised over the years, you could write a book about them?*

BILL GAINES: [laughter] Well, these things came up over such a long period of time that we never thought of it as any kind of merchandising program, until recently. Really they just happened. People would come in with these ideas and they seemed to be good so we did them. Almost none of them were ever particularly commercially successful, and we usually did them with people who weren't real business people, and most of them were sold through the magazines, one way or another. It's only where we made a deal with Parker Brothers to do the *Mad* game, which took off and became the second most popular game Parker ever put out since Monopoly, that's the first thing that ever took off and made a lot of money. Outside of that we still haven't had any really successful items. Things come and go.

GG: One of the first things you did was a black-and-white print of Alfred, sold very briefly in the magazine for 15 cents.

GAINES: Yes. My recollection is that Bill Elder did the art.

GG: I think you wrote me that about 10,000 of them were sold, does that sound right?

GAINES: I have no idea, I can't recall.

GG: It was only offered for three issues, so I thought that was quite a lot for the time. Was reader interest that high, do you think, when you introduced Alfred, that 10,000 people would want them?

GAINES: Oh, we easily could have sold 10,000; I'm just sitting here trying to figure out how we didn't lose money when you consider the envelope and the postage for a 15 cent item [laughs]. But yeah, we could have sold that many. Since we went color with it we've sold hundreds and hundreds and hundreds of thousands, so we could easily have sold 10,000 black-and-white ones.

GG: It's pretty hard to find that black-and-white one, very few of them seem to be around.

GAINES: I don't think I have any. It was run in the magazine in an early issue...

GG: Yeah, #27, on the back cover it's...

GAINES: Yeah, that's about right, and that's the only one I know of, but I know we did sell them.

GG: How did the Ballantine Mad *reprint paperbacks come about?*

GAINES: I think Ian Ballantine, who was the head of Ballantine Books, came up with the idea, and maybe Lyle Stuart was helping him, I'm not too clear, but we did five Ballantine Books and then I sent them to New American Library.

GG: As far as I know those were the first paperback books to reprint from comic books. Is that your recollection?

GAINES: Probably.

GG: They're now out of print, although they were published for many, many years.

GAINES: Well, they're probably out of print because I haven't gotten any royalties on them in a long time; I mean I get royalty statements every six months but I don't think I get royalties.

GG: I think they've been out of print since the mid-'70s sometime, and I know they went through a series where they tried different cover artwork.

GAINES: Well, there were at least three sets of covers. There was the original set, there were variations on that with different colors in the background, and then there was a whole second set that Ballantine did without telling us about it that some people liked but I thought were dreadful, and I made such a stink about it that I made them make a third set of covers that I think were all [Norman] Mingo, and that's the last set of covers I can recall.

GG: I think the set that you hated was...I think they used a National Lampoon *artist if I'm not mistaken; the guy's name is Robert Grossman, does that sound right?*

GAINES: I have no idea who he was, but if it was a *Lampoon* artist and I hated it, that figures. [laughs]

GG: Yeah, I thought that was a curious...

GAINES: At least I'm consistent. [laughs]

GG: When Al Feldstein came in, you began offering the jewelry, the T-shirts, and the "Straight Jacket." Was that a cooperative idea between the two of you, or was it your idea or more Feldstein's idea to...

GAINES: People just came in, people just come in. The jewelry people came in and wanted to do jewelry. The T-shirts as I recall were originally the sister-in-law of [EC artist] Johnny Craig who used to live here in New York and had something to do with peddling stuff at Yankee Stadium, and she came up with that idea. They never sold all that well, and...what was the other one?

GG: The "Straight Jacket."

GAINES: The "Straight Jacket." Somebody that I think Al knew came in with that. Dandy idea, and can you believe this: we must have advertised that in a million or so issues and only sold 1,500. That's how badly our merchandising did, and I thought that was a wonderful item for $4.95.

GG: It's a terrific item. My theory is that Mad *at that time sold for 25¢, but the "Straight Jacket" was $4.95, which is 20 times more than an issue of* Mad, *so it must have been too expensive for the readership.*

GAINES: Well, obviously it was, but it was an effective jacket.

GG: It had a working padlock on the back...

GAINES: It had a working padlock, and it was really a fine piece. I have a couple salted away somewhere.

GG: There's only a few of them known to exist;

there may be others out there, but...

GAINES: Well, out of 1,500, there wouldn't be too many known.

GG: What about the Mad *cufflinks, the 14 karat gold ones that sold for $66; what was the idea behind those?*

GAINES: Well, "Mr. Peepers" came in with that. What was his name?

GG: Wally Cox?

GAINES: Wally Cox, and he had a gold jewelry business. He came to us with the idea of making these cufflinks and selling them through the magazine. If they cost $66, they were something like that, I think we got them for $33. So, I bought a set for myself, which I still have, and of all the people we advertised to, one guy ordered them, and I figured "Oh, for heaven's sakes," and I just gave it to him [laughs], and to the best of my knowledge there are only two sets in existence; he got one and I had the other. Wally Cox made them on demand, like he did everything.

GG: So, very likely your set is the only set that now exists because you don't know what could have happened to the other.

GAINES: Well, I don't know who got the other, I don't remember, but I bet he's still got 'em; I don't think you throw away a thing like that.

GG: I'm a fan of the four hardback books, Mad for Keeps, Mad Forever, A Golden Trashery of Mad, *and* The Ridiculously Expensive Mad; *I think* Mad *works nicely in that format with better paper and the hardbound situation.*

GAINES: Yeah.

GG: Do you have any more plans for books along those lines?

GAINES: Oh, well, a young lady named Maria Reidelbach has written a complete history of *Mad* called *Completely Mad*, a hardcover book that's full of *Mad* material. But there are no hardcover collections in the works at the moment.

GG: In an article on Mad *in the May, 1960, issue of* Coronet, *it says that* Mad for Keeps *sold around 35,000 copies. Would that be right?*

GAINES: I think the first one, *Mad for Keeps*, sold

about 25,000, but I could be wrong. The next one sold about 20,000, and the third one sold 15,000, and they didn't go back to press with any of them to the best of my knowledge, and when it got down to a 15,000 sale they didn't think there was any point in going further with them. *The Ridiculously Expensive Mad* was a very successful book, that was a beautiful book, and full of all of those gimmicks. That sold for $9.95, and they printed 25,000, and they sold out. Unfortunately, it was so expensive to produce, they didn't want to go back to press with it, so there were never more than 25,000 of them.

GG: That's a hard book to find with all the premiums intact. Everybody ripped them out.

GAINES: Oh, sure.

GG: What about the Mad *records, particularly the one called* Alfred E. Neuman Sings "What, Me Worry," *the little 45, whose idea was that?*

GAINES: Well, again, somebody walked in with it, and it really was a blackmail thing. He walked in and he said "I have this little record, and I'm gonna put it out, do you want to be associated with it?" So I figured, "Well I might as well, because he's gonna put it out anyway." I didn't really like the idea and I wasn't crazy about the song or the rendition, but I did it. I don't think it sold anything. Aside from that, the first *Mad* record I remember was the one that Henry Morgan...

GG: Musically Mad.

GAINES: *Musically Mad*, with Henry Morgan and Bernie Greene and his Orchestra, and I think that was on RCA, and then we got into the Big Top stuff. Somebody...Sam Bobrick and, uh...

GG: Norm Blagman?

GAINES: Norm Blagman, wrote the lyrics and music, respectively. It was all done, and it had been to perhaps RCA, they thought it was too crazy, so they turned it down. Bobrick and Blagman came to us, and we loved it, so eventually it was put out through Big Top as a *Mad* record [*Mad Twists Rock 'n Roll*], and then they wrote a sequel [*Fink Along with Mad*], which was also pretty good but I never thought was quite as good

as the first one. That also went out through Big Top. We took a few bands of that and put them out as plastic records in our specials, I don't remember how many times we did it but at least twice. Then Big Top went bankrupt, and all this stuff is in limbo. We tried to get the rights to those *Mad* records so we could reissue them; Big Top, whoever owns what's left of Big Top, will not sell any part of it, they want to sell the entire thing. I don't know if anyone will buy the entire thing, so these two records are, in effect, dead.

GG: Right, and that's a shame.

GAINES: Yes.

GG: Those records really captured the early '60s Fabian, and that style dead on.

GAINES: Fabulous, fabulous.

GG: How about everybody's favorite collectible, the Mad *busts?*

GAINES: Well, once again somebody came in and wanted to make *Mad* busts, and we got, I'm not sure but it may have been Kelly Freas [Freas has confirmed this], to actually do the head, sculpt the head, and these people made the *Mad* bust in three sizes; two were put on sale, and the third one they just made a few for us. I have the set of three, and I also have one of the small ones that someone found in an antique shop that was so beautifully painted that they gave to me as a present. I have a few put away, but once again, they didn't sell particularly well through the magazine. I can't remember how many we sold, a few thousand, that's all.

GG: I remember they came out around 1960 or '61, and at that time it was popular to have these little busts of Beethoven or Mozart....

GAINES: [amused] Yes, yes.

GG: ....and I figured you'd have a whole group of these famous composers, and in the middle there would be Alfred.

GAINES: It could have been done [chuckles].

GG: The third bust, was a larger size?

GAINES: Yes.

GG: How much bigger?

GAINES: Well, probably as much bigger as it was

between one and two as it was between two and three.

GG: So it stepped up.

GAINES: It stepped up.

GG: You know, there's a Swedish Mad *bust that steps right in the middle of the two that were released.*

GAINES: [Points to large gold bust of Alfred] That it?

GG: No, that's nice though; I wonder who did that?

GAINES: That's Swedish. [the bust referred to was actually German]

GG: Is that Swedish as well? It's a bisque one, like the ones that were released, only it's exactly halfway....

GAINES: I don't think I've ever seen it. These should have been giveaways, because I have never licensed them to be sold.

GG: Is that right? Sweden has all kinds of things like that.

GAINES: Well, most of them are giveaways. They do it for publicity or subscription gimmicks, if you buy a subscription they send you one of these free, and in fact some of them are quite clever.

GG: In fact, there's a Swedish one that looks like a casting, I don't know if you've seen that, but it's probably about a foot and a half tall [shows it to Gaines, who points to the wall]. *Oh, there it is, is that the mold of it?*

GAINES: Well, it's a white one, and I think there may be one like this in the stock room. But, yeah, the Swedish do a lot of this, but as I say they're not supposed to be sold. If I ever find they've been selling them I'll jump on their heads [chuckles].

GG: Well, I'll never tell! Are you familiar with a game that Transogram put out called Screwball, the Mad Mad Mad Game?

GAINES: I think we tried to stop it, and were not successful, or else we decided we couldn't stop it so we didn't even try, I don't remember.

GG: There are two versions of the game [shows photo]; *this is the original version, and then they later made* "Screwball" *much larger, took out one of the* Mads, *and then they put a microphone in front of Alfred's face to obscure him.*

GAINES: Well, maybe that's the result of some legal action on our part, I just don't remember.

GG: Do you also know about the "What, Me Worry" doll; it came out in about 1961, well after you started using Alfred. He stands about a foot and a half or two feet tall...[shows photo]

GAINES: I don't know if I've ever seen that...the tooth is on the wrong side. I don't know. Somebody found that thing for us [points to a nicely detailed cloth Alfred E. Neuman doll on top of the *Mad* Zeppelin display case] at a flea market, but it may be a one of a kind because it's the only one I ever saw, a little rag doll.

GG: How did the foreign editions come about?

GAINES: Well, like everything that goes on around here I never seek anybody out, so they all came to me. The first one that came was the British edition, and that came about because in those days, as I recall, you could not send American magazines into Great Britain. They wanted to make sure people bought British magazines, so the only way to do it was to put out a British edition, and somebody came to us with the idea. The second oldest was Sweden, and someone just showed up with the idea of a Swedish edition, and then one by one people came. I think the Swedish people were associated with people who then put out Danish, Norwegian, and Finnish, and then all those people went by the wayside and we have a whole new set of people doing those editions.

GG: There was a French edition that lasted, what, only about six issues or so.

GAINES: There were *two* French editions, they were both failures. The first was translated...I have been told, and I don't know enough French to be able to judge, but I have been told that both of them were very badly translated, and that that's part of the reason they were failures. Another reason is that they were too tame for the French audience. There's a French lampoon-type humor magazine which so far surpasses *Mad* that nobody wanted to read *Mad*. These are things that I've been told, but both editions were failures. The first was translated by…there's a black guy, I forget his name for the moment, but you would recognize his name, he's been around Broadway for years [a checking of the foreign bound volumes turns up the name Melvin Van Peebles], and the second one was translated by a British couple, and I don't think any of them understood *Mad* humor. We had lots of failed editions; we had two Italian failed editions but we started a third. We had a Spanish but that failed. We've had a series of publishers in Holland, that's probably the third oldest foreign edition. We've had at least five or six publishers and still publishing. We had one in Argentina that ended up in jail for publishing something Wally Wood did on the Catholic Church, and the war came with England and that killed that. We do have, for some time and with two different publishers, a Brazilian edition, we've had two different Mexican editions, both dead, we had a Puerto Rican edition which didn't survive, and that's all I can think of.

GG: There was a South African edition….

GAINES: Oh, there still is, and an Australian edition which is very successful. We recently started a Chinese edition.

GG: What about the Mad *animated special that*

Bill Gaines (left) and Al Feldstein (right) in the EC offices, late 1950

was supposed to come out in the mid-'70s?

GAINES: Well, it was completed and the network, I forget which one, ABC maybe, which had commissioned it decided not to run it. One of the reasons we heard was because we had taken off on one of their big advertisers in that special, and they had just signed a big deal with that advertiser. Whether that's true or not I have no idea, that's not the kind of thing you ever know for sure.

GG: Do you have film on that, or video?

GAINES: Somebody has. You know, I loan these things out and then I forget who I loaned them to and the bastards don't return them, but there should be one of those kicking around somewhere. Then we have the Hanna-Barbera special which was like seven years in the making, and it has yet to be released and I don't know if it ever will be. It cost CBS a small fortune [chuckles]. Then there's the fiasco with the Warner Bros. movie, for which we got a quarter of a million dollar advance and which they never made. Now, I'm not talking about *Up the Academy*, that was another movie. *Up the Academy* was something they came to me and said "We have this film about to go, would you like to have *Mad* Magazine Presents…" like *Lampoon* had very successfully presented *Animal House.* So I read the script and it was not the greatest script in the world and it was also in very bad taste, and I made the deal on the theory that Warners would eliminate all the stuff that was bad. They did none of this, and since we're co-owned by Warner Communications there was nothin' I could do about it. If it had been anybody but Warner Bros. I would have sued. The worst we could do was run an article on the thing in *Mad* warning people not to see it [laughs]. It was a flop, but since that was a flop they're afraid to make *The Mad Movie*, and so we got a quarter of a million dollars for nothing.

GG: What kind of a movie would The Mad Movie *have been?*

GAINES: Well, who knows, we never got that far!

GG: With regard to Shock Illustrated #3, *I was comparing cover dates and* Shock Illustrated #3 *has the same cover date as* Confessions Illustrated

#2, which made it out. Did it just happen that Shock *came off the press second?*

GAINES: Well, it was the ninth Picto-Fiction book, and by the time that was printed Leader News had gone bankrupt and I literally did not have the money to bind the issue. The insides were printed, the covers were printed, and all I had to do was bind them and I could release it. They were selling so badly that I don't know if it would have been worthwhile, but I literally didn't have the money to do it, so I had 100 copies hand bound, and I threw away a quarter of a million *Shock* #3's, not bound. And of course those 100 copies have become collector's items.

GG: *Right, I have one.*

GAINES: You have one? Oh, fantastic. Where did you get it and what'd you pay for it?

GG: *Well, I got it from a dealer here in New York who got it somehow, and I paid about two and a half, you know, 250 bucks.*

GAINES: That's all? Oh my, what a buy!

GG: *Yeah, I've had it a while, I go back a long time with this stuff.*

GAINES: Yeah, well, I kept twelve of them like I kept twelve of everything, and when Russ Cochran first wrote me, a long time ago, he said how his EC collection was almost complete, but he did not know how he would ever get a *Shock* #3, so I said well, you complete your collection and when you have it completed tell me and I'll give you one. So he completed his collection, he wrote me very happily that it was completed, so I opened my package and pulled one out, I still have eleven, and I sent it to him. I know he has one and I have eleven and you have one, so that's thirteen, and I don't know where the rest of them are [laughs].

GG: *So you couldn't afford to bind* Shock*, but you could afford to bind the next issue of* Mad*. Was it just that you were putting all your resources into* Mad *at that point, or were they with different distributors, or...*

GAINES: No no no....it's hard for me to remember the exact chronology....I think when Leader News went bankrupt I wouldn't have had the money to print *Mad* either, in fact I think I owed the printer a large quantity of money. What happened is my mother and I put $110,000 into the business to keep *Mad* going, but we didn't spend any of that on *Shock* which, as far as I was concerned, was a dead issue. That $110,000, you know, was enough to keep *Mad* going long enough until it caught on and started making money, and we were able to pay off all the debts and get back in the black.

GG: *What about the EC cufflinks that you gave to the staff?*

GAINES: Well, those were just gold-plated, and they didn't cost more than about ten or fifteen bucks a pair, if that much. I got them someplace down in the Bowery, and actually you could get any initials in that particular format. You know, people would use that format and just put their own...like I could put a "BG" in there for Bill Gaines, but I used "EC", and since it was similar, coincidentally, to the EC emblem it made a nice present. They're very rare because they weren't very well made and I think most of them broke, but a few people never used them and just put 'em away and have them pristine. There couldn't have ever been more than fifty of them [EC historians usually put the figure at twenty-four sets].

GG: *It would be interesting to know who still has them, or do you know offhand?*

GAINES: [Shakes head no] I gave 'em to the staff. Then I also for the girls had made a much nicer item. It was a charm, a large EC charm which they could put on a bracelet. Lyle Stuart's first wife died, and I had given her one of these, and Lyle very kindly gave the charm to my wife, and she hooked it on her gold bracelet, so now Annie has an EC bracelet which is even rarer than the cufflinks, because I don't think there were more than a dozen or so of them.

GG: *The Nostalgia Press book, I heard they were working on another one, a science fiction volume. Is that true?*

GAINES: I don't remember that story. It's not impossible. There have been so many different collections; I think [Nostalgia Press publisher]

Woody Gelman's was the first, and the second that came along was by those two guys where they actually put out twelve or fifteen reprints of EC Comics.

GG: East Coast Comix.

GAINES: Right, what were their names?

GG: Um, Ron Barlow and Bruce Hershenson.

GAINES: Right, absolutely, you've got a good memory. And they were probably the second people, and then Russ [Cochran] came on the scene, and he started...first he had big EC albums, and then he went into these things [points to the *Complete EC Library* sets], and then he went into the $4.95 color things of which he did a dozen or so, and then the thing with Bruce [Hamilton], the Gladstones. I don't recall if there was anything in between there or not, that's all I can think of off the top of my head.

GG: That sounds about right. Were you disappointed when the East Coast Comix reprints failed after twelve issues?

GAINES: Oh, sure, but I think they were overpriced; I mean they hadda be. When you publish as few copies as they were printing, the printing costs and the engraving costs are so high that...in a comic book the nut is very large, and unless you can print a couple hundred thousand, it's tough. I'm talking about what ordinarily used to be called a ten cent comic, I don't know what they go for today.

GG: Probably twenty dollars!

GAINES: No no no, they're still publishing these things for the newsstand but, you know, you can't do it for anything like a dime anymore, probably might be a buck, I dunno.

GG: Right.

GAINES: What does DC charge for a comic today?

GG: I dunno, I think it's about a buck and a half, for a lot of them.

GAINES: [incredulous] Really?

GG: I think so, between a buck and a buck and a half, I'm pretty sure.

GAINES: My God, for a thirty-two page comic that's half full of ads! [laughs]

GG: I don't buy 'em, so...

GAINES: No, I don't either.

GG: I was a fan of the Ballantine EC paperbacks; in fact, that's how I first knew about EC, as a kid.

GAINES: We had...I think we had five of them, which included two Ray Bradbury's, and...what did we have, two horror, a science fiction and two Bradbury's?

GG: Yeah, and it seemed like they were part of a series, because they were numbered on the spines; is it just that they didn't sell well enough to continue the series?

GAINES: Well, I don't think they sold well enough or they would have continued coming out, it's the old story; when something stops it isn't selling well enough. That's the best of my recollection.

GG: Those were important books; I think they laid a lot of the groundwork for the later reprints that came about. It was close to ten years between the time you stopped publishing the EC comics and when these came out, so that's just about a generation there, and I think that got a lot of people into EC, like "Hey, what is this stuff, this is not like anything we've ever seen before."

GAINES: Well, you're probably right. The first Ballantine *Mad* book came out in 1954, wasn't it?

GG: That sounds right.

GAINES: I dunno when the EC stuff came out, it must have been a little later...

GG: I think it was '64.

GAINES: Oh well...but the *Mad* books were the first ones to use the old comic plate, in effect, and chopped it in three pieces so you could put it on three consecutive pages, and I think they continued to do the same thing when they did the EC stuff.

GG: You saved virtually all the artwork, and twelve copies of everything...

GAINES: Well, I saved twelve but over the years, for one reason or another, I seem to have taken some out. Well, you know about Russ Cochran?

GG: He's selling the mint ECs.

GAINES: Yeah, well we opened them up...

GG: That must have been fun!

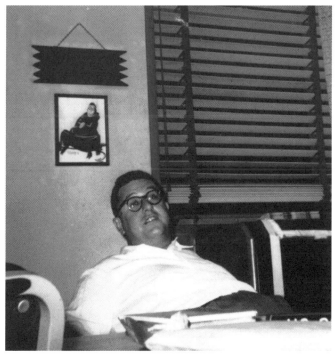

Bill Gaines in his office, December 1955. The plaque on the wall reads "Everything I like is illegal, immoral, or fattening---Woollcott."

GAINES: It was very exciting because first of all, I had no idea what I was going to find; this stuff had not been opened for many, many years, and I was afraid that some of this might be yellow. It wasn't. Bob Overstreet said it was the finest collection of ECs that exists. I didn't do anything special; we wrapped them in butcher paper, you know, just brown paper, and sealed them with tape, and put 'em away, and that's all I did. I didn't have enough sense to put them in mylar....

GG: Which didn't exist, by the way.

GAINES: Well, which didn't exist, but there were sleeves around to use, but I didn't do that. I just wrapped them up, twelve of 'em, and every once in a while I apparently opened a package, took one out and resealed it, to the point that there was only one copy of *Vault of Horror* #12 [actually the first issue], which would be the most valuable of them all and that's the one I had one copy of. We have almost complete runs of four, five, six, seven copies, I don't know how many, but only one complete run which includes *Vault of Horror* #12, that's the only one.

GG: Did you save the Pre-Trend stuff as well, or did you begin with Vault of Horror?

GAINES: No, I never bothered. I saved enough to bind them, and I have bound volumes of everything. They're at home. This is just *Mad*. I took 'em home 'cause one day something disappeared and it scared the hell out of me; turned out it hadn't disappeared, it was misplaced, but all my "Picto-Fiction" was gone. This so scared me that I took the whole collection home; I mean, this is just laying around, anybody could come in and take 'em. All my ECs are safe at home now.

GG: In an interview you did years ago with Rich Hauser you were talking about Shock Illustrated *#3, and you said "I wrapped twelve copies, and I kept three for my bound volumes and Al's bound volumes." I was curious about that; does that mean you have two sets....*

GAINES: Not three, really two; if I said three, I don't know what I was thinking. I have one set of bound volumes, and Al [Feldstein] has a set of bound volumes, which I hear he sold. Al [ironic laugh], Al is not at all nostalgic about this stuff...

GG: Well, to tell you the truth, since you heard that I'll tell you that I bought the foreign Mads, *I now have his volumes.*

GAINES: You bought them from Feldstein?

GG: I bought them from a dealer who got them from Feldstein. So, it was supposed to be a secret; you know about it, so I'll tell you.

GAINES: [Shakes his head] Well, I knew that he sold them, I didn't know who got them; I'm glad you got them! Al seems to have no nostalgic feeling for all this old stuff. Excuse me... [John Ficarra comes in; he and Gaines go over wording for a subscription form...]

GG: So, now, the secret's out; the dealer that I bought these volumes from said "Well, you can't tell anybody, I don't care who it is, he doesn't want it to get back to Bill that he sold these things."

GAINES: I heard about it already, but I don't know who I heard it from, and I'm not surprised. Did he sell all his ECs too?

GG: No, he kept those, he refused to sell those...

GAINES: Really? That's surprising.

GG: *I did ask about them; I wanted those too.*
GAINES: Did somebody get his American *Mads*?
GG: *No, he kept those; he kept all his ECs, and his American* Mads.
GAINES: I see, so he just sold all the foreign ones. Aw, well, that's...what's he gonna do with them anyway? No, I had heard he sold everything.
GG: *Well, to my knowledge he kept that stuff.*
GAINES: I'm glad to hear it. [laughs]
GG: *In fact, I inquired about his EC cufflinks and the story I heard was that they were broken and he threw them away.*
GAINES: I don't believe he ever had a set of the gold ones. I mean, I paid cash for mine, I think I paid $33....
GG: *No, I'm talking about EC cufflinks...*
GAINES: I know what you're talking about. These

Bill Gaines at 225 Lafayette Street circa 1957. Longtime EC and Mad staffer Jerry De Fuccio appears at left.

were EC cufflinks but they were gold EC cufflinks, I think the ones he threw away were the gold-plate. The solid gold ones were EC cufflinks, weren't they?
GG: *No, they just had a big "14 karat" written on them, the ones that were offered in* Mad....
GAINES: Oh, right, I'm sorry! Well, then, there's something else. I think I had a set of EC cuff-links made up in solid gold, now where the devil are they?
GG: *Did you make them for yourself?*
GAINES: Yes. I have to think about that, I really don't know...gee, that's something I've forgotten, and I'll have to check that out, and I'm not sure how many I made of them; I might have had a set

made for Al...
GG: *What about the idea of doing some new EC stories?*
GAINES: Oh, this idea has come up and been...I wouldn't even consider it unless I did it with Al, and I don't think he has the slightest interest in it. I've been carrying around a plot for the last thirty years or so, waiting for the opportunity to use it, but I don't know if it will ever happen.
GG: *I wanted to ask you, what were you thinking when you wrapped twelve copies of everything, did you just love it so much that you wanted to keep it...*
GAINES: Yeah.
GG: *That was just basically it, you didn't have any regard that in twenty years it would be worth....*
GAINES: Who knew? [laughs]
GG: *I think it's exceptional that you saved all of it.*
GAINES: Well, I saved all the art, I saved all the issues, I bound issues so I really had thirteen copies of everything, I just did it because I loved the stuff and I felt that's what you're supposed to do. My father didn't do that, and I was always quite angry. If he'd been on the ball we would've had twelve copies of *Action Comics* #1, just for example [laughs], and I think he blew it. I was a kid when that stuff came out, but I remember they were all around the house and we used to sweep them up every once in a while and throw 'em all away [shakes his head].
GG: *What a memory to have! It would have been great to have bound volumes of all that stuff, as well.*
GAINES: Well, he did make bound volumes of his stuff, so I've got things like *All-American Comics, Wonder Woman, Sensation,* and so on.
GG: *Oh, that's nice.*
GAINES: Yeah, I have them, but he never bound any of the DC comics, which he was associated with too. He just never bothered and he certainly never saved anything aside from those bound volumes; that's all he ever did save...and he had so many things before that, like *Picture Stories From the Bible,* not in comic form but in a the form of a black and white, this size [indicates oversize

volume]. He did "We Want Beer!" ties which I'd give an arm and a leg for...

GG: "We Want Beer!" It said that on the ties?

GAINES: Yeah, this was during Prohibition, with a big mug of beer foaming over, and oh lordy, I mean, where are you gonna find one of these?

GG: Well, you never know; I'm gonna make a note of it.

GAINES: That goes back to 1933, I think...well, pre-Roosevelt, because when Roosevelt came in, one of the first things he did was repeal the 18th Amendment, but until then we had no alcohol.

GG: Some of the art from the EC stuff seems to be missing, particularly the house ads and things; I don't think I've ever seen them come up at auction.

GAINES: Well, Russ [Cochran] has some of them, and some of them are missing. We used to cannibalize that stuff, unfortunately. We'd rip all the lettering off one ad to make the next ad, that kind of thing. Nobody took proper care of those ads, I must admit, but some of them are kicking around; I'm not sure where.

GG: The trick when you're a collector is to figure out where.

GAINES: Yeah.

GG: Were the Mad *imitations a thorn in your side?*

GAINES: Oh, yeah, still are. 'Course they're all gone but *Cracked*, but oh, there were many, many, many.

GG: They seemed to use Alfred E. Neuman with reckless abandon, particularly...you know the one Marvel put out called Crazy *[Gaines nods]. It seemed like about every tenth issue they'd put Alfred E. Neuman on the cover somewhere.*

GAINES: Somebody did that and they finally went too far, and I sued 'em, and I got an injunction, and they hadda throw, like, 150,000 paperbacks away. This made me very happy. I don't remember the details 'cause it's a long, long time ago.

GG: Can you clarify for me...I know the story about the lawsuit over Alfred E. Neuman in the early '60s, and I can understand how you could defend your use of Alfred, because there were so many different versions of him and he was everywhere, but what I'm not clear on is how you were able to

use him exclusively from then on; does it have to do with trademark law?

GAINES: It's "unfair competition." We are now so identified with Alfred, and vice versa, that if someone else used it, it would be considered unfair competition with *Mad* because a purchaser might think it was a *Mad* product.

GG: To wrap this up...I would say that you've led a pretty remarkable life...

GAINES: I'm content with it [laughter]!

GG: I wanted to ask, do you ever look around at all the things you've done and think to yourself, "How the hell did I ever get here?"

GAINES: Yeah! I started out to be a chemistry teacher, and, god, what a dull life that would have been! No, I've been remarkably lucky, and I've just had so much fun doing everything I've done. The most fun I had was the old ECs; I really loved that stuff because I was involved in the editorial. Since I took over *Mad,* I mean, since *Mad* is my only thing left after dropping everything else, I was strictly in the business end, you know, I had very little creative input in the magazine. I have staffs who do it much better than I could. I had a talent for the old EC comics, I don't have a talent for *Mad*, and, you know, it's not as much fun any more because now I'm ninety-five percent business. It was just more fun from 1950 to '54 [laughs]. But, I've been very lucky with it. It's made me wealthy and I love my life and I'm sixty-eight and I have no plans to retire, because I think if you retire, you die.

GG: That's good news; I think everybody will be happy to hear that, that you're not retiring.

GAINES: Nah. They'll either carry me out or they'll fire me; I'm not gonna retire [laughter]!

WILLIAM M. GAINES
PUBLISHER & CHIEF BIGOT

485 MADISON AVE. • NEW YORK 10022

Bill and Anne Gaines with Grant Geissman. Anne is holding the 14 karat gold Mad *staff logo pin Bill gave to the author for his work on* Collectibly Mad.

Photo by Lydia Geissman

Sadly, Bill Gaines died in his sleep on June 3, 1992. True to his word, he never retired, working in the office until a few days before his demise. They nearly did have to carry him out; his schedule called for him to work at the office the day after his death.

Although Bill did not get to see this book as a finished product, he had read and approved every word, and stated that he "couldn't wait to see it with all the pictures." In February, 1992, I had the manuscript bound as a keepsake, and sent it to him for signing. What he wrote was this: "Thank you, dear Grant, for this fabulous compendium! Without you, of course, it would never have existed!" I was greatly flattered. But without *Gaines*, of course, none of it would ever have existed.

Gaines had a knack for hiring talented people and giving them the freedom to do what they did best. He encouraged artists and writers to develop their own styles, while paying some of the highest rates in the industry. With unprecedented foresight he stored virtually every scrap of original art he published, ensuring that his beloved publications would live on in the form of high-quality reprints. Bill created an environment where artists, writers, and staff felt appreciated, and in return many of them produced the best work of their careers.

With Gaines's passing comes the end of an era. Like Hollywood movie moguls David O. Selznick and Jack Warner, publishing mogul Gaines ran his business on his own terms. He published what he liked, championed projects he believed in, and did what pleased him, all while keeping his eye firmly on the bottom line. Had there never been a Bill Gaines it might have been necessary to invent one, for the careers of many of the most highly regarded talents in comics and magazine illustration were launched or furthered in his publications.

It is to the fond memory of Bill Gaines, the ultimate Keeper of the Flame, that this book is respectfully dedicated.

—Grant Geissman
June 5, 1992

Photo by Larry Stark/Fred von Bernewitz collection

The EC stock room in December, 1955. Visible on the bottom shelf at lower left are what look to be bundles of *Mad* #14, 15 and 18. Also showing are stacks of Ballantine paperbacks: *The Mad Reader*, *Mad Strikes Back*, and *Inside Mad*. The other bundles and boxes are the remaining stock of *Mad* and other EC comics, business stationery and manila envelopes. One of Nick Meglin's favorite memories of working at *Mad* (late 1956) is of the work table in the stock room being elevated to a more convenient height with foot-high bundles of mint copies of *Mad #1*.

PRE FACE

Welcome to *Collectibly Mad–The Mad and EC Collectibles Guide,* a compilation of virtually all *Mad* and EC ephemera and collectibles.

At the beginning of this project, author Grant Geissman did not want to include a price guide within its pages. Price guides, he felt, often reflect artificial values; that is, prices for collectibles are often arbitrarily set by the compiler, either because there are no reported sales, or the compiler wants to serve his own self-interest. Geissman wanted *Collectibly Mad* to be an honest tribute to a unique and colorful publishing house, and even though he can now lay claim to being the pre-eminent expert in the field of *Mad* and EC collectibles, he did not want to "tarnish" the book with a price guide.

But something happened during production which convinced him to add prices, both with the pictured objects and in a separate section. Several reports surfaced relating how certain dealers gouged naive collectors. Ultimately, of course, an item is worth whatever someone is willing to pay for it, and prices on *Mad* and EC collectibles have been escalating rapidly. What was needed was an indexing of prices realized to aid collectors and dealers alike in buying and selling this memorabilia. Since Geissman was the one person in a position to do something about the problem, he consented to include a price guide.

Only it had to be honest.

The prices here reflect actual, legitimate prices paid for collectibles. Pricing for pieces that fall outside the comic book market have been researched through collectors in various other specialized fields (doll, toy, slot machine, advertising, postcard, and political). The prices here reflect the cost for materials in like-new condition. If a user of this guide should encounter a piece of merchandise in less-than-new condition, the price should be downsized accordingly.

It should be noted that some items listed here are of such scarcity that they rarely change hands, making accurate price information difficult. In addition, where no reported sales of an object have been recorded, the guide states that, without any artificial, arbitrary price pegged to it.

So once again, welcome to *Collectibly Mad– The Mad and EC Collectibles Guide*, both a loving tribute, and an honest price guide.

—Dave Schreiner, editor

SECTION ONE: EC COLLECT iBLES

The "GhouLunatic" photos

The first EC premiums (something you have to send away for) were 5" x 7" black and white photos of the hosts of EC's horror comics, the three "GhouLunatics." They were offered in letters columns beginning in late 1950, and continued for two years. The photos were originally offered separately at 10¢ each, but later sold as a set of three for 25¢. The photos are heavily retouched shots of artist Johnny Craig (in costume and make-up) taken by editor Al Feldstein. About 10,000 sets were eventually sold, and they are quite rare. An article on their creation appears in the EC fanzine *Squa Tront* #5 (section 1, chapter 4). The photos were the idea of staff "gofer" Paul Kast, and Gaines donated the proceeds from them to help pay Kast's way through law school. Kast mailed out the photos from his home in Merrick, N.Y., in a small manila envelope, and the "V.K., O.W., C.K." on the return address denotes the Vault Keeper, Old Witch, and Crypt Keeper. The envelope is even rarer than the photos. The photos were reprinted around 1969; the reprints are photo glossies, while the originals were printed with a fine dot screen.

GhouLunatic photos: set of three $250-$300

single photo $75-$100 each   mailing envelope $25-$50

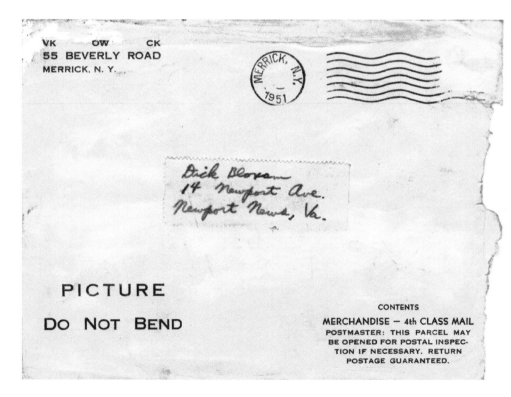

The original "EC Fan-Addict Club" kit

One of the elements that separated EC from its competitors was the sense of "family" the company imparted; EC's publishing of reader mail created the feeling of a direct link between the fans and the creators. The logical extension was starting a fan club, which was done in mid-1953.

The first announcement of the "Fan-Addict Club" appeared on a flyer inserted into subscribers' copies. This flyer is scarce, and has never been reprinted before its appearance here.

"EC Fan-Addict Club" announcement (1953): $50

Failure to carry this card at all times will result . . .

In case of accident . . . tch, tch!

This is to certify that

_____
INVALID IF SIGNED

is a life member in good standing of

THE NATIONAL E.C. FAN-ADDICT CLUB

and is therefore entitled, upon presentation of this card, to purchase any 32 page E.C. magazine for the special membership newsstand price of 10c.

11961   *Melvin*

PRESIDENT

If this card is lost . . . tough!

If you find this card, kindly drop it . . .

Wallet ID card

An Announcement

As we shall shortly begin announcing in our letter columns, we've decided to form a national fan organization. And we feel it's only fair that our subscribers be the first to learn of this. So read on . . . this is hot and exclusive!

Before launching into the sordid details of the club, however, we would like to sketch in a little background. We started out with two conditions that positively *had* to be met:

1) Our club would have to be a *different* kind of fan club . . . a continuously active club that would provide long-range interest, enjoyment and benefits for its members! And . . .

2) Our club would have to be a *non-profit* fan club! Incredible as it may seem, the only income we at E.C. derive . . . or care to derive! . . . from our efforts comes from the *newsstand sales* of our 10c mags. We actually *lose a little* on subscriptions, and *make very little* on the annuals . . . both are primarily offered as *services* to promote good will! If you readers want a fan club, we're more than happy to oblige . . . but, again, as a *service, not* for *profit!*

So here's what we've come up with . . .

1) THE NAME: As one reader wrote a while back, "E.C. magazines are habit-forming." So what could be more logical than to call the organization, "THE E.C. FAN-ADDICT CLUB"?

2) THE SET-UP: The E.C. Fan-Addict Club will consist of the national "parent" organization, and local chapters. *Everyone* who joins will be a member of the *national* organization. In addition, *any group of five or more* prospective members may join as an *authorized chapter* of the national organization. Each such chapter will be assigned a charter number. The name and address of the elected president of each authorized chapter will be made available to all members, so that those who are not already a member of a chapter will be able to join the one nearest them if they wish to.

3) *WHAT YOU GET:* Each member will receive a full-color 7½ by 10½ membership certificate, suitable for framing; a wallet-size

membership identification card; a striking membership patch for sweaters, jackets, etc.; and a very distinguished-looking membership pin!

4) *COST OF JOINING:* Membership in THE E.C. FAN-ADDICT CLUB will set you back two bits . . . 25c! This 25c represents the exact cost *to us* (plus or minus a fraction of a cent!) of one *envelope,* one *stamp,* and the above mentioned four items . . . *certificate, card, patch,* and *pin!* (The cost of Ruby's and Nancy's loving labor in packing and mailing is lovingly donated by E.C.)

5) POSSIBLE FUTURE PLANS: We are considering publishing an E.C. FAN-ADDICT CLUB BULLETIN, containing such features as national and local chapter news; advance inside information on new titles, future stories, and special issues, etc.; articles and stories submitted by members; and a "back-issue trading post!" *Only club members would be eligible to subscribe,* with the price and frequency of publication yet to be decided upon.

We are also considering some sort of "E.C. Surprise-of-the-Month" plan for members. What the surprises might be, and what we might have to clip you for THIS one, is also as yet undetermined.

6) IF YOU'RE STILL INTERESTED: For an individual membership, send 25c, along with your clearly printed name and address, to:

THE E.C. FAN-ADDICT CLUB
Room 706
225 Lafayette Street
N.Y.C. 12, N.Y.

If *five or more* of you wish to join as an *authorized chapter,* enclose each member's name and address, along with 25c for each name, and indicate the name of the elected president. We will notify each *president* of his chapter's *charter number* . . . but each chapter *member* will receive his membership credentials, etc., *individually.*

So that's it! Meet new friends. Make new enemies. See the world. Spend money. Join THE E.C. FAN-ADDICT CLUB!!!

The "EC Fan-Addict Club" kit consisted of a full color 7 1/2" x 10 1/2" membership certificate, a wallet-size ID card, a cloth patch, and a bronze relief pin (mailed together in a large manila envelope), for 25¢. EC later published five issues of a club newsletter, the *EC Fan-Addict Club Bulletin*, and raised membership price to 50¢ to cover additional postage. The complete kit is difficult to find; single items are more frequently encountered. The rarest item is the bronze relief pin.

Cloth patch

"EC Fan-Addict Club" kit ('53):

complete kit $400-$500

pin $150-$250

patch $50-$75

card $50

certificate $75-$100

bulletins $25 each

Bronze relief pin

Membership certificate

The National E.C. Fan-Addict Club BULLETIN

Nov. 1953   Number 1

Dear Fan-Addict,

Well, here the silly thing finally is! Our first bulletin! Took a long time coming, eh? We're truly sorry. Actually, we've been so busy with so many new projects that we honestly haven't had the time to sit down and get this off before today. But new projects mean news...and that's one of the things this bulletin is for. And since you're a Fan-Addict, you're entitled to the scoops.

<u>3-D</u>: At this writing, there are two E.C. 3-D mags kicking around. As usual, we've tried to outdo the field. We have included in each mag, two 3-D viewers, with <u>four</u> earpieces. No other <u>3-D</u> mag can make that statement! And are these viewers versatile! Adjustable ear-pieces for egg-heads; adaptable for four-eyed egg-heads; and, once assembled, able to be folded and placed in pocket or mag for safekeeping...without bending earpieces! Only "molten-dyed" optically clear acetate color filters are used...far superior to the type made by printing the color upon clear acetate, which results in fogging and mottling.

<u>THREE DIMENSIONAL EC CLASSICS</u> (3-D No. 1) contains four of E.C.'s best yarns in the fields of humor, science-fiction, war, and suspence...completely rewritten and redrawn especially for 3-D...by <u>Wood</u>, <u>Krigstein</u>, <u>Evans</u>, and Ghastly Graham <u>Ingels</u>. Four truly gorgeous pieces of work! Cover masterpieced by Kurtzman.

<u>THREE DIMENSIONAL TALES FROM THE CRYPT OF TERROR</u> (3-D No. 2) features four of E.C.'s top horror stories...lovingly turned out by <u>Davis</u>, <u>Elder</u>, <u>Craig</u>, and <u>Orlando</u>. Four more gems of 3-D art! Cover dreamed up by <u>Feldstein</u>.

The 3-D process used was invented by an old gentleman by the name of Freeman H. Owens, and patented seventeen years ago. Most 3-D comics appear to have utilized this process, and Mr. Owens is in the process of instituting patent infringement proceedings against the various publishers of same. E.C. was the only publishing company to obtain a license from Mr. Owens. Printed with 3-D inks especially manufactured for E.C. by the Superior Ink Co. of N.Y., on extra-heavy 45 pound bleached stock, these mags contain only one page of inside advertising...and that's in 3-D. The <u>price</u>? Two bits!

<u>Read all 3-D mags under good strong light</u>. Reading 3-D mags sharpens up your stereo vision...If eye-strain results, it's probable that your eye muscles need a little working with. So don't be discouraged...take it slowly, and read a little every day till you get used to it. But remember...<u>strong light</u>!

<u>Gossip</u>: George Evans is the proud papa of a new baby daughter, his second. Name's Janice Ruth. <u>Feldstein</u>'s leading the pack...just had his third gal, Jamie Lynn. The <u>Craigs</u>' third addition is a Scotch terrier, name of "Scruff." The Jack <u>Kamens</u> are expecting their third...they already have two sons. Jack and Deena <u>Davis</u>...as well as Johnny and Mickey <u>Severin</u>...are expecting their first! The Wally Woods moved into a new apartment, migrating into mid-town Manhattan from the wilds of Queens. Al <u>Williamson</u> just broke his eleventh engagement...he's so fickle!

Our business manager, Frank <u>Lee</u>, has retired...At present, cruising around the Caribbean. Our new business mgr. is <u>Lyle Stuart</u>. Our beloved <u>Ruby Kast</u> is no longer with us...she's expecting shortly. Added two gals to the mail-order, subscription, and fan-mail department: Jackie Abrams and Shirley Norris. But boss-gal Nancy Siegel still swamped.

<u>Weird Science-Fantasy</u>: Now being engraved, E.C.'s combined 15¢ science-fiction quarterly will blossom forth with a radically new and different cover design. The stories are some of the very best we've done to date in s-f. <u>Wood</u> does the cover, and then leads off with an alien civilization yarn. <u>Krigstein</u> follows with a shocker about outer-space colonization. <u>Williamson</u> takes care of third spot with an adaptation of Ray Bradbury's "The Flying Machine," the original of which appears in Ray's new book, "The Golden Apples of the Sun." Joe <u>Orlando</u> winds up with a "twist-ending" tale that'll tickle your fancy. We think this is one swell issue...and we've got our fingers crossed that the extra nickle tariff won't scare away our regular readership...'cause we'd like to continue publishing s-f.

<u>New Mag</u>: Also being engraved, the first issue of E.C.'s new humor mag... The cover (this issue,drawn by Feldstein) follows the same format as companion mag, MAD! (MAD, incidently, is selling like wildfire all over country...and the imitations are springing up, as always, like weeds!) ...Orlando, Kamen, and Elder will chuckle your ribs in that order with latest lampooning efforts. See it...buy it...create a PANIC!

<u>Back Issue Trading Post</u>: Seems just about all of you Fan-Addicts want back-issues. To print a list of all of you that want them would virtually mean to reproduce the entire membership roll of the club...which, incidently, numbers this writing close to 9000...and we obviously haven't the room. So this is how it'll work. We're gonna attack the problem from the other end! If you've got back issues you want to get <u>rid</u> of...either by selling or trading...fill out the coupon below and mail it in. We'll print as many names as possible in the second issue of this bulletin.

E.C. Fan-Addict Club
Room 706; Trading Post Dept.
225 Lafayette Street
N.Y. 12, N.Y.

☐ I got MAD
☐ I got s-f
☐ I got horror
☐ I got war
☐ I got SuspenStories
☐ I got measles

I got back issues I wanna sell or trade.

Name _____

Address _____

City _____ Zone ___ State ___

<u>Plug</u>: One of our old fans...Bobby Stewart, Route 4, Kirbyville Texas...beat us to the punch and got out two issues of "The EC Fan Bulletin" before we got around to writing our first. He sells 'em for a dime apiece. Seems to have hotter news than we do...revealed the title PANIC at a time we thought only three people knew it! Still haven't figured out how he knew!

<u>Bulletin price</u>: Eventually we'll be forced to charge a pittance or so for a subscription to this rag. Membership is growing so fast that the postage will soon become a sizable item, to say nothing of printing. But this issue is on the house!

<u>Covers</u>: The above will give you a rough idea what the mags mentioned will look like. More news next issue. Till then... <u>GO MAD!</u> Your Grateful Editors,

E-C... join the E.C. FAN-ADDICT CLUB

The E.C. Fan-Addict Club Bulletin
Room 706
225 Lafayette Street
New York City 12, N.Y.

<u>Third Class Mail</u>

Marvin Durfee
Fairville Road
Newark, N. Y.   226

EC Fan-Addict Club Bulletin #1

The National
E.C. Fan-Addict Club
BULLETIN

Number 2

March 1954   So without

Dear Fan-Addict,

Well, here it is! The second issue of our Bulletin. So without further ado, let's get right into it!

NEWS: To replace the now dead Frontline Combat and Weird Fantasy, we at E.C. are contemplating two new titles. A meeting of all our writer-editors and artists was held recently in order to discuss the problem of just what to put out. The following are under consideration: (1) a fourth horror mag starring the three GhouLunatics, called the Crypt of Terror; (2) some sort of private-eye mag; (3) a magazine of sea stories; (4) a mag of airplane stories; (5) a few highly intriguing new-type ideas that we'd rather not mention, as some rival editors might be members of this fan-club! We'd like to hear from you fan-addicts re what YOU'D like to see us do. Who knows... what evil ideas lurk in the hearts of you fan-addicts?!

GOSSIP: The Jack KAMENS, who were expecting their third little fan-addict, forged ahead of the pack with a pair of twins...a boy and a girl...Mitch and Terry. Congratulations, congratulations...Mary Frances. Deena DAVIS presented hubby Jack with a new son and heir, Jack Jr. Johnny and Mickey SEVERIN are now into their own ivy-covered Jersey cottage. Joe ORLANDO present gorgeous wife Gloria with a new fluttering 30 inch T.V. set! The Harvey KURTZMANS are expecting their second. Al WILLIAMSON just broke his twelfth engagement...still fickle!

BACK ISSUE TRADING POST: Coupons from the last issue have been pouring in from fan-addicts eager to sell or trade back issues of E.C. mags with you other slap-happy creeps. (Incidently, at this writing, the club membership stands at approximately 17,700. So the following ought to receive plenty of inquiries.) If you're interested in back issues, these fan-addicts claim to have them:

Name	Address	City
David Dechard	5902 Anita	Dallas 6, Tex.
Carl Shapiro	3495 Boulevard	Jersey City, N.J.
Richard Dzenis	317 North East	Indianapolis, Ind.
Dick Tabb	5069 Courbille	Detroit, Mich.
Letha Joe Evans	Box 258	Jonesville, N.C.
Edward Schaller	401 W. Fern St.	Philadelphia, Pa.
Edward Wigelius	3557 Valencia Rd.	Jacksonville 4, Fla.
Betty Maino	198 Idaho Rd.	Youngstown 9, Ohio
Richard Lederer	6116 18th Ave.	Brooklyn 4, N.Y.
George Ormisten	1417 N.W. 21	Oklahoma City, Okla.
Ted Watkins	626 E. Lyndon	Flint 5, Mich.
Robert Ridolphi	948 S. Lawrence	Montgomery 6, Ala.
Joe Wagner, Jr.	51 Jersey St.	Trenton 10, N.J.
Wayne Fenner	226 Thurbers Ave.	Providence, R.I.
Roberta Cook	96 Norway St.	Newark 6, N.J.
Juliet Nagel	242 Rosedale Ave.	Bronx, N.Y.
John Giglio	31-37 43rd Street	Long Island City, NY
Bert DuPont	2955 Dexter St.	Denver, Colo.
Ivan Goldman	2972 E. 78 St.	Chicago 49, Ill.
Jim Kropp	8317 Monroe	St. Louis 4, Mo.
James Wills	2011 Edgeland Ave.	Louisville 4, KY.
Sonny Myers	4407 Colonial Dr.	Columbia 3, S.C.
J.L. Richman	1064 Caroll Place	Bronx 56, N.Y.
Steve Francis	2150 34th Ave.	Oakland, Calif.
Henry E. Johnson	2519 Pierce Ave.	Houston 3, Texas
William S. Cobun	2731 Harrison Ave.	Cincinati, Ohio
Abe Hoffman	10234 Sentinal Ave.	Los Angeles, Calif.
Joe Caldwell	587 S. Crest Rd.	Chattanooga, Tenn.
Stanford Grossman	22508 Kane (South)	Detroit, Mich.
Paul Ayan	80 Alleghany St.	Boston 20, Mass.
Pauline Bobbett	3627 Southward Dr.	Gulfport, Miss.
Michael Bogost	5317 Uhiuhi St.	Honolulu 16, Hawaii
James Brown	661 Ave. A	Reading, Pa.

EC Fan-Addict Club Bulletin #2

Name	Address	City	M SF H W SS
John Berman	15 Overlook Road	White Plains, N.Y.	M SF H W SS
Jimmy Tuten	612 Lee Ave.	Waycross, Ga.	M SF H W SS
John Fugler	2001 Cherokee Ave.	Baton Rouge, La.	M SF H W SS
Jerry Drescher	65 Lillian Ave.	Freeport, N.Y.	SF
Mickey Cawthon	2218 Pickett St.	Greenville, Tex.	M W
Edwin Lilveholm	12 Sutherland Rd.	Brookline, Mass.	M SF H W SS
Allan Katz	7730 Main St.	Flushing, L.I., N.Y.	H
Charles Callahan	131 Chestnut St.	Marlboro, Mass.	W SS
Joseph Langlois	568-82 St.	Brooklyn 9, N.Y.	M SF H W SS
Carl McGregor	679 Cottage St.	New Bedford, Mass.	H SS
Allan Burke	4405 W. Jackson Blvd.	Chicago 24, Ill.	H W SS
Sheldon Hack	4259 Clements	Detroit, Mich.	M SF
Jerry Gibbons	212 E. Goodall	Marion, Ill.	M SF H W
Danny Kemper	4017 Karlisle Ave.	Baltimore, Md.	W
Billy Meyers	102 Sequoia Dr.	Chattanooga, Tenn.	SF H SS
Jeffrey Allen	16202 Delrey	Cleveland, Ohio	H W
Ron Wheeler	20456 Keating	Detroit, Mich.	H W
Ronald Johnson	5 E. Ozburn St.	Pinckneyville, Ill.	M SF H W SS

* M - Mad; SF - Weird Science, Weird Fantasy; H - Haunt of Fear, Tales from the Crypt, Vault of Horror; W - Two-Fisted Tales, Frontline Combat; SS - Crime SuspenStories, Shock SuspenStories.

CLUB MEMBERSHIP PRICE AND BULLETIN: Good news for all you fan-addicts! We have decided not to charge a subscription price for this Bulletin. But you can imagine what the cost is for printing and mailing 17,700 (and rising fast) copies of this Bulletin. So rather than charge extra for it, we will in part defray the costs by raising the membership price FOR NEW MEMBERS to 50¢. All you charter members get in under the wire! The date for the switch-over will be June 1st, 1954. No 25¢ memberships will be accepted if the letter is post-marked after that date. So if you want to get your friends in cheap, get 'em in now!

FAVOR: How would you like to be a road-man for E.C.? How would you like to have a hand in increasing our sales, and insuring our continued success? We feel we can sell our mags if they're displayed properly. You can, with very little effort, help us get better display...if you care to! Everytime you pass your newsstand, fish out the E.C.'s from the bottom of the piles or racks and put 'em up on top or front...BUT PLEASE, YOU MONSTERS, DO IT NEATLY! And if your newsdealer does not carry all the E.C. titles, ask him to order them from his wholesaler...BUT PLEASE, YOU MONSTERS, DO IT POLITELY! With good distribution and prominent display, your chances of continuing to be entertained by us will be that much greater.

More trading-post names next issue...and perhaps addresses of local chapters for those of you who may wish to join. Till then...

E-C-ing you! - Your Grateful Editors

The E.C. Fan-Addict Club Bulletin
Room 706
225 Lafayette Street
New York City 12, N.Y.

Third Class Mail

GO MAD!
join the
E.C.
FAN-ADDICT CLUB

Marvin Durfee
Fairville Road
Newark, N.Y.

226

The National E.C. Fan-Addict Club BULLETIN

June 1954

Dear Fan-Addict,

Number 3

THIS IS AN EMERGENCY BULLETIN!

This is an appeal for action!

THE PROBLEM: Comics are under fire...horror and crime comics in particular. Due to the efforts of various "do-gooders" and "do-gooder" groups, a large segment of the public is being led to believe that certain comic magazines cause juvenile delinquency, warp the minds of America's youth, and affect the development of the personalities of those who read them! Among these "do-gooders" are: a psychiatrist who has made a lucrative career of attacking comic magazines, certain publishing companies who do not publish comics and who would benefit by their demise, many groups of adults who would like to blame their lack of ability as responsible parents on comic mags instead of on themselves, and various assorted headline hunters. These people are militant. They complain to local police officials, to local magazine retailers, to local wholesalers, and to their congressmen. They complain and complain and threaten and threaten. Eventually, everyone gets frightened. The newsdealer gets frightened. He removes the books from display. The wholesaler gets frightened. He refuses shipments. The congressmen get frightened...November is coming! They start an investigation. This wave of hysteria has seriously threatened the very existence of the whole comic magazine industry.

WE BELIEVE: Your editors sincerely believe that the claim of these crusaders...that comics are bad for children...is nonsense. If we, in the slightest way, thought that horror comics, crime comics, or any other kind of comics were harmful to our readers, we would cease publishing them and direct our efforts toward something else!

And we're not alone in our belief. For example: Dr. David Abrahamsen, eminent criminologist, in his book, "Who Are The Guilty?" says, "Comic books do not lead to crime, although they have been widely blamed for it...In my experience as a psychiatrist, I cannot remember having seen one boy or girl who has committed a crime, or who became neurotic or psychotic...because he or she read comic books." A group led by Dr. Freda Kehm, Mental Health Chairman of the Ill. Congress of the P.T.A., decided that living room violence has "a decided beneficial effect on young minds". Dr. Robert H. Felix, director of the National Institute of Mental Health, said that horror comic books do not originate criminal behavior in children...in a way, the horror comics may do some good...children may use fantasy, as stimulated by the "comics" as a means of working out natural feelings of aggressiveness.

We also believe that a large portion of our total readership of horror and crime comics is made up of adults. We believe that those who oppose comics are a small minority. Yet this minority is causing the hysteria. The voice of the majority...you who buy comics, read them, enjoy them, and are not harmed by them...has not been heard!

EC Fan-Addict Club Bulletin #3

WHAT YOU MUST DO: Unless you act now, the pressure from this minority may force comics from the American scene. It is members of this minority who threaten the local retailers, who threaten the local wholesalers, who have sent letters to the Senate Subcommittee on Juvenile Delinquency (now investigating the comic industry).

IT IS TIME THAT THE MAJORITY'S VOICE BE HEARD!

It is time that the Senate Subcommittee hears from YOU...each and every one of you!

If you agree that comics are harmless entertainment, write a letter or a postcard TODAY...to:

The Senate Subcommittee on Juvenile Delinquency
United States Senate
Washington 25, D.C.

and in your own words, tell them so. Make it a nice, polite letter! In the case of you younger readers, it would be more effective if you could get your parents to write for you, or perhaps add a P.S. to your letter, as the Senate Subcommittee may not have much respect for the opinions of minors.

Of course, if you or your parents disagree with us, and believe that comics ARE bad, let your sentiments be known on that too! The important thing is that the Subcommittee hear from actual comic book readers and/or their parents, rather than from people who never read a comic magazine in their lives, but simply want to destroy them.

It is also important that your local newsdealer be encouraged to continue carrying, displaying, and selling all kinds of comics. Speak to him. Have him speak to his wholesaler.

Wherever you can, let your voice and the voices of your parents be raised in protest over the campaign against comics.

But first...right now...please write that letter to the Senate Subcommittee.

Sincerely,
Your grateful editors
(for the whole E.C. Gang)

The E.C. Fan-Addict Club Bulletin
Room 706
225 Lafayette Street
New York City 12, N.Y.

Third Class Mail

GO MAD!
join the
E.C.
FAN-ADDICT CLUB

Marvin Durfee
Fairville Road
Newark, N. Y.

336

The National E.C. Fan-Addict Club BULLETIN

September 1954   Number 4

Dear Fan-Addict,

With school about to start, and you miserable, we thought we'd cheer you up with another bulletin!

NEWS: Now that you're cheered up, this'll make you miserable again...we're certainly miserable about it! As will shortly be announced in our Horror and SuspenStory mags on sale in October, we at E.C. are giving up! WE'VE HAD IT! As a result of what we believe to be hysterical, injudicious, and unfounded charges leveled at crime and horror comics, many retailers and wholesalers throughout the country have been intimidated into refusing to handle this type of magazine. Magazines that do not reach the newsstands cannot sell. Economically our situation is acute. So we are forced to capitulate. We are dropping Tales from the Crypt, The Vault of Horror, The Haunt of Fear, Crime SuspenStories, and Shock SuspenStories.

However, along with this obituary notice comes a birth announcement. E.C. IS PLANNING A NEW NEW TREND! In January of 1955, we hit! In fact, we hit with five (5) sensational new titles. They won't be horror magazines and they won't be crime magazines...they'll be utterly new and different - but in the old reliable E.C. tradition! Naturally, we can't tell you what they'll be YET...some of our competitors may be Fan-Addict Club members...but when the new titles are ready to go, you'll be the first to know, via the next bulletin.

GOSSIP: The Harvey Kurtzman's new arrival arrived...a furshlugginer boy...Peter John (pronounced Potrzebie). Beloved Ruby Kast is back part-time, helping Nancy Siegel in the subscription department. Gloria Orlando, Joe's beautiful wife, is also pitching in part-time in the sub dept. Dick Polenberg, executive vice-president in charge of the stock room, enters college this fall. How we'll get along without this kid, we don't know! Business manager Lyle Stuart has a new assistant, who doubles as circulation manager...Bob Salomon. Dick Smith is another new addition to the editorial staff...research assistant to Kurtzman and Feldstein. Dick, and wife Barbara, are expecting their second. Al Williamson just broke his thirteenth engagement... perpetually fickle!

PLUGS: Quite a few privately printed E.C. Fan Magazines have sprung up around the country. We're amazed at the info some of these sheets contain. Even our own mothers don't know the things these guys dig up. You might be interested in subscribing to a few. We are not connected in any way with any of them:

POTRZEBIE
E.C. FAN JOURNAL   c/o Ted E. White   1014 N. Tuckahoe St.   Falls Church, Va.
E.C. SLIME SHEET   c/o Mike May   9428 Hobart St.   Dallas, Texas
E.C. SCOOP   c/o Ernie Crites   6000 S. Wood St.   Chicago, Ill.
                     c/o Barry Cronin   955 Walton Ave.   N.Y.C.

Any publishers of E.C. Fanzines not mentioned above who would like a plug in the next F.A.C. Bulletin, send in a copy!

GRATEFUL THANKS: We would like to thank, most sincerely, all of you FAN-ADDICTS who volunteered to be road-men for E.C. Good distribution and prominent display is always reflected in better sales. Our sales during the recent and continuing comic slump have not been good, but compared to the catastrophic sales being experienced by the rest of the industry, they are high! It is probable that your efforts have been the deciding factor in keeping E.C. alive. So please continue to make sure that E.C. mags are getting better display by fishing them out from the bottoms of the piles or racks and putting them up on top or front. And if your newsdealer does not carry all of the E.C. titles, continue to ask him to order them from his wholesaler.

EC Fan-Addict Club Bulletin #4

BACK ISSUE TRADING POST: If you're interested in back issues, these Fan-Addicts claim to have them:

o Valdes, Jr.	3814 Porter Ave.	El Paso, Texas	*M	SF	H	W	SS
yle Henson	8401 S. Tacoma Way	Tacoma 9, Wash.	M				
gh Redmon	25 Webb Ave.	Stamford, Conn.	M	SF	H		SS
arles Varcie	1020 N.W. 81 St.	Oklahoma City 14, Okla.	M		H		
y Hoover	17591 Riopelle	Detroit 3, Mich.	M	SF	H	W	SS
ge Venetis	Route 2	Manchester 3, Tenn.	M	SF	H	W	SS
illiam Stover	2812 N. Sacramento	Chicago 18, Ill.	M	SF	H	W	
ie Silveira	215 S. Russell	Monterey Park, Calif.			H	W	SS
y Zounes	3347 Thomas Blvd.	Port Arthur, TExas	M	SF		W	SS
neth White	164 Hillcrest St.	Waltham 54, Mass.		SF	H		SS
er Branson	636 E. Street	Chula Vista, Calif.				W	SS
en Harris	A.P.O. 696	c/o P.M., N.Y., N.Y.	M	SF	H	W	SS
ie Smith	RFD #1	Greenwich, Ohio	M	SF			SS
Chavannes	441 Ocean Pkway.	Brooklyn 18, N.Y.	M	SF			SS
e Horvath	Box 233	Paris, Ky.		SF			
man Benedict	1825 N. Mozart St.	Chicago 47, Ill.					SS
hael Reynolds	2071 Vyse Ave.	Bronx, N.Y.	M	SF	H	W	SS
nk Freeman	1913 Rosemary	Columbia, Mo.		SF	H	W	SS
y Floh	122 E. Union St.	Somerset, Pa.	M	SF	H	W	SS
Bollinger	915 N. President St.	Wheaton, Ill.	M	SF	H	W	SS
n Berkowitz	2068 Vyse Ave.	Bronx, N.Y.	M	SF	H	W	SS
Swanson	726 Maple St.	Annville, Pa.	M	SF			
ard Hallowell	66 Ave. A	N.Y.C. 9		SF	H	W	SS
th Weisbaum	18 Rosehill Ave.	Smethport, Pa.		SF			SS
ard Long	133 Water St.	Hallowell, Maine		SF	H		
Lavash	1115 Intervale Ave.	N.Y.C. 59		SF		W	
in Seybold	310 E. Vine St.	Reading 15, Ohio	M		H		
tin Schneider	6 Overlook Rd.	Waltham, Mass.	M				SS
es Ruggiero	203 Mulberry St.	Mt. Carmel, Ill.			H		
Strattan	362 Linden Blvd.	Brooklyn 3, N.Y.			H		
Kramer	2034 S. 17th St.	Philadelphia, Pa.	M				SS
es Mizell	221 S. 41st St.	Louisville, Ky.					
Reiss	55 Kassebaum Lane	Lemay, Mo.			H		
ene Needham	1102 Fretwell	Anderson, S.C.				W	
Wikstrom	RFD #2, Box 542	Westwood, N.J.		SF	H	W	SS
my Urban	1625 Sunset Dr.	Logan, Utah	M	SF	H	W	SS
Goldsworthy	Blackpoint Rd.	Ticonderoga, N.Y.	M	SF	H	W	SS
k Buchheim	207 N. 6th St.	Pottsville, Pa.		SF	H		SS
rt Bennett	2207 W. 78th St.	Inglewood, Calif.	M		H		SS
Scherman	67-64 150th St.	Flushing, L.I., N.Y.		SF	H	W	SS
	603 S. Jefferson	Zilwaukee, Mich.	M	SF	H	W	SS
	1038 Clay Ave.	Pelham Manor, N.Y.	M	SF	H	W	SS
			M	SF	H	W	SS

Mad; SF-Weird Science, Weird Fantasy; W-Two-Fisted Tales, Frontline Combat; H-Haunt of Fear, Tales from the Crypt, Vault of or; SS-Crime SuspenStories, Shock SuspenStories.

That's it for this issue.

E-C-ing you! - Your Grateful Editors

The E.C. Fan-Addict Club Bulletin
Room 706
225 Lafayette Street
New York City 12, N.Y.

Lee Swanson
1015 Boston Post Rd.
Marlboro, Mass.   6121

The National
E.C. Fan-Addict Club
BULLETIN

December 1954

Number 5

Dear Fan-Addict,

Well, here it is! As we promised in the last Bulletin, you would be the first to know the titles and subject matter of E.C.'s six sensational new magazines.

Five years ago, we at E.C. started our "New Trend" line. With it, we revitalized the entire comic magazine industry. Other publishers, in order to compete with us, had to raise the quality of their product. We feel that we can state, without fear of contradiction, that E.C. changed the entire complexion of the comic magazine industry!

We hope now to revitalize and change the complexion of the comic industry once again with our "NEW DIRECTION" magazines. And here they are:

EC Fan-Addict Club Bulletin #5

IMPACT: Stories unlike anything you've ever read before! Yet designed to carry an al "impact" with E.C.'s traditional surprise endings.

OR: Tales in the E.C. tradition, painted against the historical background of ancient ome, medieval Europe, and other exciting eras.

A: The thrilling adventures of special correspondents covering all newsfronts for ress".

HIGH: The gallant exploits of the men who flew the combat skies in fabric and wood ing the fabulous era of World War I aviation.

ANALYSIS: The most revolutionary idea ever presented in comics! Fictional case eople undergoing psychoanalysis.

ories of people seeking health and happiness through the grim but stirring world ine.

OFFER: Because you're E.C. Fan-Addicts...and because we love you...we're ecial subscription offer. For a limited time only (your letter must be postmarked er 15, 1954), you can receive, for the usual eight-issue subscription price, any E.C. New Direction magazine. Just fill out the coupon (or a copy) below, r each special Fan-Addict subscription, and mail to:

mics
"Special"
reet,

send me NINE of the magazine(s) I have checked. I enclose one dollar ($1.00) for each special subscription.

☐ IMPACT ☐ ACES HIGH

☐ VALOR ☐ PSYCHOANALYSIS

☐ EXTRA ☐ M.D.

NAME _____

ADDRESS _____

CITY _____ ZONE NO. _____

STATE _____

FAN-ADDICT NUMBER _____

Look for E.C.'s NEW DIRECTION magazines on your local newsstands. They'll be on sale throughout the month of January. Sometimes wholesalers and retailers are hesitant to handle new titles, so if your newsdealer fails to display them, ask him to order them from his wholesaler.

E-C-ing you! - Your Grateful Editors

The E.C. Fan-Addict Club Bulletin
Room 706
225 Lafayette Street
New York City 12, N.Y.

Lee Swanson
1015 Boston Post Rd.
Marlboro, Mass.   6121

Sec. 34.66 P. L. & R.
U. S. Postage
PAID
Permit No. 8239
New York, New York

The Entertaining Comics Group

225 LAFAYETTE STREET, NEW YORK 12, N. Y., CAnal 6-1994-5

EC stationery and envelopes

EC had several types of business letterheads over the years. The most notable version was used from about mid-1954 until EC ceased publishing comic books at the end of 1955. This 8 1/2" x 11" stationery featured the latter-day EC logo and four full color panels of Jack Davis art, representing the crime, humor, science fiction, and horror comics.

EC stationery, with Jack Davis art: $200-$300 (unused sheet)

THE ENTERTAINING COMICS GROUP
225 LAFAYETTE STREET
NEW YORK 12, N. Y.

GO MAD!
join the
E.C.
FAN-ADDICT CLUB

NEW YORK
DEC 18 '53
N. Y.

U.S. POSTAGE
03

PB METER
P.B.171280

Marvin C. Murfee
Fanville Rd.
Newark, New York

E. C. Publications, Inc.
225 Lafayette Street
New York 12, New York

E.C. Creations, Inc.
225 Lafayette Street, New York 12, N.Y.

The two examples of "Entertaining Comics" and "EC Publications" envelopes have the return address printed in blue. Note the postmark on the legal size version of Dec. 18, 1953, and the postal meter ad for the "EC Fan-Addict Club."

The "EC Creations" envelope dates from about the mid-1950s; the logo and return address are printed in tan and moss green, respectively. EC was (and still is with regard to *Mad*) actually comprised of two companies, "EC Publications" and "EC Creations," each handling separate aspects of the overall business.

CHAPTER TWO

E. C. CREATIONS, INC.
850 THIRD AVENUE
NEW YORK 22, N.Y.

The matching "EC Creations" and "EC Publications" envelopes with the 850 Third Avenue return address date from the early 1960s; the lettering is printed in blue.

E. C. PUBLICATIONS, INC.
850 THIRD AVENUE
NEW YORK 22, N.Y.

Envelope, Entertaining Comics (legal size): $25

Envelope, EC Publications (small size): $20

Envelope, EC Creations, mid-1950s: $25

Envelope, EC Creations, 850 Third Avenue: $10-$15

Envelope, EC Publications, 850 Third Avenue: $10-$15

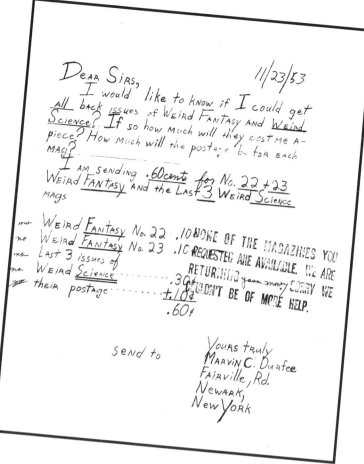

The writer of this 1953 request for EC back issues
received his own letter back with a rubber stamped reply,
a practice Gaines followed until his death.

EC postcards, sent to subscribers of *Weird Science-Fantasy*
(postmarked April 11, 1955) and *Incredible Science Fiction*
(postmarked Nov. 2, 1955).

EC postcards: $25-$35

WSF —
Our production schedule for this quarter has been
completed due to a speed-up program. All books
up-to-date have appeared on the stands. There
will be a delay of a few weeks before our books
will hit the stands again. Be patient and stick
with us!

THE ENTERTAINING COMICS GROUP
225 Lafayette St., New York 12, N. Y.

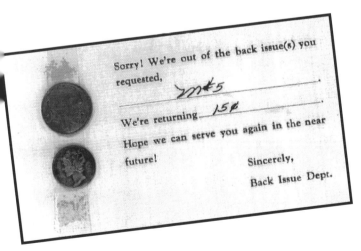

Sorry! We're out of the back issue(s) you
requested, _____

We're returning _15¢_

Hope we can serve you again in the near
future!

Sincerely,

Back Issue Dept.

This "back issue" insert card was sent in response to an
order for *Mad* #5, and still has the original coins
refunded by EC.

Back issue insert card: $25

ENTERTAINING COMICS GROUP
225 LAFAYETTE STREET, NEW YORK 12, N. Y.

Dear Reader,

We are dropping Incredible Science-Fiction. Your subscription has .... issues to run. So that you receive full value for your
money, we're going to finish out your subscription with .../....copies
of the NEW 25¢ MAD.

(If you are already receiving MAD, please return this postcard to us so that we may extend your MAD subscription rather
than send you duplicate copies.)

Yrs,
ye editors

ENTERTAINING COMICS GROUP
225 LAFAYETTE STREET, NEW YORK 12, N. Y.

EC mailing envelopes

Much ado was made in the EC letter columns about subscription copies being sent in "manila envelopes." There are at least three logo variations known, the earliest being "Educational Comics, Inc." (a holdover from the M.C. Gaines era) and the more familiar "Entertaining Comics Group." Remarkably, a substantial number of these mailing envelopes exist, because many EC subscribers used them to store their ECs. Note the postmarks on the examples shown of 1951 and 1952, respectively.

EC mailing envelopes (8" x 11"): $5-$10

ENTERTAINING COMICS GROUP, 225 LAFAYETTE STREET, NEW YORK 12, N. Y.

The magazine you hold in your hand may become a collector's item. It is the last issue of this title.

We're as sorry as you are.

So it shouldn't be a total loss, we're dropping your stencil into the subscription file of one of our NEW NEW magazines, and will finish your sub with that title.

That's okey with you . . .

EC-ing you,

The Editors

ENTERTAINING COMICS GROUP, 225 LAFAYETTE STREET, NEW YORK 12, N. Y.

The "Last Issue" and "New *Mad*" cards

Changes in 1955 necessitated these two 3 1/4" x 5 1/2" cards, inserted into subscriber's copies. The first was included with the last issues of some of the New Trend comics to announce their end. The second was included with copies of *Mad* #23, announcing its transformation from a 10¢ comic to a 25¢ magazine. The cards were printed on heavy, rose-colored stock; the type is light blue. (Cards found in the "Gaines file copies" of *Mad* #23 are on white stock with black ink.)

"Last Issue" card: $25-$35, "New *Mad*" card: $25-$35

Dear Reader:

This, alas and alack, will be the last issue of Mad as a 10¢ comic magazine.

So, be careful of the accompanying magazine. Treat it gently. Make it last.

In three months or so you will receive your first issue of the re-born Mad . . . which will be a 64-page 25¢ slick.

You lucky fellow. Your sub will be transferred to the new NEW MAD — and we're sending you one 25¢ magazine for every 2 10¢ magazines.

Keep grinning.

Ye Editors

The "Thank you for writing" flyers

As a gesture of thanks, EC sent flyers in response to reader mail, along with a canny reminder that subscriptions were available. There are three different designs, with art by John Severin, Will Elder, and Marie Severin, respectively. The flyers measure 8 3/4" x 15 5/8". The John Severin version was used in early 1952, the Will Elder version circa mid-1954, and the Marie Severin version circa early 1955. Of the three, Elder's is hardest to find.

"Thank you for writing" flyers:

John Severin $100

Will Elder $100-125

Marie Severin $100

Shock Illustrated #3

One of the rarest of all EC collectibles. *Shock Illustrated* was a title in EC's "Picto-Fiction" line, a unique but ultimately unsuccessful combination of prose fiction and black and white artwork. Other titles were *Crime Illustrated*, *Terror Illustrated*, and *Confessions Illustrated* (a romance title). These magazine-size titles ran from October, 1955, to May, 1956—the last books Bill Gaines published before turning his full attention to *Mad*. The contents of *Shock Illustrated* #3 had been printed and were ready to be bound. With his distributor bankrupt and himself deeply in debt to the printer, Gaines couldn't afford to bind the issue and had to order the full print run of 250,000 copies destroyed. As a favor, the bindery hand-bound 100 copies for the EC archives, and after filing perhaps 15 copies, the rest were given out at the office or sent to fans who knew about and requested the issue. It is not known how many survive, but *Shock Illustrated* #3 is very difficult to find and has long been one of the "crowning touches" of EC collections. (There is still a question of the number of hand-bound copies made. Ted E. White in *Hoohah!* #6 [Sept. 1956] stated 200 existed; Gaines recalled 100.)

Shock Illustrated #3: $900

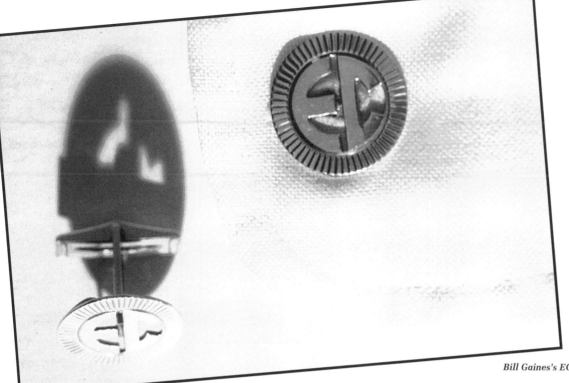

Bill Gaines's EC cufflinks

EC Cufflinks and Charm Bracelet

Few collectors have ever seen a pair of EC cufflinks; they have become a somewhat legendary collectible. Gaines had roughly 24 pairs made in the early 1950s as Christmas gifts for the EC staff and other associates. It is not known how many survive as they were not very well made and many of them broke and got thrown away. A few pairs have found their way into private collections. Gaines had the gold-plated links made by a jeweler out of existing letters that happened to be similar to the EC emblem. There is also an EC charm bracelet that was given to women; Gaines believes there were no more than twelve made. Marie Severin recalls that the charm and bracelet were given as gifts on successive Christmases. He also had a set of EC cufflinks made for himself (and perhaps for Al Feldstein) from 14 karat gold.

EC cufflinks: one pair sold at auction in November 1994 for $2,185

EC charm bracelet: no reported sales

Anne Gaines's EC charm bracelet

41

CHAPTER FOUR

The Complete EC Checklists

In June, 1955, Fred von Bernewitz published (via mimeograph) *The Complete EC Checklist*, an exhaustive indexing of EC's New Trend comics. The first printing was a grand total of 50 copies; the second, 200 copies, January, 1956; and a third of 75 in June, 1956. Single copies were 25¢, which also entitled the buyer to the *Supplement* (March, 1958, 250 copies), which listed the subsequent New Direction comics. *The Full Edition of the Complete EC Checklist*, updated to include all the Pre-Trend comics, appeared in July, 1963; single copies were $1.50. In 1970 Joe Vucenic compiled an updated edition in the same format, and in 1974 Vucenic issued a "big second printing" which also contained a reprint of "Zombie Terror" (from *Moon Girl* #5), the first EC horror story; both sold for $5. All editions of the *Checklist* measure 5 1/2" x 8 1/2". Von Bernewitz's checklists are highly regarded, and were considered indispensable by the EC staff. (In the late 1960s an unauthorized version titled *The Complete EC Index* was published; it was retyped to 8 1/2" x 11" size.)

Complete EC Checklist:
1955 1st printing $100

2nd and 3rd printings $50-$75

Supplement $50

1963 edition $75

1970 edition $25

1974 edition $25

The Complete EC Checklist and original mailing envelope (1956)

Supplement (1958)

The Full Edition of the Complete EC Checklist (1963)

1970 and 1974 editions

Bill Gaines, Fred von Bernewitz, and Ted E. White in December, 1955, gathering data from Bill's Pre-Trend bound volumes.

Photo by Larry Stark/Fred von Bernewitz collection

EC fanzines

A close-knit but geographically separated group of fans produced numerous fanzines during EC's heyday and for several years after. These were printed via hectograph or mimeograph, with print runs from 25 to 200 copies per issue. Some first-rate writing is to be found in many of these magazines. An analysis of these early fanzines was serialized in the latter-day EC fanzine *Squa Tront* (issues #5, 1974; #7, 1977; #8, 1978; and #9, 1983), with cover reproductions. Titles included *Potrzebie, Good Lord!, Spoof, Concept, The EC Slime Sheet, Scoop, Fanfare, The EC Fan Bulletin, The EC World Press, Graham Backers* (dedicated to the work of Graham Ingels), *Squatront* (Mike Britt), *The EC Fan Journal, ECcch!,* and what many consider the best, *Hoohah!* They are rarely offered for sale, and some issues of the more obscure titles are thought not to have any surviving copies.

EC fanzines, 1950s: rarely offered for sale, roughly $30-$50 each, $75-$100 for issues of *Hoohah!*

*Examples of 1950s
EC fanzines*

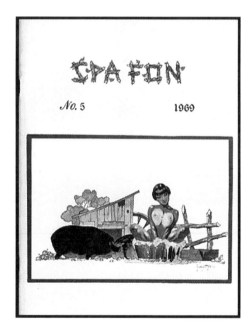

Spa Fon #1-5

The first wave of EC fanzines had all but died out by the early 1960s, but in 1966 a group of second generation EC fans picked up the torch. The first of the new fanzines, *Spa Fon* (January, 1966; 125 numbered copies), was printed via mimeograph with an offset cover. Subsequent issues were all offset-printed. *Spa Fon* got better with age; the fifth and last issue (September, 1969) had a full color cover by Frank Frazetta and an interview with Gaines by publisher Rich Hauser. (*Spa Fon* #1's cover was originally printed for a fanzine called *Outre* #4; the title was changed with paste-overs, but over the years these paste-overs have tended to fall off.)

Spa Fon: #1 (1966) $50, #2-4 $25, #5 $30

Squa Tront #1-9 with early
advertising flyer and original
mailing envelope

The best second generation fanzine, *Squa Tront*, published by Jerry Weist, appeared in September 1967; the first issue had a full color EC homage cover by Roger Hill. Issue #2 (September 1968) had a color cover by Al Williamson and a color back cover featuring EC characters by Reed Crandall; vintage photos of the *Mad* staff and offices appear as well. Issue #3 (1969) had a full color Al Feldstein oil painting cover and #4 (1970) a Graham Ingels full color oil, both gifts to Gaines in the 1950s. (The first printing of *Squa Tront* #1 was done on single sheets and stapled from front to back; 750 copies were printed. It was later reprinted with a saddle-stitched spine in an edition of 2,000. *Squa Tront* #2 was saddle-stitched and had a press run of 1,000; a 2,000 copy reprinting was identical except the price of 75¢ was opaqued.)

Starting with issue #5 (1974), John Benson took over as editor, and later became editor/publisher. Under Benson, five issues of *Squa Tront* have appeared, the most recent #9 (1983). The nine issues belong in the collection of every serious EC fan. (A deluxe reprinting of the best of *Squa Tront*, plus additional material, to be called *Squa Tront, the EC That Never Was*, is being planned by Weist.)

Squa Tront : #1 (1967) 1st printing $50-$75, 2nd $30, #2 $30, #3 $30, #4 $30, #5-9 $10-$15 each

Several other EC fanzines appeared in the late 1960s and after. The longest running was *The EC Fan Addict,* published by Tom Veilleux, with the all-dittoed first issue appearing around the end of 1967. Issue #2 (1968) was offset-printed and had an article on *Mad* by Bill Parente and a checklist of Al Williamson's EC work. Issue #3 (circa 1968) had a cover by Reed Crandall and an article by Jerry Weist. Issue #4 (1969) brought a title change to *Seraphim* and the final issue, #5 (1970), had an Al Williamson front cover and art by Berni Wrightson, Kenneth Smith and Roy Krenkel.

EC Fan Addict : #1-3 $20 each

Seraphim: #4 and #5 $10-$20 each

Other EC fanzines:

225 Lafayette St., 1979-80, Gary Arlington one-page flyers, approximately 165 issues
Best of Hoohah!, The, Ron Parker, 1984, excellent, reprints many features from this 1950s fanzine
Best of Weird Science-Fantasy, The, Bob Brosch, circa 1971, reprints five EC sf stories in black and white
Comic Book Vid-Scene, vol. 1, Ken Kaffke, 1992, EC related videos, artwork, interviews
Dimension Conventions program book, March 1982, book for con that featured several EC artists as guests
EC Collector Illustrated, The, #1, 1972, history of EC with art repros, but no new information
EC Comics Story, The, by James Van Hise, 1987, history of EC with many art repros
EC Lifeline #1, 2, and 3 (others?), Don Edwards, 1978-1979, poorly produced Xerox fanzine, interesting news
Fans of EC, The, #1 (others?), Tom Crouss, Spring 1985, poorly produced Xerox fanzine
FMZ #1, Mike Britt, March 1970, reprints from the 1950s EC fanzines *Fanfare* and *Squatront*
Good Lord!, 1993-present, Xeroxed EC newsletter from Abner Doon Productions
Horror from the Haunt of Fear #1-present, 1994, produced by third-generation EC fans, with permission of the Gaines estate
Lucky Fights It Through, 1979, black and white reprint of 1949 EC anti-venereal disease comic by Harvey Kurtzman
Qua Brot #1, Kyle Hailey, 1985, excellent one shot issue, similar to *Squa Tront*

225 Lafayette St. flyers: no reported sales; *The Best of Hoohah!*: $10-$20

The Best of Weird Science-Fantasy: $20; *Comic Book Vid-scene* vol. 1: $20

Dimension Conventions program book, March 1982: $10-$20

The EC Collector Illustrated, #1: $10-$15, with mailing envelope $20

The EC Comics Story: $5; *EC Lifeline* #1, 2, and 3 (others?): $5 each

The Fans of EC, #1 (others?): $5; *FMZ* #1, Mike Britt, March 1970, $10-$20

Good Lord! #1-present: $2-$3; *Horror from the Haunt of Fear* #1-present (1994): $2-$3

Lucky Fights It Through, 1979 black and white reprint: $10; *Qua Brot* #1: $10

The Best of Hoohah!

FMZ #1

The Best of Weird Science-Fantasy

The EC Comics Story

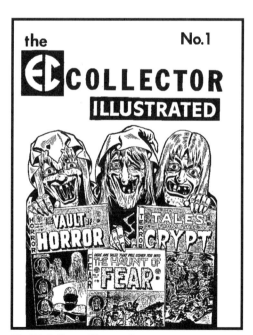

The EC Collector Illustrated

225 Lafayette St. #43

CHAPTER FOUR

Fan-oriented publications with EC-related articles

A Talk with B. Krigstein, 1963, Bhob Stewart and John Benson interview, EC references (200 copies printed)
A Talk with H. Kurtzman, 1966, John Benson interview, EC and *Mad* references (200 copies)
Al Williamson: His Work, 1971, Jim Vadeboncoeur checklist, EC art repros
Amazing World of DC #6, May 1975, special Joe Orlando issue, Orlando interview, reprints EC sf story "Judgement Day" in black and white
Animation Magazine, Spring 1989, review of *Comic Book Confidential,* Gaines mentioned
Blab! #1 (Monte Beauchamp, ed.), 1986, "Notes from the Underground" part one: various underground artists discuss EC's influence on them
Blab! #2 (Monte Beauchamp, ed.), 1987, "#1 EC fan" Gary Arlington interview, "Notes from the Underground" part two
Blab! #3 (Monte Beauchamp, ed.), 1988, miscellaneous EC references
Blab! #4 (Monte Beauchamp, ed.), 1989, miscellaneous EC references
Blab! #5 (Monte Beauchamp, ed.), 1990, "4-Color Frenzy" by Ray Zone and interview with Joe Coleman, various EC covers reproduced and EC references
Blab! #6 (Monte Beauchamp), 1991, "Alcoholic Cartoonists": Graham Ingels and Wally Wood bios
Cartoonews #20, 1979, George Evans issue
Cinefantastique, January 1990, HBO *Tales from the Crypt* cover and feature article, Gaines featured
Collector's Showcase vol. 12, no. 10, Oct. 1992, EC horror comics article, Russ Cochran quoted
Collector, The #13, Fall 1973, EC SF tribute cover by Ken Barr
Comedy #1, Summer 1980, "Help! I'm a Prisoner of the Future ," Kurtzman interview, focus on *Help!* magazine but EC and *Mad* tie-in
Comic Book Collector #6, June 1993, horror comics article, EC covered
Comic Book Marketplace #2, 1991, feature on *Squa Tront* publisher Jerry Weist, Weist pictured with Bill Gaines
Comic Book Marketplace #3, 1991, piece on opening of Gaines "file copies" by Bob Overstreet
Comic Cellar #1, 1980, Canadian, EC homage cover and short article
Comic World, The, #12, 1970, "Johnny Craig, the Master of Horror and Intrigue" by Bob Overstreet
Comickazi #1, Sept. 1969, reprints splash of "Dance Hall Racket" (*Crime Patrol* #10) from original art not in Gaines's archives.
Comics Buyer's Guide #839, Dec. 15, 1989, Gladstone EC reprints announced
Comics Buyer's Guide #867, June 29, 1990, "Gaines File Copy" story and photos
Comics Buyer's Guide #877, Sept. 7, 1990, "Spawn of the Son of M.C. Gaines ," part 1 (Don Thompson)
Comics Buyer's Guide #881, Oct. 5, 1990, "Spawn of the Son of M.C. Gaines," part 2
Comics Buyer's Guide #902, March 1, 1991, Gladstone EC license revoked
Comics Buyer's Guide #914, May 24, 1991, obit and bio of Graham Ingels by Roger Hill
Comics Buyer's Guide #918, June 21, 1991, "Extra-Large EC Comics dead after one issue"
Comics Buyer's Guide #926, August 16, 1991, "*Two Fisted Tales* returns" (new Kurtzman series)
Comics Buyer's Guide #962, April 24, 1992, "Cochran Changes Format of EC Reprint Comics"
Comics Buyer's Guide #972, July 3, 1992, Byron Preiss, Dark Horse plan *New Two-Fisted Tales*
Comics Collector #2, Winter 1984, "The EC Legend, a Brief History" by Lawrence Watt-Evans
Comics Feature #17, June 1981, article on history of EC by Chuck Wooley, focus on Pre-Trend ECs
Comics Interview #42, 1987, Frank Frazetta interview, several reprints of EC art
Comics Journal #60, November 1980, "The Life, Death, and Resurrection of EC Comics," overview tied to *The Complete EC Library* sets
Comics Journal #67, October 1981, major Harvey Kurtzman interview with many EC and *Mad* repros,and "The EC Progressives, part one: Harvey Kurtzman"
Comics Journal #71, March/April 1982 "The EC Progressives, part two: Bernard Krigstein"
Comics Journal #77, November 1982, "Censorship in Comics Panel," Bill Gaines on panel
Comics Journal #81, May 1983, major interview with Bill Gaines (cover by Wm. Stout), and "The Recognition of Shock" by Bhob Stewart (many EC art repros)
Comics Journal #91, July 1984, H. Kurtzman interview from 1982 Creation Con
Comics Journal #96, March 1985, Howard Nostrand interview (Bhob Stewart), EC and *Mad* references
Comics Journal #100, July 1985, Gaines and Kurtzman interviews
Comics Journal #142, June 1991, Arnold Roth interview re: *Mad*, Kurtzman, *Humbug, Trump, Help!*
Comics Journal #150, May 1992, Mark Schultz interview, EC references and art repros
Comics Journal #153, Oct. 1992, cover caricature of H. Kurtzman by Jack Davis, section on Kurtzman re: EC, "Annie Fanny", *The New Two-Fisted Tales*, etc.
    Reprints "Rubble" from *Two-Fisted Tales* #24.
Comics Journal #157, March 1993, Harvey Kurtzman tribute
Comics Scene #8, 1989, feature on HBO *Tales from the Crypt*
Comics Scene #21, 1991, feature on Gaines (with photos), EC and *Mad* covered
Comics Scene #35, July 1993, Bill Elder interview, "last" Bill Gaines interview, both with art repros
Comics Scene #47, November 1994, Harvey Kurtzman "final interview" with art repros
Comics Scene Spectacular #1, 1989, has fold out photo of HBO's Crypt Keeper
Comics Scene Spectacular #7, 1992 "The EC Story," Gaines interview, updates on EC artists.
Crimmer's, Spring 1976, Harvey Kurtzman interview, panel repros from *Mad* and EC war comics
Fandom Annual #1, 1967, Kurtzman interview, and "Capsule History of *Weird Science*" (Bill Spicer)
Fandom Annual #3, 1972, "EC Revisited" by Rich Hauser and misc. EC covers and art reprinted
Fandom's Agent #6/7, 1968, EC homage cover, "The Evolution of EC Horror" article, cover repros
Fanfare #1, Spring 1977, Al Feldstein interview by Ed Spiegel
Fanfare #4, Summer 1981, "The Pulp Art of Graham Ingels," EC references and art repros
Fangoria #84, 1989, cover and feature on HBO's *Tales from the Crypt*
Fangoria #94, 1990, feature on second season of HBO's *Tales from the Crypt*
Fangoria #104, 1991, feature on third season of HBO's *Tales from the Crypt*
Fangoria Horror Spectacular #4, 1991, feature on HBO *Tales from the Crypt* cinematography
Fangoria Horror Spectacular #7, 1992, feature on fourth season of HBO's *Tales From the Crypt.*
Fangoria Horror Spectacular #10, 1994, episode guide to fifth season of HBO's *Tales From the Crypt.*

Fantastic Exploits #19, circa 1971, reprints three stories from EC sf comics in black and white

Fantastic Exploits #22, circa 1971, reprints "Upheaval" (Williamson) and cover to *Valor* #2 in black and white

Fantastic Fanzine Special #2, February 1972, report on Harvey Kurtzman from the 1971 Comic Art Convention (reprints cover to *Frontline Combat* #7), "The Living Spirit of EC" panel with Al Williamson, Bill Gaines, Joe Orlando, Russ Cochran, Roger Hill (with photos and a drawing of the Three GhouLunatics by Berni Wrightson)

Flashback #1: Wood and EC, 1971, reprints three stories from EC sf comics in black and white

Golden Age #3, 1968, analysis of Kurtzman's EC war comics by Tom Fagen

Golden Age #5, 1969, "The Horror of EC" (folio of art repros), "The EC Quiz"

Graphic Fantasy #2, August 1971, EC inspired SF comic magazine, contains folded and tipped-in full color poster of *Incredible Science Fiction* #33 cover (12" x 16 1/2")

Graphic Illusions, Summer 1971, reprints "Inside EC" by Jerry Kolden from *YMIR* vol. 2, #1

Graphic Story Magazine #13, Spring 1971, John Severin interview with misc. reprints from EC

Graphic Story Magazine #15, Summer 1973, Harry Harrison interview, EC references and art repros

Graphic Story Magazine #16, Summer 1974, classic EC parody "The Wishing World"

Graphic Story World #6, July 1972, review of *The EC Horror Library* (Nostalgia Press) by Bill Spicer and "Are You An EC Fan?" article by John Benson

Graphic Story World #7, September 1972, photos and quotes from the 1972 "EC Fan Addict Convention," assembled by John Benson

Graphic Story World #8, December 1972, expanded coverage of the 1972 "EC Fan Addict Convention" by John Benson

Guts #4, September 1968, "Violence in the Entertainment Media" article, reprints "Baseball Is Ruining Our Children" from *Mad* #34 and the EC "Are You A Red Dupe?" editorial

I'll Be Damned #1, 1970, "The EC Answer to Comic Book Originality" by Meade Frierson III, analysis of EC's "borrowed" story ideas for the SF comics

Illustrated Harvey Kurtzman Index, The, 1976, Glenn Bray, many reprints from EC and *Mad*

Infinity #4, 1972, reprints EC SF story "A New Beginning" in black and white

Inside Collector, The, #4, Oct. 1990, article on EC reprint publisher and collector Russ Cochran

Inside Comics #2, Summer 1974, "Conversations with Harvey Kurtzman," EC and *Mad* references

Masquerader #6, 1964, "EC, the New Trend" by Ed Lahman

Media Sight Magazine #3, Fall 1983, Gaines interview

Monster Times, The, #4, March 15, 1972, preview of Amicus' *Tales from the Crypt* film

Monster Times, The, #9, May 17, 1972, article on sf comics, EC covered with reprints

Monster Times, The, #10, May 31, 1972, EC issue

Monster Times, The, #14, July 31, 1972, article on Peter Cushing re: Amicus' *Tales from the Crypt*

Monster Times, The, #19, February 1973, one page article on the East Coast Comix reprints

Monster Times, The, #22, May 1973, article on Amicus' *Vault of Horror* film

Monster Times, The, #29, Dec. 1973, "EC Lives," article and interview re: Russ Cochran's *EC Portfolios*

Nightmare #8 (Skywald magazine), 1972, Amicus' *Tales from the Crypt* covered, EC art repros

Ophemera (Bhob Stewart), 1977, "Feldstein," analysis by Bhob Spicer

Overstreet Comic Book Price Guide #9, 1979, EC tribute issue, Wood cover and many EC cover repros

Panels #2, Spring 1981, "Is War Hell?," analysis of Kurtzman's war comics

Rocket's Blast Special #7, 1967, EC issue, "The End of an Era" by William Parente

Rocket's Blast, The, #16, March 1963, "A Capsule History of EC's *Weird Science* by Bill Spicer (reprinted in *Fandom Annual* #1, 1967), has Spicer's stencil tracing of *Weird Science* #12 (#1)

Rocket's Blast, The, #19, June 1963, "A Capsule History of *Frontline Combat* by Bill Spicer, has Spicer's stencil tracing of *Frontline Combat* #1 cover

Rocket's Blast, The, #47, 1966, "An Interview With Harvey Kurtzman" by Alan Hewetson, reprints covers to *Two Fisted Tales* #18, *Mad* #1, and *Frontline Combat* #1

Rocket's Blast, The, #51, 1966, article by Russ Cochran on comics, EC covered

Rocket's Blast, The, #126, April 1976, "The EC Pre-Trends" by J. B. Clifford, cover and panel repros

Rocket's Blast, The, #131, Oct. 1976, "Ray Bradbury and EC," several panel reproductions from EC

Rocket's Blast, The, #153, June 1983, "What's So Funny About Comics," analysis of *Mad* comics

Spirit Magazine #31, June 1984, "Shop Talk" with Harvey Kurtzman by Will Eisner.

Styx #2, 1973, "A Tribute to EC," reproduces 37 EC comic covers in black and white

Vanguard #1, 1966, Harvey Kurtzman interview

Voice of Comicdom #16, 1970, "Graphic Critique: Frank Frazetta," reprints splash from "Squeeze Play" and cover to Ballantine *Tales from the Crypt*

Wallace Wood Treasury, The, 1980, checklist of Wood's work, reprints from EC comics and *Mad*

Will Eisner's Quarterly #6, Sept. 1985, Jack Davis/Harvey Kurtzman interview

Witzend #6, 1969, first publication of "The Spawn of Venus" story (Wallace Wood art) intended for the never published EC 3D science fiction comic

Wonderworld (formerly *Graphic Story World*) #10, November 1973, more "EC Con" coverage (excerpts from the War Comics Panel), and "The Rime of the Valiant Publisher," a poetic tribute to Gaines by Jerry De Fuccio with art by Don Martin

YMIR, Vol.2, #1, circa 1966, "Inside EC" by Jerry Kolden, interesting revisionist history giving Harry Harrison and Wallace Wood most of the credit for the success of EC

Fan-oriented publications with EC-related articles: various prices, average $5-$25 each

Fandom's Agent #6

Monster Times #10

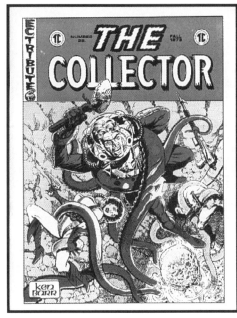

The Collector #28

Blab! #1

Cinefantastique, Jan. 1990

The Comics Journal #67

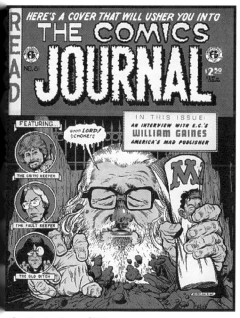

The Comics Journal #81

from "The Wishing World," Graphic Story Magazine #16

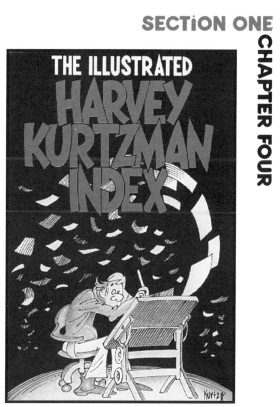

The Illustrated Harvey Kurtzman Index

Graphic Fantasy #2

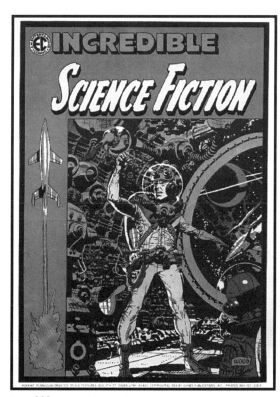

*Incredible Science Fiction #33 poster
from Graphic Fantasy #2*

from Rocket's Blast #19 (Bill Spicer re-creation)

CHAPTER FiVE

Seduction of the Innocent

Although anti-comics sentiments had been in the wind since the 1940s, it was Dr. Fredric Wertham and his 1954 book *Seduction of the Innocent* that galvanized these forces, and which ultimately became the rallying point of efforts to "clean up the comics." Wertham's basic theory was that since juvenile delinquents read comic books, comic books cause juvenile delinquency. Excerpts from the book were published in the November 1953, issue of *Ladies' Home Journal* ("What Parents Don't Know About Comic Books") and the May 1954, issue of *Reader's Digest* ("Comic Books—Blueprints for Delinquency"). Several panel reprints from EC appear in the book, including "Foul Play" (*Haunt of Fear* #19), "Right On the Button" (*Weird Science* #19), and a detail from the cover of *Crime SuspenStories* #20. Gaines testified before a Senate subcommittee, defending his comics (detailed in *The Mad World of William M. Gaines*: section two, chapter eight; film footage of some of Gaines's testimony appears in the film *Comic Book Confidential*: section one, chapter eleven). Wertham and his book were directly responsible for the premature burial of EC, and so the book occupies a place of dishonor in EC collections.

Seduction of the Innocent: with dust jacket and bibliography $200-$300, without bibliography $100-$150

The Ladies' Home Journal, Nov. 1953 (Wertham article): $35

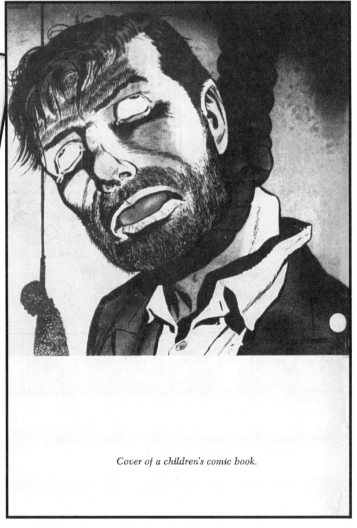

Cover of a children's comic book.

A comic-book baseball game. Notice the chest protector and other details in the text and pictures.

EC reprints from
Seduction of the Innocent

A young girl on her wedding night stabs her sleeping husband to death with a hatpin when she realizes that he comes from a distant planet and is a "mammal."

from The Ladies' Home Journal Nov. 1953, note Haunt of Fear #19 in photo

THE NEW YORKER

MARCH 24, 1951

•

INCIDENTAL INTELLIGENCE: Educational Comics, Inc., 225 Lafayette Street, issues the following publications: *Vault of Horror, Tales from the Crypt, Weird Fantasy, Weird Science, Haunt of Fear*, and *Crime SuspenStories*.

Several magazine pieces related to EC appeared in the early 1950s:

A paragraph in the March 24, 1951 *New Yorker* under the heading "Incidental Intelligence," prompted a schizophrenic but clever response from Gaines (dictated to Al Feldstein) in the April 7, 1951 issue.

New Yorker, The, March 24 and April 7, 1951 (Gaines letters): $5-$10 each

THE NEW YORKER

APRIL 7, 1951

DEPARTMENT OF CORRECTION
(JEKYLL AND HYDE DIVISION)

EDUCATIONAL COMICS, INC.
PUBLISHERS AND LICENSORS OF
PICTURE STORIES FROM THE BIBLE
"COMPLETE OLD AND
NEW TESTAMENT" EDITIONS
PICTURE STORIES FROM
AMERICAN HISTORY,
SCIENCE AND WORLD HISTORY
225 LAFAYETTE ST.
TELEPHONE CANAL 6-1994-5
NEW YORK 12, N.Y.
MARCH 28, 1951

The Editors, *The New Yorker*,
SIRS:

ON page 20 of the March 24th, 1951, issue of your publication, you stated that this organization, Educational Comics, Inc., of 225 Lafayette St., publishes the following magazines: *The Vault of Horror, Tales from the Crypt, Weird Fantasy, Weird Science, The Haunt of Fear*, and *Crime SuspenStories*.

This information is erroneous, and I, as vice-president of Educational Comics, Inc., demand an immediate retraction. Educational Comics, Inc., does not publish any of the six magazines which you listed in your defamatory item. We are engaged in publishing the highly educational material listed on this letterhead. I consider your comments a personal insult, since I, as vice-president of Educational Comics, Inc., would have absolutely nothing to do with magazines dealing with such shocking and distasteful subject matter as those which you list.

I am awaiting your immediate action and response in this matter.
Very sincerely yours,
WILLIAM M. GAINES
Vice-President

WMG/af

THE E-C COMICS GROUP
"THE BETTER SELLING COMICS"
225 LAFAYETTE ST.
NEW YORK 12, N.Y.
TELEPHONE CANAL 6-1994-5
MARCH 28, 1951

The Editors, *The New Yorker*,
SIRS:

ON page 20 of the March 24th, 1951, issue of your publication, you stated that Educational Comics, Inc., of 225 Lafayette Street, publishes the following magazines: *The Vault of Horror, Tales from the Crypt, Weird Fantasy, Weird Science, The Haunt of Fear*, and *Crime SuspenStories*.

Educational Comics does not publish these magazines. This information is erroneous, and I, as vice-president of the E-C (Entertaining Comics) Group, of 225 Lafayette Street, demand and insist upon an immediate retraction and correction.

Having worked very hard to build up a reputation for the very finest entertaining comic magazines in the field, I note with much chagrin that our years of labor and achievement are credited to a company which is not in any way responsible for this fine work. I am proud of our publications, and our sales attest to their popular acceptance.

As vice-president of the E-C Group, I would have absolutely nothing to do with magazines dealing with such dry, unentertaining, and obviously *educational* material as Educational Comics, Inc., publishes.

I am awaiting your immediate action and response in this matter.
Very sincerely yours,
WILLIAM M. GAINES
Vice-President

WMG/af

•

The first issue of the mini-sized magazine, *Tops* (March 1954) had a two page feature on Gaines and EC that included a reprint from the story "...In Gratitude" from *Shock SuspenStories* #11.

Tops #1, March 1954 (Gaines article): $25

JEKYLL-HYDE of the COMICS

In 1947, William Gaines inherited $1,000,000 and an unsuccessful group of comic magazines. He was 25 years old, and the combination of youth and money proved irresistible. He decided to try to revamp the magazines into money-making propositions.

How? His answer: horror stories!

Purveying horror to the kiddies has earned Gaines the enmity of rival publishers, PTA's, and prominent psychiatrists. But it also boosted the sales of his magazines to over a million copies per month.

When asked to defend the lurid contents of such comics titles as *Vault of Horror*, *Tales from the Crypt*, etc., Gaines replies:

"Our magazines are written for adults. It isn't our fault if the kids read 'em, too."

However, there is a Jekyll-Hyde personality at work in Gaines' magazines.

For along with frankly sensational, often revolting "horror stories," Gaines also publishes comics stories which make a bold and welcome plea for racial tolerance. (*See illustration opposite*).

These stories which appear in his regular horror monthlies, are, by contrast, well written, well plotted, ruthless in their revelation of a kind of horror that lies close beneath the surface of life in modern America. **38**

In this story, a Korean veteran denounces fellow-townsmen who have refused decent burial to his comrade.

39

The June 1954, issue of *Pageant* (a digest-size magazine) had a feature on *Mad* comics with Will Elder art done for the article, and four pages of reprints from *Mad*. A subsequent job offer from *Pageant* to Harvey Kurtzman was a deciding factor in turning *Mad* into a 25¢ magazine, thereby keeping Kurtzman in the fold a little longer, and indirectly assuring *Mad*'s survival.

Pageant, June 1954 (Mad article): $20

Other EC-related Magazine and Newspaper Articles:

Galaxy, May 1955, review of *The Mad Reader*
Magazine World (trade publication), May 15, 1946, back cover ad for EC Pre-Trend comics
New York Daily News, Sept. 15, 1954, "Crime-Comics Pioneer to Drop Horror Books," Gaines quoted.
New York Daily News, Sept. 17, 1954, editorial: "The Only Right Censorship" (subheaded "Publisher Bows to Public Opinion")
New York Post, Sept. 14, 1954, "Pioneer of Horrors in Comics Quits Them"
New York Times, April 22, 1954, "No Harm In Horror, Comics Issuer Says," Gaines quoted
New York World-Telegram & Sun, Sept. 14, 1954, "Crime Comics Out, Publisher Decides," Gaines quoted.
Newsdealer (trade publication), July 1948, ad for EC Pre-Trend comics
Newsdealer, July 1949, photo of Bill Gaines with Henry E. Schultz of A.C.M.P., ad for EC Pre-Trends
Parents, Oct. 1953, annual rating of comic books; *Mad* listed as "objectionable"
Parents, Aug. 1954, annual rating of comic books; *Mad* and *Panic* listed as "objectionable"
Picture Post (London), Nov. 20, 1954, "Horror Comics: Is This the End?" article, British *Tales From The Crypt* comic shown
Publishers Weekly, Jan. 10, 1986, piece by Lyle Stuart on comic book censorship and comics code
Reader's Digest, June 1954, T. E. Murphy article, gives plots of several EC stories (uncredited)
Reader's Digest, Nov. 1954, T. E. Murphy article, describes cover of *Crime SuspenStories* #22
Reader's Digest, Feb. 1956, Gaines mentioned in article about "cleaning up" comics by T. E. Murphy
San Francisco Examiner Image, April 18, 1993, tribute to Harvey Kurtzman with EC art repros
Spin, August 1988, EC covered in article about comics
Tikkun, March/April 1992, "Of Mice and Menshun: Jewish Comics Come of Age," *Mad* comics covered, "Mickey Rodent" splash reprinted
Writer's Digest, August 1953, Gaines quoted in article about writing for comic books
Writer's Digest, Feb. 1954, "Madman Gaines Pleads for Plots," article by Gaines (with Feldstein?) to recruit outside writers to EC

See section two, chapter sixteen for further article listings on Gaines

Galaxy, May 1955, review of *The Mad Reader* : $3
Magazine World (trade publication), May 15, 1946, back cover ad for EC Pre-Trend comics: $20
Newsdealer (trade publication), July 1948, ad for EC Pre-Trend comics: $20
Newsdealer, July 1949, photo of Bill Gaines with Henry E. Schultz of A.C.M.P., ad for EC Pre-Trends: $20-$25
Parents, Oct. 1953, Aug. 1954, annual rating of comics: $5-$10
Reader's Digest, June 1954, gives plots of several EC stories (uncredited): $3
Reader's Digest, Nov. 1954, describes cover of *Crime SuspenStories* #22: $3
Reader's Digest, Feb. 1956, Gaines mentioned: $10
Writer's Digest, August 1953, Gaines quoted: $10
Writer's Digest, Feb. 1954, "Madman Gaines Pleads for Plots:" $25
Other EC-related Magazine and Newspaper Articles: $3-$25

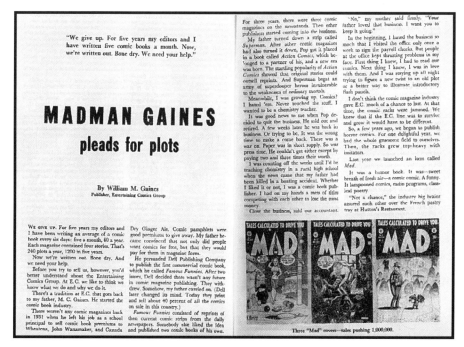

Writer's Digest, February 1954

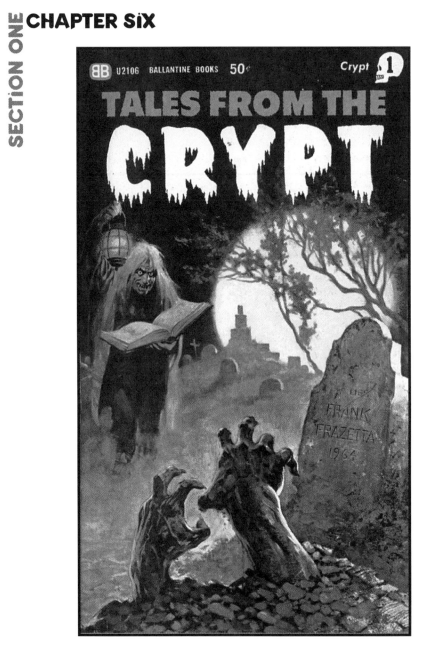

Ballantine Books paperback EC reprints

In December 1964, the first of five black and white Ballantine Books paperbacks of EC reprints, *Tales From the Crypt*, appeared. It was followed in March 1965, by *Tales of the Incredible* (EC science fiction reprints), and in August 1965, by *The Vault of Horror*. Under Ray Bradbury's name, *The Autumn People* (October 1965) and *Tomorrow Midnight* (June 1966) appeared, consisting of Bradbury stories EC had adapted. The books were 50¢ each, had an excellent cross section of EC stories and boasted front cover paintings by Frank Frazetta, who had become a highly successful commercial artist (movie posters, album jackets, and book covers). The reprints introduced a new generation of fans to EC, and set the stage for a remarkable series of reprint efforts in the 1970s, '80s, and '90s.

Ballantine Books paperback EC reprints: $20 each

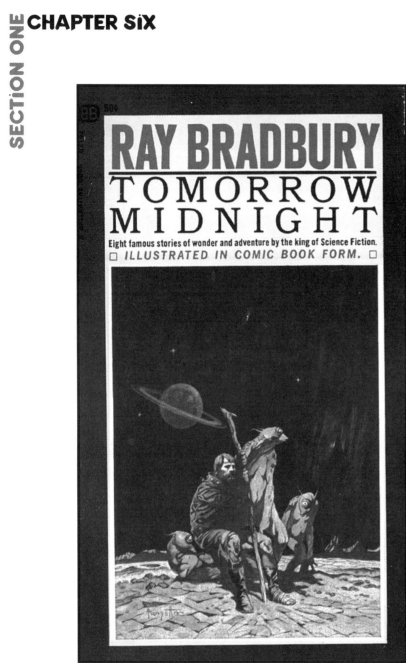

Nick Meglin in 1964 with Frazetta's roughs for the *Tales From the Crypt* paperback. Photo by Frank Frazetta/Nick Meglin collection

Nostalgia Press hardback *EC Horror Library*

In 1971, Nostalgia Press issued a 10" x 14" full color hardcover book (with dust jacket) of EC reprints, under the titles *The EC Horror Library of the 1950's* and *Horror Comics of the 1950's*. The "horror" label was something of a misnomer as the book also contained stories from EC's "shock" and sf comics. The book boasted superior production values and sold for a then astronomical $19.95. The book contained new artwork by Joe Orlando, an introduction by Bhob Stewart (who also co-edited with Ron Barlow), and a reprint of EC critic Larry Stark's "Elegy" (from the 1956 EC fanzine *Hoohah!* #6). Especially noteworthy was the final story, "An Eye for an Eye," which appeared for the first time after being rejected in 1955 for the final issue of *Incredible Science Fiction* (#33) by the Comics Code Authority. According to Stewart, due to a mix-up the book was remaindered at a price higher than the original list price, and remained available until the late 1970s. A companion volume devoted to EC science fiction stories was being developed, but the death of publisher Woody Gelman spelled the end of the project. Bhob Stewart generated inked roughs for the unpublished EC science fiction book, which were given to Roy Krenkel to create the final art. Krenkel finished at least four pieces, including a title page border, a scene of nuclear devastation in Manhattan, and a copyright page illustration. The whereabouts of this artwork is unknown.

EC Horror Library : with dust jacket, $100

EC Horror Library pre-publication announcement

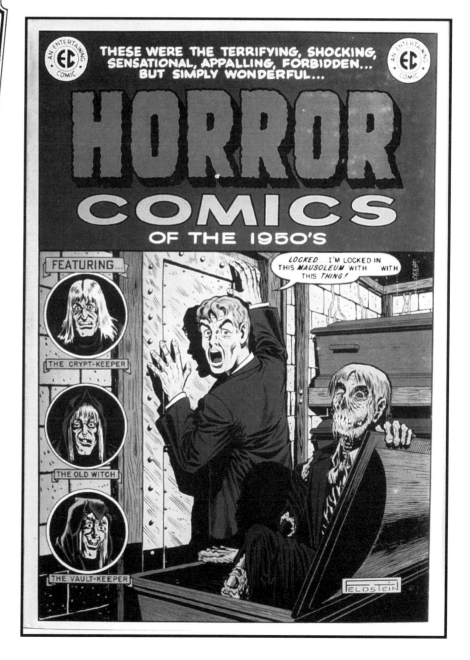

61

Haunt of Fear #18 poster

The first EC reprint item from Russ Cochran was a black and white "fine art" poster of the cover to *Haunt of Fear* #18. Printed on heavy paper, the print measured about 15" x 21", and was shot from the original Graham Ingels art, which Gaines had given to Cochran in 1966 after considerable prodding. A notice reading "Copyright © 1953 Fables Publishing Co., Inc." appears at the bottom left corner. The poster was produced in 1971 and sold for $1.00. Cochran recalls that about 1,000 copies were printed, and evidently it was not a sellout, for as recently as 1990 some dealers were offering them in quantity at $10.00 each. Shortly after the print's release, Marie Severin hand colored a number of them, with ten signed (by Severin), numbered and dated versions made; no two are exactly alike. Each sold for $100.

Haunt of Fear #18 poster: $10-$15

Haunt of Fear #18 Marie Severin hand-colored print: $450

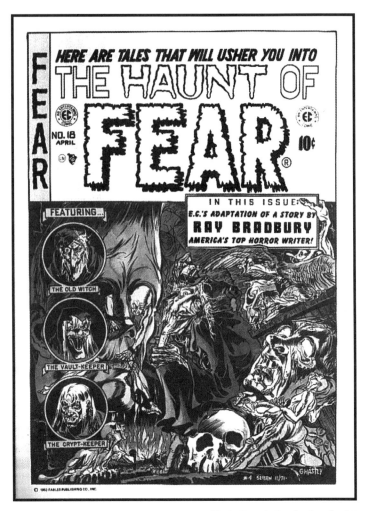

Marie Severin hand-colored print

Black and white unsigned poster

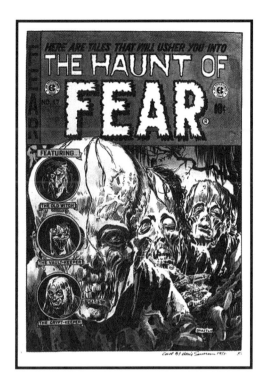

Marie Severin hand-colored prints

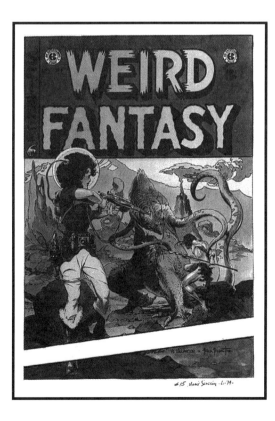

Marie Severin hand-colored prints

The success of the hand-colored *Haunt of Fear* #18 print led Cochran to offer a second series of prints. The image area measured about 10" x 14 1/2" on the eleven covers offered, including *Weird Fantasy* #15 and 21, *Tales From the Crypt* #35, *Haunt of Fear* #14, 17 and 24, *Weird Science* #6 and 9, *Weird Science-Fantasy* #25 and 27, and *Two Fisted Tales* #30. Twenty of each print were offered for sale, but most sold about twelve or less. No two were exactly alike, and each was signed, dated and numbered by Severin; the price for each was $75. In an interview in the *Complete EC Library* edition of *Psychoanalysis,* Severin stated (good-naturedly) that the project was "a pain in the neck." The prints occasionally surface and are quite desirable.

Marie Severin hand-colored prints: average price $300 each

Frank Frazetta
Weird Science-Fantasy #29 print

In 1972, Cochran released a print of the cover to *Weird Science-Fantasy* #29, colored and signed by Frank Frazetta. Considered one of Frazetta's best, the art was originally done as a *Buck Rogers* cover for Famous Funnies but was rejected as being too violent; Gaines used it (with changes) but paid a usage fee only so Frazetta could keep the original art. As with the Marie Severin prints, no two are exactly alike. An edition of fifty was announced, but only about forty were made. Each is signed, dated, and numbered, and most (if not all) have a small drawing at the bottom as well. The prints originally sold for $150 apiece. A smaller black and white print, signed by the artist, was made available for $5. (Two of the prints were used as the front and back covers of *EC Portfolio* #2.)

Frank Frazetta *Weird Science-Fantasy* #29 print: last reported sale in 1988, $2,000

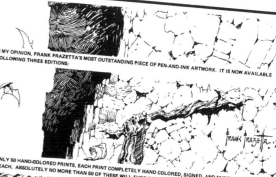

Original flyer for *Weird Science-Fantasy* #29 print

EC Portfolio #1-6

EC Portfolios

On the heels of Nostalgia Press's *EC Horror Library*, Cochran issued the first in a series of large (11 1/2" x 16") portfolios of black and white EC stories, shot from original art. Detailed line work that dropped out in the cheaply-produced original comics is wonderfully clear in the portfolios. Six volumes were produced between 1971 and 1977, reprinting 29 stories and 27 covers. Portfolio #1 had a large EC logo embossed on the front; issues #2-6 had alternate Marie Severin colorings of various covers. Portfolio #1 cost $10; subsequent volumes were $15. Print runs were 800 copies of #1, 1,100 copies of #2, and about 1,500 copies each of #3-6. The portfolios led to Cochran's *Complete EC Library* (section one, chapter 14).

EC Portfolios: #1 $75-$100

#2 $50-$75

#3-6 $25 each

The East Coast Comix reprints

In 1973 Ron Barlow and Bruce Hershenson launched the first in a series of full color comic book-size *EC Classic Reprints*, published by East Coast Comix. These were reprints of full issues of various EC comics, minus ads and with editorial comment (some original letter pages and text stories appeared in later issues). The goal was to reprint every EC comic, but only twelve issues were printed. The final issue, *EC Classic Reprint* #12 (reprinting *Shock Suspenstories* #2) appeared in 1975. The first nine issues were $1.00, issues 10 and 11, $1.25, and #12, $1.50. While the books were attractively produced, distribution was limited to the few comics shops then in existence, record stores, and "head" shops where they were displayed alongside underground comix and rolling papers. Readership apparently hovered at around 15,000, not enough to sustain the series. The most interesting issue historically was the first, *The Crypt of Terror*. This book originally appeared in 1955 as the final issue of *Tales From the Crypt* (#46) but was actually slated to be the first issue of EC's planned but aborted fourth horror title, *The Crypt of Terror*. The East Coast Comix version was the first (and so far only) publication of the cover as planned.

East Coast Comix EC reprints: #1 $10

#2-12 $5 each

EC Classic Reprints #1-12 (East Coast Comix)

EC IS BACK!
EXACTLY AS IT WAS

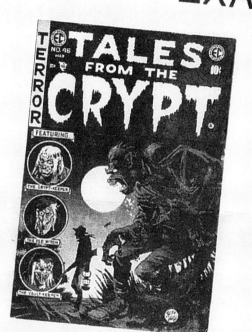

Bill Gaines has finally said yes and E.C. is back! Not as expensive hardcover collections and not as expensive art folios, but as inexpensive full color comic books! That's right, East Coast Comix has been given permission from Bill Gaines to reissue exact full color duplicates of the original E.C.'s.

Just as E.C. guaranteed the highest standards of quality, we at East Coast Comix are doing the same. We have journeyed to the legendary vault with Bill Gaines to unearth the original art to reproduce from and we are preparing perfect color for color reprints of each book. . . . but naturally without ads.

To start with, we'll be releasing Tales From The Crypt #46 in February 1973 with Weird Science #15 and Shock Suspenstories #12 shortly thereafter.

We're offering this opportunity to start with E.C. again with a 3 or 6 issue subscription. A 3 issue subscription will cost you $3.00 and a 6 issue subscription only $5.00! Remember!, by subscribing you're guaranteed of getting your E.C.'s HOT OFF THE PRESSES and you're showing your support for this important project.

Full Color!!
1⁰⁰ each

Dealer rates on request

EAST COAST COMIX
P.O. BOX 1290   GREAT NECK, N.Y. 11023

( ) Find $1.00 for Crypt No. 46 (Plus 25¢ postage)
( ) Find $3.00 for first three issues.
( ) Find $5.00 for first six issues.

Name _____

Address _____

City _____ State _____ Zip Code _____

Original announcement for the
East Coast Comix reprints

The duplicate EC Fan Addict Kit

In 1971 EC fan Dave Gibson issued an "original duplicate EC Fan Addict Kit." The kit was a facsimile of the the 1953 version, down to the paper color of the "Bulletins" and the two-color cloth EC patch. The only item not duplicated was the bronze pin; an EC sticker was included in its place. In addition, coloring on the new certificate differs from the original. Each piece of the kit bears a copyright notice that does not appear on the original items, making them easy to identify. Only a few hundred were made, and were sold through the mail or at conventions.

Duplicate EC Fan Addict Kit: complete kit in envelope, $50-$75

THIS IS THE ONLY ORIGINAL DUPLICATE

EC
FAN ADDICT KIT

Failure to carry this card at all times will result...

This is to certify that

INVALID IF SIGNED

is a life member in good standing of

THE NATIONAL E.C. FAN-ADDICT CLUB

and is therefore entitled, upon presentation of this card, to purchase any 32 page E.C. magazine for the special membership newsstand price of 10c.

© Copyright 1971 WILLIAM M. GAINES   PRESIDENT

In case of accident ... tch. tch!

If this card is lost ... tough!

If you find this card, kindly drop it ...

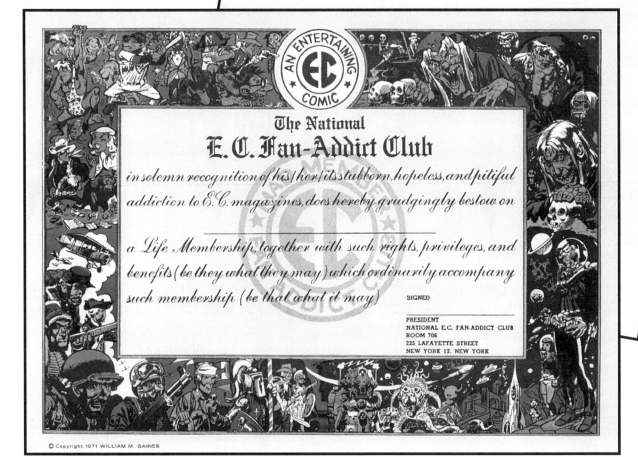

AN ENTERTAINING EC COMIC

The National
E.C. Fan-Addict Club

in solemn recognition of his/her/its stubborn, hopeless, and pitiful addiction to E.C. magazines, does hereby grudgingly bestow on

_____

a Life Membership, together with such rights, privileges, and benefits (be they what they may) which ordinarily accompany such membership (be that what it may)

SIGNED

_____

PRESIDENT
NATIONAL E.C. FAN-ADDICT CLUB
ROOM 706
225 LAFAYETTE STREET
NEW YORK 12, NEW YORK

© Copyright 1971 WILLIAM M. GAINES

The National E.C. Fan-Addict Club BULLETIN

Number 5

...cember 1954

...an-Addict,

...ell, here it is! As we promised in the last Bulletin, you ...
...and subject matter of E.C.'s six sensational new magazin...

...ive years ago, we at E.C. started our "New Trend" line. Other publishers, in order t...
...re comic magazine industry. We feel that we can state, without...
...quality of their product. We ...
...nged the entire complexion of the comic magazine industry...

...We hope now to revitalize and change the complexion of th...
...r "NEW DIRECTION" magazines. And here they are:

The National E.C. Fan-Addict Club BULLETIN

September 1954   Number 4

Dear Fan-Addict,

...to start, and you miserable, we thought we'd cheer you up with another

...you're cheered up, ...
...s will shortly be ...
...are giving up! ...
..., and unfounded ...
...s throughout the ...
...gazines that do ...
...we are forced t...
...unt of Fear,

The National E.C. Fan-Addict Club BULLETIN

Number 3

June 1954

Dear Fan-Addict,

THIS IS AN EMERG...

This is an appeal f...

THE PROBLEM: C...
...in particular. Due to the eff...
...a large segment of the publi...
...cause juvenile delinquency...
...development of the personal...
...are: a psychiatrist who has ...
...certain publishing compani...
...their demise, many groups ...
...as responsible parents on ...
...assorted headline hunters. ...
...police officials, to local m...
...congressmen. They comp...
...everyone gets frightened. ...
...from display. The whole...
...congressmen get frighten...
...This wave of hysteria has ...
...comic magazine industry...

WE BELIEVE: ...
...crusaders...that comics ...
...slightest way, thought th...
...comics were harmful to ...
...our efforts toward some...
...And we're not a...
...eminent criminologist, ...
...do not lead to crime, al...
...perience as a psychiatri...
...has committed a crime...
...she read comic books. ...
...man of the Ill. Congres...
..."a decided beneficial e...
...the National Institute of ...
...originate criminal beh...
...some good...children ...
...means of working out ...
...We also belie...
...and crime comics is ...
...are a small minority...
...the majority...you w...
...by them...has not be...

The National E.C. Fan-Addict Club BULLETIN

March 1954

Dear Fan-Addict,

Well, here it is! The second issue of our Bulleti...
further ado, let's get right into it!

NEWS: To replace the now dead Frontline Combat ...
E.C. are contemplating two new titles. A meeting o...
and artists was held recently in order to discuss t...
to put out. The following are under consideration...
starring the three GhouLunatics, called the Crypt ...
of private-eye mag; (3) a magazine of sea stories;...
stories; (5) a few highly intriguing new-type idea...
mention, as some rival editors might be members o...
to hear from you fan-addicts re what YOU'D like t...
what evil ideas lurk in the hearts of you fan-add...

GOSSIP: The Jack KAMENS, who were expecting ...
forged ahead of the pack with a pair of twins...
Terry. Congratulations, congratulations. Johnn...
the proud parents of a baby girl...Mary Frances...
hubby Jack with a new son and heir, Jack Jr. ...
into their own ivy-covered Jersey cottage. Joe...
wife Gloria with a new fluttering 30 inch T.V. ...
are expecting their second. Al WILLIAMSON ju...
still fickle!

BACK ISSUE TRADING POST: Coupons from the ...
from fan-addicts eager to sell or trade back ...
other slap-happy creeps. (Incidently, at thi...
stands at approximately 17,700. So the follo...
of inquiries.) If you're interested in back ...
claim to have them:

David Decherd	5902 Anita
Carl Shapiro	3495 Boulevard
Richard Dzenis	317 North East
Dick Tabb	5069 Courbille
Letha Joe Evans	Box 258
Edward Schaller	401 W. Fern St.
Edward Wigelius	3557 Valencia Rd.
Betty Maino	198 Idaho Rd.
Richard Lederer	6116 18th Ave.
George Ormisten	1417 N.W. 21
Ted Watkins	626 E. Lyndon
Robert Ridolphi	948 S. Lawrence
Joe Wagner, Jr.	51 Jersey St.
Wayne Fenner	226 Thurbers Ave.
Roberta Cook	96 Norwa.. St.
Juliet Nagel	242 Rosedale Ave
John Giglio	31-37 43rd Stree
Bert DuPont	2955 Dexter St.
Ivan Goldman	2972 E. 78 St.
Jim Kropp	8317 Monroe
James Wills	2011 Edgeland
Sonny Myers	4407 Colonial Dr.
J.L. Richman	1064 Caroll Place
Steve Francis	2150 34th Ave.
Henry E. Johnson	2519 Pierce Ave.
William S. Cobun	2731 Harrison Ave.
Abe Hoffman	1023½ Sentinal Ave.
Joe Caldwell	587 S. Crest Rd.
Stanford Grossman	22508 Kane (South)
Paul Ayan	80 Alleghany St.
	3627 Southward Dr.
	... St.

The National E.C. Fan-Addict Club BULLETIN

Nov. 1953   Nu...

Dear Fan-Addict,

Well, here the silly thing finally is! Our first bulletin! Took a ...
time coming, eh? We're truly sorry. Actually, we've been so busy with ...
new projects that we honestly haven't had the time to sit down and get th...
off before today. But new projects mean news...and that's one of the thi...
this bulletin is for. And since you're a Fan-Addict, you're entitled to ...
scoops.

3-D: At this writing, there are two E.C. 3-D mags kicking around. As ...
we've tried to outdo the field. We have included in each mag, two 3-D vi...
with four earpieces. No other 3-D mag can make that statement! And are t...
viewers versatile! Adjustable ear-pieces for egg-heads; adaptable for fou...
eyed egg-heads; and, once assembled, able to be folded and placed in pocke...
mag for safekeeping...without bending earpieces! Only "molten-dyed" optic...
clear acetate color filters were used...far superior to the type made by ...
printing the color upon clear acetate, which results in fogging and mottli...

THREE DIMENSIONAL EC CLASSICS (3-D No. 1) contains four of E.C.'s best ...
yarns in the fields of humor, science-fiction, war, and suspence...complete ...
rewritten and redrawn especially for 3-D...by Wood, Krigstein, Evans, and ...
Ghastly Graham Ingels. Four truly gorgeous pieces of work! Cover masterpi...
by Kurtzman.

THREE DIMENSIONAL TALES FROM THE CRYPT OF TERROR (3-D No. 2) features fo...
of E.C.'s top horror stories...lovingly turned out by Davis, Elder, Craig, s...
Orlando. For more gems of 3-D art! Cover dreamed up by Feldstein.

The 3-D process used was invented by an old gentleman by the name of ...
Freeman H. Owens, and patented seventeen years ago. Most 3-D comics appear ...
to have utilized this process, and Mr. Owens is in the process of instituting ...
patent infringement proceedings against the various publishers of same. E.C. ...
was the only publishing company to obtain a license from Mr. Owens. ...
Printed with 3-D inks especially manufactured for E.C. by the Superior In...
of N.Y., on extra-heavy 45 pound bleached stock, these mags contain only one ...
page of inside advertising...and that's in 3-D. The price? Two bits!

Read all 3-D mags under good strong light. Reading 3-D mags sharpens up ...
your stereo vision...if eye-strain results, it's probable that your eye ...
muscles need a little working with. So don't be discouraged...take it slowly, ...
and read a little every day till you get used to it. But remember...strong ...
light!

Gossip: George Evans is the proud papa of a new baby daughter, his second. ...
Name's Janice Ruth. Feldstein's leading the pack...just had his third gal, ...
Jamie Lynn. The Craigs' third addition is a Scotch terrier, name of "Scruff." ...
The Jack Kamens are expecting their third...they already have two sons, Jack ...
and Deena Davis...as well as Johnny and Mickey Severin...are expecting their ...
first! The Wally Woods moved into a new apartment, migrating into mid-town ...
Manhattan from the wilds of Queens. Al Williamson just broke his latest ...
engagement...he's so fickle! ...
Our business manager, Frank Lee, has retired...At present, cruising around ...
the Caribbean. Our new business mgr. is Lyle Stuart. Our beloved Ruby Kast ...
is no longer with us...she's expecting shortly. Added two gals to the mail-...
order, subscription, and fan-mail department: Jackie Abrams and Shirley Norris. ...
But boss-gal Nancy Siegel still swamped.

Weird Science-Fantasy: Now being engraved, E.C.'s combined 15¢ science-...
fiction quarterly will blossom forth with a radically new and different ...
design. The stories are some of the very best we've done to date in s-f. ...
Wood does the cover, and then leads off with a shocker about outer-space ...
colonization. Williamson follows with an alien civilization yarn. Krigstein ...
takes care of third spot with an adaptation of Ray Bradbury's "The Flying ...
Machine," the original of which appears in Ray's new book, "The Golden Apples ...
of the Sun." Joe Orlando winds up with a "twist-ending" tale that'll tickle ...
your fancy. We think this is one swell issue...and we've got our fingers ...
crossed that the extra nickle tariff won't scare away our regular readership...
'cause we'd like to continue publishing s-f.

Bronx ...,						
Oakland, Calif.	M					
Houston 3, Texas	M	SF	H	W	SS	
Cincinati, Ohio	M	SF	H	W	SS	
Los Angeles, Calif.			SF	H		SS
Chattanooga, Tenn.	M	SF	H		SS	
Detroit, Mich.			SF	H	W	
Boston 20, Mass.	M			H		SS
Gulfport, Miss.				H		
Honolulu 16, Hawaii				H	W	SS
... Pa.						

Graphic Masters posters

Also in 1971, a company called Graphic Masters, run by
Bruce Hershenson and Ron Barlow, released two full color
EC posters: *Tales From the Crypt* #38 and *Vault of Horror*
#32. These measured 22" x 28" and were shot from the
original artwork with new coloring added. This was the
first uncensored publication of these particular EC covers
(apart from a few small house ads), as the original art had
been toned-down with paste-overs. Each poster cost $2.50.
The paper was uncoated (non-glossy) stock, and posters
that have been exposed to sunlight for any length of time
have not fared well, showing substantial yellowing;
carefully stored or protected posters show little or no
deterioration.

Graphic Masters posters (**Crypt** #38 and **Vault** #32): $25 each

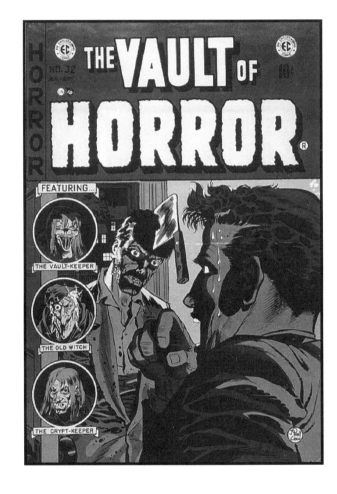

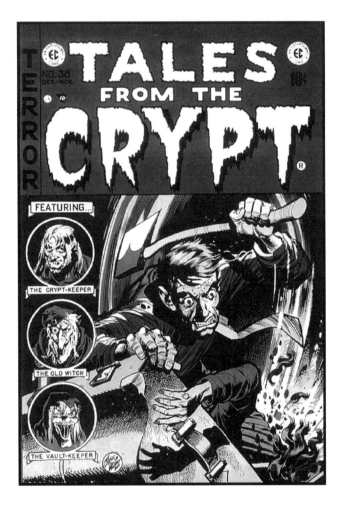

Original flyer for the Graphic Masters posters

Membership kit envelope

E. C. Fan-Addict Convention

Membership Kit

SEDUCTION of the INNOCENT

Admission badges

E. C. Fan-Addict Convention
SATURDAY
MAY 27
1972
THE VAULT-KEEPER
NAME

E. C. Fan-Addict Convention
SUNDAY
MAY 28
1972
THE OLD WITCH
NAME

E. C. Fan-Addict Convention
MONDAY
MAY 29
1972
THE CRYPT-KEEPER
NAME

EC Fan-Addict Convention 1972

Pinback button

1972 EC Fan-Addict Convention

In 1972 Bruce Hershenson and Ron Barlow produced the first and only major convention devoted solely to EC, the "EC Fan-Addict Convention." Held in New York over a Memorial Day weekend, the con had a full schedule of panel discussions, films (including the 1972 Amicus *Tales from the Crypt* film and Harvey Kurtzman's 1953 home movies showing the EC staff at play), an exhibit of original art, and the requisite dealer's room. Advance membership entitled one to a $5 discount on the *EC Horror Library* hardcover, the two Graphic Masters posters, a three day admission, a convention "progress report," and the program book *EC Lives*. A 2 1/4" convention pinback button was given at the door. Edited transcriptions of most of the discussions were later published in *Squa Tront* #8 (see section one, chapter four), along with photos taken at the con. The convention was a success, but plans to make it an annual event were abandoned. Most of the EC staff attended, with many of them participating in the panels.

EC Fan-Addict Convention: complete membership kit with button $50-$75

program $20, progress report $15, *EC Lives* book $20-$25

Convention book

1972 FAN ADDICT CONVENTION

Program

THE OLD WITCH

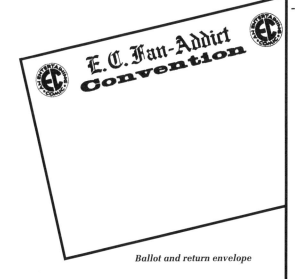

Ballot and return envelope

E.C. Fan-Addict **Convention**

E.C. Fan-Addict **Convention**
MAY 26-29, 1972

Dear E.C. Fan Addict Convention Member,

    This is to confirm receipt of your membership fee of $........
We are glad to know that you will take part in this historic event.

    This letter, however, serves another purpose. Reproduced below is the priliminary ballot for the first annual E.C. FAN ADDICT CONVENTION AWARDS. This ballot will determine the candidates on the final ballot to be voted upon at the convention itself.

    REMEMBER! you are the judge and jury, so make your decisions carefully.

**** B A L L O T ****

Print your nomination for each category in the blank space.

<u>E.C. HORROR BOOKS</u>:

    1)   Best artwork in an individual story ....
        Give name of story and artist

    2)   Best script for an individual story ....
        Give name of story only

    3)   Best overall Horror artist ....

<u>E.C. SCIENCE-FICTION BOOKS</u>:

    1)   Best artwork in an individual story ....
        Give name of story and artist

    2)   Best script for an individual story ....
        Give name of story only

    3)   Best overall Science-fiction artist ....

                  MAIL COMPLETED BALLOT TO:

                    Bruce Hershenson
                    8 Wooleys Lane
                    Great Neck, N.Y.
                        11023

Let us entertain you at the first annual...

E.C. Fan-Addict Convention

HOTEL McALPIN—NEW YORK CITY
MAY 26-29, 1972
MEMORIAL DAY WEEKEND

Membership
JOIN NOW AND ENJOY THESE BONUSES

- A $5.00 DISCOUNT ON THE E. C. HORROR LIBRARY
- FREE — 2 FULL COLOR E. C. POSTERS
- FREE — THE E. C. CONVENTION BOOK
- ADMISSION TO THE CONVENTION FOR ALL 4 DAYS
- ADMISSION TO THE MOVIE "TALES FROM THE CRYPT"

Advance registration is $7.50 until April 1, 1972. Before you drop your drool cups at this seemingly exorbitant price, wait and listen to what you get! First of all you receive RIGHT NOW in the mail both of the FULL COLOR E.C. POSTERS (by Graphic Masters), a $5.00 VALUE!! NEXT . . . . you will have the privilege of purchasing the E.C. HORROR LIBRARY book (by Nostalgia Press) at $15.00 . . . . . a $5.00 DISCOUNT!!!! (No need to wait! If you enclosed an additional $15.00 you will get your E.C. book hot off the press in the mail OR you can wait it out until the convention and buy your copy when you arrive!)

SUDDENLY the $7.50 doesn't seem like so much . . . does it?? PLUS you'll get admission to the convention for all four days, including all activities. AND.....as a SPECIAL BONUS you'll receive ABSOLUTELY FREE our really ghoulish convention book which will far surpass any of the fanzines.

After April 1, admission will be accepted on a day to day basis ONLY, ($2.00 a day) specify which day(s) you plan to attend. There will be NO MORE FREE POSTERS and NO MORE DISCOUNTS on the E.C. book and the convention book will have to be purchased separately at a cost of at least $2.00.

In consideration for those of you who may have already purchased either the posters or the E.C. Horror Library or both, you may register at the special membership fee of $5.00. This entitles you to admission for all four days as well as a free copy of the convention book. This $5.00 registration offer ends on April 1, 1972.

Supporting membership is $2.00. This entitles you to all of the progress reports and to the program book. You can convert to a full membership at any time by sending an additional $5.50.

GUESTS

At the present time the following E.C. personalities have agreed to attend the E.C. convention . . . .

BILL GAINES WILL ELDER
AL FELDSTEIN JACK DAVIS
JOHNNY CRAIG WALLY WOOD
MARIE SEVERIN JOE ORLANDO
ROY KRENKEL GEORGE EVANS
HARVEY KURTZMAN AL WILLIAMSON
JACK KAMEN

ORIGINAL E.C. ART

Through special arrangement with Bill Gaines . . . the convention will feature an entire room overflowing with ORIGINAL E.C. ART!!! Yes you heard right!! Original art will be on display by all of your favorite E.C. artists from some of the most famous E.C. stories. This will be perhaps your only opportunity to see these beautiful pages by: . . . WOOD, DAVIS, WILLIAMSON, FRAZETTA and INGELS and many others.

ACTIVITIES

Unlike most conventions, the E.C. FAN ADDICT CONVENTION will be your convention. While there will be a large dealer's room, where considerable activity will take place, this will not be the primary function of the convention. Our main concern will be to provide you with the opportunity to meet and talk with those E.C. personalities you've long admired.

FRIDAY, MAY 26

6:00 P.M. — DEALER ROOM SET-UP (Dealers Only)
GENERAL REGISTRATION (Avoid the Saturday Rush)

SATURDAY, MAY 27

9:00 A.M. — REGISTRATION BEGINS (Register before the activities begin so you won't miss a thing.)
11:00 A.M. — DEALER'S ROOM OPENS TO THE PUBLIC
1:00 P.M. — E.C. HORROR PANEL (Questions and answers with Bill Gaines, Al Feldstein, Johnny Craig, Jack Davis and Others)
4:00 P.M. — "TALES FROM THE CRYPT" movie (First Showing). Don't miss this First Run Feature Film adapting 4 E.C. stories!
5:00-6:00 P.M— DEALER'S ROOM CLOSES FOR DINNER HOUR
6:00 P.M. — E.C. WAR PANEL (Questions and answers with Harvey Kurtzman, Bill Elder, Jack Davis, George Evans and Others)
8:00 P.M. — "THE KURTZMAN MOVIES" (Actual Home movies taken back in 1953 at the E.C. Halloween Party and the E.C. Boat Cruise, featuring all of the old E.C. staff including Ghastly Graham Ingels!)
9:00 P.M. — DEALER'S ROOM CLOSES FOR THE DAY
9:30 P.M. — FIRST AUCTION (E.C. Material Only)
10:00 P.M. — "TALES FROM THE CRYPT" movie (2nd Showing)

SUNDAY, MAY 28

10:00 A.M. — DEALER'S ROOM OPENS
1:00 P.M. — E.C. SCIENCE-FICTION PANEL (Questions and answers with Bill Gaines, Al Feldstein, Wally Wood, Al Williamson, Joe Orlando, and Others)
4:00 P.M. — "TALES FROM THE CRYPT" movie (3rd Showing)
5:00-6:00 P.M.— DEALER'S ROOM CLOSES FOR DINNER HOUR
6:00 P.M. — AWARDS PRESENTATION (The first Annual E.C. Awards will be presented for best achievements in both art and script. Be sure to place your ballot at the immediate entrance of the convention.
9:00 P.M. — DEALER'S ROOM CLOSES FOR THE DAY
9:30 P.M. — 2ND AUCTION (All types of material)

MONDAY, MAY 29

10:00 A.M. — DEALER'S ROOM OPENS
1:00 P.M. — SURPRISE E.C. PANEL
5:00 P.M. — THE FIRST ANNUAL E.C. FAN-ADDICT CONVENTION WILL BE OFFICIALLY ENDED.

THE HOTEL

The convention will take place at the HOTEL MC ALPIN, located at Broadway and 34th Street in downtown Manhattan. It is only one block east of Penn Station and can be easily reached via subway.

We have obtained sensational room rates for the convention, FAR LOWER than the regular rates. In order to take advantage of these rates, however, you MUST be a member of the convention.

Postpaid reservation cards will be sent to you upon receipt of your membership fee. The rates are as follows:

SINGLE — $14.00
DOUBLE — $18.00
3 IN A ROOM — $21.00
4 IN A ROOM — $24.00

HOTEL MC ALPIN — NEW YORK CITY
MAY 26-29, 1972
MEMORIAL DAY WEEKEND

E.C. CONVENTION BOOK

No doubt you have ideas as to what a convention book is like. Usually a hastily assembled conglomeration of endless pages of ads, schedules of activities and listings of members. The E.C. Convention book will hopefully start a new trend. While the final contents are still in the planning, this first year's book will highlight the artists and writers that made E.C. what it was. For each artist and writer there will be a complete UP-TO-DATE biography, an interview, photos now and then, and reproductions of his finest E.C. art, plus added features still in the planning.

All members of the convention will receive the book FREE. Non-members will be able to obtain the book only after the convention is over. The price of the book will be at least $2.00, but the final cover price will not be set until publication.

DEALERS

There will be a spacious dealer room accommodating at least 75 3x6 tables, while there will be a huge assortment of E.C. comicbooks for sale, there will be other types of comicbooks available . . . such as is usually found at comic conventions.

Reservations for tables are now being accepted at the advance rate of $25.00 per table up until April 1, 1972. After April 1 the table rate will be $30.00 per table. The placement of your table(s) will be determined on a first come — first serve basis starting at the immediate entrance to the dealers room. Reservations for all tables or requests for additional information is to be sent to:

BRUCE HERSHENSON
8 Wooleys Lane
Great Neck, N.Y. 11023

E. C. FAN-ADDICT CONVENTION
2623 Silver Court
East Meadow, N.Y. 11554

( ) Find $7.50 registration
( ) Find $22.50 for E.C. Book and registration
( ) Find $5.00 registration
( ) Find $2.00 for supporting membership

Name
Address
City _____ State _____ Zip Code _____

original flyer announcing convention

EC Masks of the "Three GhouLunatics"

One of the more imaginative items to be offered at the 1972 convention were these plastic "life masks" of the hosts of the horror comics. Commissioned by Dave Gibson, the masks were sculpted by Bob Cabeen and measure about 9" x 15". They were available in two versions: clear plastic at $15 per set, or in extremely limited hand-painted (by Cabeen) sets. The price on this version is no longer certain. About 200 of the clear plastic sets were made; about six were hand-painted. Gibson recalls that he never got around to signing a contract with Gaines for the masks, and Gaines told security not to let Gibson into the convention without a fully-executed agreement. Contracts were duly signed, and the masks were allowed to take their place in EC history.

EC Masks: set of three, unpainted
$50-$75

set of three, painted:
no reported sales

"Old Witch" mask (1985)

This latex "half head" mask of the Old Witch was made in 1985 as a prototype for an intended set of three GhouLunatics. Fashioned by Steve Fiorilla of East Arlington, Mass., Death Studios of LaPorte, Indiana (run by Jeff Keim) made test molds in anticipation of a full production run, but the masks were never made. Evidently, Gaines liked it, but could not grant the rights as Joel Silver, Walter Hill and company already had options on all three GhouLunatics as part of the deal that led to the HBO *Tales From the Crypt* series. A single painted mask was completed; some unfinished test models also exist.

Old Witch Mask: no reported sales

CHAPTER ELEVEN

Amicus Films' *Tales From the Crypt* and *Vault of Horror* films

In 1972, Amicus Films, a British production house, released a feature film anthology of five stories taken from EC's horror comics, entitled *Tales From the Crypt*. The cast included Peter Cushing, Nigel Patrick, Patrick Magee, Joan Collins and Sir Ralph Richardson as the Crypt Keeper, and the film enjoyed good reviews and revenues. The following year Amicus released a sequel entitled *The Vault of Horror*, with Terry-Thomas and Glynis Johns, but this film was not as well received either critically or at the box office. As with all films, a number of promotional items exist.

Tales from the Crypt (Amicus Films): one sheet $30, lobby cards $5 each, stills $2.50 each

Tales from the Crypt paperback novelization (Jack Oleck): $5

Vault of Horror, The (Amicus Films): one sheet $25, lobby cards $5 each, stills $2.50 each

Vault of Horror, The home video (Nostalgia Merchant): $15

Vault of Horror, The paperback novelization (Jack Oleck): $5

There are eight different color lobby cards (in two different sizes) and a number of black and white stills showing scenes from the film.

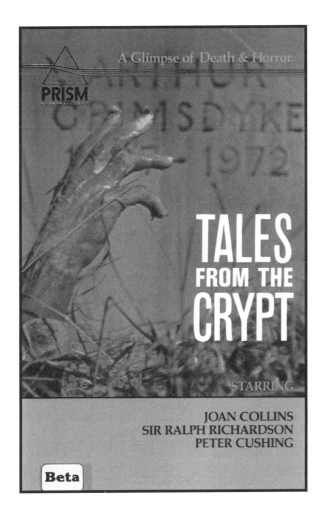

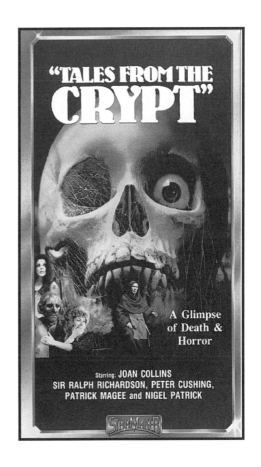

Two different home video tapes of *Tales From the Crypt*; the version on the right is a budget tape that is still available at $9.99, quite a bargain considering the earlier version (on left) listed for about $75.

Novelizations of *Tales from the Crypt* and *The Vault of Horror* by sometime EC script writer Jack Oleck.

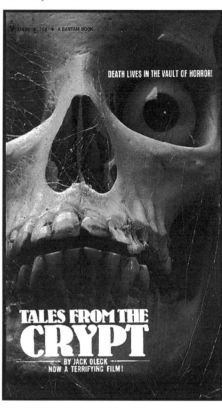

★ PAGE 9

THE OLD WITCH

THE VAULT KEEPER

THE CRYPT KEEPER

The yarn-spinning trio of horrendous hosts in the E.C. comic line-up

SIR RALPH RICHARDSON
The cinematic version of the Crypt Keeper

MOVIES

The Creative Horror of E.C. Now Haunts the Film Crypt

By John Stanley

THERE WAS a period, in the early 1950s, when the practice of pictorial storytelling in four colors reached a pinnacle of art — at least art within the limited domain of the ten-cent comic book. The publishing house responsible for these offbeat magazines was called Entertaining Comics (shortened to E.C. by its editors and fans) and, unlike the funny animals and superhero rags of that day, they dealt with adult themes that were written and drawn by some of the best illustrators then in the business.

While E.C.'s "new trend" themes included suspense, science-fiction, war and satiric humor, it was really the horror titles that left the deepest impact on young and old alike.

Publisher W. C. Gaines is usually given credit for Mad magazine and the E.C. line, but it was Harvey Kurtzman who created Mad and it was really the ingenuity of Alfred Feldstein, writer and artist, that breathed freshness and innovation into the pages of "Tales From the Crypt" and "The Haunt of Fear." Johnny Craig handled "The Vault of Horror" and stayed up to Feldstein's high writing and artwork standards.

If the morbidity had a tongue-in-cheek quality that went over the heads of the kids, it was savored by the thousands of adults who faithfully read these magazines from 1950-55.

(Ironic that despite their very moral attitude, and their involvement with themes of bigotry and social injustice in "Shock Suspenstories," E. C. Comics were to be attacked for their liberal viewpoints and banned from most newsstands during the comic book witch hunt of 1954. When the new Comics Code was formed, E.C. died. With them died an era of innovation and creativity.)

Now, however, Amicus Films of England has chosen five of the E.C. horror tales and produced "Tales From the Crypt," which is currently at the Warfield. Although not in strict keeping with the format of the magazines, the tales are told by the Crypt Keeper (played by Sir Ralph Richardson, if you can believe that). Each retains most of the plotting techniques of Feldstein and Craig and, in some episodes, an attempt has been made to duplicate the horror, panel by panel.

"... And All Through the House" (Vault of Horror No. 35, Feb.-March 1954), drawn by Johnny Craig, Joanna Clayton has just "whomped" her husband to death with a poker on Christmas Eve, while daughter Carol dreams of sugar plums in her upstairs room. As Joanna is getting rid of the corpse, a radio newscaster reports an escaped homicidal maniac in the area, dressed in a Santa Claus suit. Sure enough, a man in a Santa Claus suit promptly knocks on the door. Frantically, Joanna rushes to lock all the doors and windows. She sighs with relief, feeling she's safe. In the E.C. tradition, the ending is a snapper.

"Reflection of Death" (Tales From the Crypt No. 23, April-May 1951), drawn by Alfred Feldstein. Al and Carl are speeding through the night when suddenly a car hits them head-on. When Al awakens, lying by the side of the road, there is no sign of Carl or the wreck. He seeks help, but each time a passer-by screams and flees — even a tramp. Al, who is never shown in the panels (the point-of-view technique is used), finally makes his way to Carl's house, where he finds his friend blind, having survived a car accident two months before. Horrified, Al goes to a mirror to find a decomposed face staring back at him. It is then Al wakes up in the car . . . the whole thing was a nightmare. But the tale doesn't end there . . . as usual, Feldstein has his double twist ending.

"Poetic Justice" (Haunt of Fear No. 12, March-April 1952), drawn by Graham 'Ghastly' Ingels, an artist still master of horrendous, grotesque style. A friendly garbage collector in a small town is loved by everyone for his kindliness until the town's richest man and his son decide they want the oldtimer's property. They begin a campaign that turns the entire town against the garbage man, culminating on St. Valentine's Day when several insulting Valentine cards are sent to the old man. His world completely shattered, he hangs himself. One year later, the old man rises from his grave in moldy fashion and . . . well, the millionaire is in for a St. Valentine's Day surprise of his own as only Feldstein could have imagined it.

"Wish You Were Here" (Haunt of Fear No. 22, November-December 1953), also drawn by Ingels. This is a variation on Jacobs' "The Monkey's Paw," in which a couple on the verge of bankruptcy realize an old jade statuette in their collection of objets d'art has the power to grant three wishes. The first is for money, whereupon the husband is killed in a car crash and the wife enriched by a double indemnity insurance policy clause. Not wanting to make the same mistake as the characters in "Monkey's Paw" (asking that a rotting corpse return from the grave), she selects her last two wishes with care . . . but, of course, the tables are turned. In some ways, Feldstein's ending surpasses Jacobs' for its horror.

"Blind Alleys" (Tales From the Crypt No. 46, February - March 1955), drawn by George Evans. The setting is a rundown, terribly managed home for the blind. The food is rotten, rats scamper down the hallways, heating and sanitation are inadequate, and the cruel director delights in teasing the patients, sometimes tripping them in the corridors. The director and his vicious dog are finally locked in separate cells as the patients begin constucting a weird labyrinth of horror. The director is set loose in this passageway, the walls of which are embedded with thousands of razor blades.

Amicus is one of today's most respected producers of horror films, in some ways surpassing Hammer's horrific capabilities. Among Amicus past hits are "Torture Garden" and "The House That Dripped Blood," both based on short stories by Robert Bloch.

The gore and blood are excessive but in relative taste. Production standards are high, and in the case of "Tales From the Crypt" the attention to atmospheric detail results in a first-rate horror film.

Americans may have been responsible for the original E.C. stories, but it took the British to bring them to the screen in a suitable fashion. Since there are scores of more E.C. stories, let us hope a film of this kind becomes an annual offering from the people at Amicus.

DECAYING CORPSE, as drawn by Alfred Feldstein in the pages of E.C. comics, has been duplicated to perfection by Peter Cushing (right) in Amicus' "Tales From the Crypt"

Datebook, Sunday, March 19, 1972.

A full page review of *Tales From the Crypt* from the *San Francisco Examiner,* Sunday, March 19, 1972.

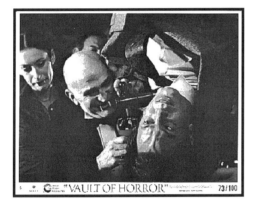

As with *Tales From the Crypt*, there are eight different color lobby cards (in two different sizes) and a number of black and white stills for *The Vault of Horror*.

A home video of *The Vault of Horror* was released in 1981 by Nostalgia Merchant; this company was absorbed into another in the mid-'80s and the title has been unavailable since.

HBO's *Tales From the Crypt*

In 1989 producer Joel Silver (*48 Hours, Die Hard*) contracted with Home Box Office for a *Tales from the Crypt* television series. Directors such as Bob Zemekis, Richard Donner and Walter Hill have directed segments of the show, and actors have included Beau Bridges, John Astin, Demi Moore, Joe Pesci, Don Rickles, Sandra Bernhard, and Carol Kane. Numerous 8" x 10" black and white publicity stills have been issued, and several videotape collections were released for sale by HBO video, along with a "one sheet" style poster. The full color brochure sent to retailers about the first of these videos contains three mock-up *Tales from the Crypt* covers done for the series, illustrated by Mike Vosburg. In 1992 Big Screen Records released a soundtrack album of music from the series.

Tales from the Crypt, HBO: poster $10, stills $2.50, home video $30, soundtrack CD $12

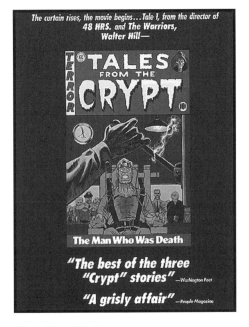

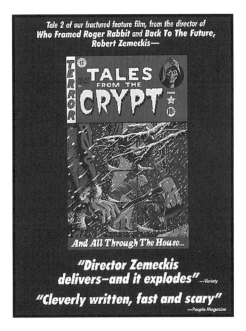

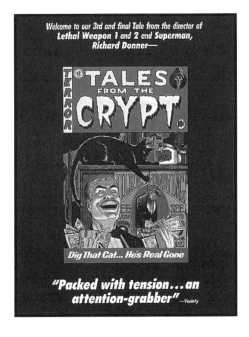

Two-Fisted Tales
Another Joel Silver production, the *Two-Fisted Tales* two-episode pilot aired on the Fox network in 1992. The series apparently has not yet sold.

Other film related items:

Creepshow
Horror novelist Stephen King conceived the 1982 film *Creepshow* as an homage to EC's horror comics, down to the twist endings and ghoulish retribution. A magazine sized comic book based on the film had interior art by Berni Wrightson and had a specially-commissioned cover by EC stalwart Jack Kamen. A pre-release one-sheet poster has the same Kamen art. A sequel, *Creepshow II*, was released in 1987 with a similar format, but no comic version was released, nor were any EC artists involved in rendering the promotional materials.

Creepshow: pre-release one sheet $25

comic book (first printing) $15-$20

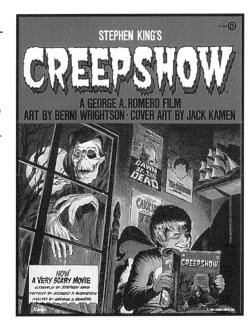

Comic Book Confidential
Canadian filmmaker Ron Mann directed this 1989 documentary about comics and their creators. Gaines is featured in several interview segments, and black and white newsreel footage of his testimony before the Senate Subcommittee on Juvenile Delinquency in 1954 appears. Also included are interviews with Al Feldstein and Harvey Kurtzman. The one-sheet movie poster for the film (with Paul Mavrides art) is quite attractive, and a promotional pinback button with the likeness of Alfred E. Neuman was also made. A home video of the film was released in 1991 by Streamline Pictures, and Voyager is releasing a CD-ROM version as well.

Comic Book Confidential: one sheet $20, button $15-$20, home video $25

While the City Sleeps
In what is probably the first appearance of EC on film, the cover to *Tales From the Crypt* #32 appears in this 1956 Fritz Lang *film noir* classic; John Barrymore, Jr., playing a psychopath, is shown reading the issue.

Psychoanalysis
Steve Allen adapted two stories from *Psychoanalysis* to live TV in 1955 or '56; a full page ad appeared in *Variety* with various psychologists and other professionals offering praise for the work.

The Fisherman
This 1966 short film was based on "Gone...Fishing" from *The Vault of Horror* #22. The film was shown at theatres in New York, Hollywood, and elsewhere. *The Fisherman* was an unauthorized production, which Gaines discovered quite by accident while sitting at the movies one night. As the film unreeled, Gaines got more and more uneasy as he realized that the story was one he and Feldstein had concocted years before. Gaines sued, and the hapless producers were compelled to put in an "adapted from EC Comics" credit and pay Gaines's legal fees. In spite of its dubious origins, *The Fisherman* was the first theatrical film to be adapted from an EC story.

EC-related Videos
Masters of Comic Book Art, The, Rhino Video, 1987, H. Kurtzman interview, *Mad* #1 shown on cover

The Masters of Comic Book Art: $20

Underground Comix homages to EC

EC's horror, crime, science fiction and humor comics had a great influence on many of the underground and alternative comix creators, and many of these artists returned the favor by producing covers, stories and entire issues of comix that were inspired by (or parodied) EC. A sampling follows:

Underground Comix homages to EC various issues, average price $5-$20

Boogeyman #1

Tales from the Tube #1

The Barn of Fear #1

Weird Fantasies #1

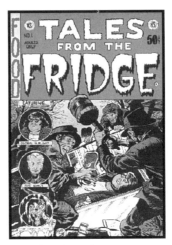

Tales from the Fridge #1

Bijou #8

Mod #1

Death Rattle #4

Harold Hedd #2

Skull #4

Skull #6

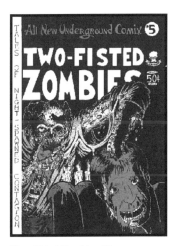

Two-Fisted Zombies #5

Four-Fisted Tales #1

Slow Death #5

Slow Death #6

Slow Death #7

Normalman #3

CHAPTER THiRTEEN

EC T-shirts

A number of EC-related T-shirts have been issued over the years. The first were offered at the 1972 convention; they were white with a red and black logo, manufactured by a company called Cheez Louize. Shirts of the same design were later offered in the East Coast Comix reprints at $3.00 each.

Another shirt at the convention was for the staff. These shirts were orange with the EC emblem on the front and the Vault Keeper (reading *Seduction of the Innocent*) on the back. Only about two dozen were made.

Russ Cochran produced a T-shirt picturing the cover to *Weird Science* #16 in the mid-1980s, selling for $15.

A *Tales From the Crypt* shirt was made for the HBO series; these were given to the staff, and used as prizes in a 900 number telephone game (you dialed "900-CRYPT" to answer questions about the series and horror books and movies).

Cheez Louize T-shirt: $65

EC Fan-Addict Convention staff
T-shirt: no reported sales

Weird Science #16 T-shirt: $15

HBO *Tales from the Crypt*
T-shirt: $25

Arnold Schwarzenegger wears a Tales from the
Crypt *shirt while hanging out with the "Crypt
Keeper." Schwarzenegger directed an episode
of the HBO series.*

CHAPTER FOURTEEN

The Complete EC Library

In 1978 Russ Cochran announced that he and Gaines had reached an agreement to reprint the entire EC line in hardcover volumes, packaged in illustrated slipcases. Complete titles were to be offered; all covers were to be reproduced in color with the stories in black and white. Prices ran from about $50 to $120, depending on the number of volumes in a particular set and when the books were purchased. The news was met with excitement and some skepticism that such a project could be completed. Happily, all titles are now in print with the exception of the Pre-Trend romance and western volumes. Also offered were sets of the color covers, suitable for framing, packaged in white, illustrated envelopes. Prices ran between $4 and $15 a set. (The *Mad* comics set was issued in two versions; one with black and white interior pages [1,000 sets], and one with full color interior pages [10,000 sets]. Covers to *Mad* #7-12 were botched at the printer, so Cochran sent these mis-prints as a gift to his ever-patient subscribers. A softbound edition of *Mad* #1-6 was issued in 1991 with new covers at $20, with other volumes to appear if sales warrant. 16,000 copies of this softbound edition were printed.)

The Complete EC Library: all titles still in print (except black and white **Mad** set): $175

Mad mis-printed cover set: in envelope: $10-$20

Mad #1-6 softcover: still in print at $20

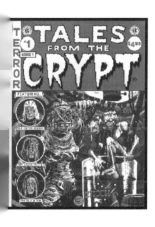

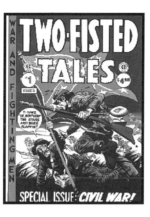
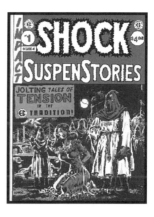

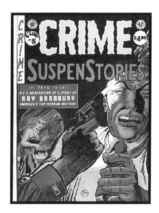

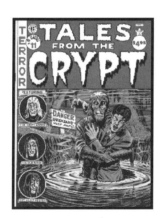

EC Classics

In response to complaints about the price of the Complete EC Library sets, and the lack of interior color, in August, 1985 Cochran began publishing a companion comic book line entitled EC Classics. Selling for $4.95, these 8 1/2" x 11" magazines had heavy cover stock and used quality white paper for the color interior pages. The series lasted twelve issues, terminating in 1989. Early issues reprinted stories selected at random (with eight stories and two covers per issue), but later numbers reprinted specific EC issues (again two per issue). Unlike the Complete EC Library, none of these books reprinted original EC letter pages or house ads. Also available for $5 was an illustrated EC Classics cardboard display stand.

EC Classics: #1 $8 #2-12 still in print at $4.95 each

EC Classics display stand: $5-$10

CHAPTER FOURTEEN

EC Original Art Auctions

Because of the agreement to reprint the entire line in *The Complete EC Library*, in 1979 Gaines decided to sell the original art at auction, with Cochran handling the catalogs and sales. As each EC title was published, the artwork was offered for sale, first through seven issues of an "Original Art List," begun in 1979. These were replaced by the "Comic Art Auction" catalogs, which began in 1980. The catalogs are also worth collecting, for all the covers and the splash pages of individual stories are reprinted (in black and white), along with a "prices realized" list from the prior auction. All pieces sold through Cochran's auctions have rubber-stamped copyright notices on the page backs.

Auction catalogs: $3 each

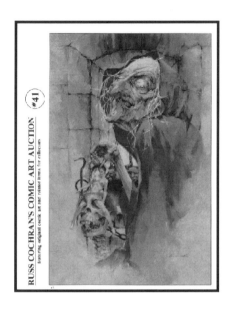

Auction catalogs

Original cover art to *Crime SuspenStories* #2 (Johnny Craig)

EC-inspired Oil Paintings

Johnny Craig was commissioned to paint several EC-inspired oil paintings in the mid-1970s. Two were sold through Cochran's auction in 1985 (one appears as the cover of *Squa Tront* #9). Craig later produced an oil re-creation of the cover to *Vault of Horror* #23 for the Sotheby's Comic Art Auction held December 18, 1991; the pre-auction estimate was $1,500-$2,000, and the piece went for $1,760 ($1,600 plus 10% Sotheby's surcharge). For the September 30, 1992, Sotheby's auction Craig contributed a re-creation of his cover to *Vault of Horror* #17. In addition, Craig was commissioned by the author to do a painting featuring the Three GhouLunatics and Drusilla; this piece, entitled "Group Portrait," was completed in December of 1991. A second commission, featuring the GhouLunatics and Drusilla stretching Alfred E. Neuman on a rack, was completed in November 1992.

Johnny Craig oil paintings: $1,500-$2,200

Johnny Craig

Graham Ingels

Graham Ingels, after decades of seclusion, agreed in 1989 to produce oil paintings featuring "The Old Witch" for sale through the Cochran auctions; four large and ten smaller works were sold through February 1991 (Ingels died April 4, 1991).

Graham Ingels oil paintings: large size $5,000 to $7,500, smaller size $1,000 to $2,100

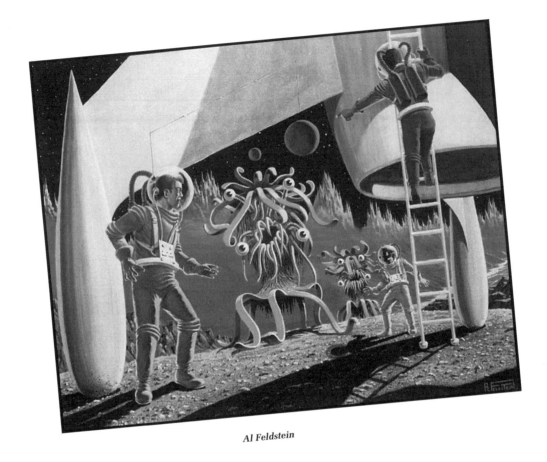

Al Feldstein

Al Feldstein did an oil painting especially for the Sotheby's December 18, 1991 auction, re-creating the cover to *Weird Fantasy* #15. It marked the first time Feldstein offered a piece for sale, and the pre-auction estimate was $5,000-$8,000; the painting sold the day after the auction for just under the $5,000 reserve. For the September 30, 1992 Sotheby's auction Feldstein created two more oil paintings: a re-creation of the cover to *Weird Science* #8, and a panorama of an alien landscape. These sold at $4,125 and $4,400 (includes 10% Sotheby's surcharge). For the June 26, 1993 Sotheby's auction three more pieces were offered: re-creations of the covers to *Weird Fantasy* #8 and 16, and a vertical alien landscape. The June 18, 1994 Sotheby's auction saw two more Feldstein pieces: re-creations of the covers to *Weird Fantasy* #13 and *Tales from the Crypt* #24.

Al Feldstein oil paintings: $4,000 to $5,000

Will Elder also did a new oil painting for the September 30, 1992 Sotheby's auction, re-creating his cover to *Mad* #5. Due to a copyright question, the painting had to be withdrawn.

Wallace Wood re-created his covers to *Weird Science* #14 and 15 in 1978 for the Collector's Bookstore/Howard Lowery auction. The covers were done in India ink and watercolor.

Wallace Wood cover re-creations: no resales reported

George Evans also did a piece for the Collector's Bookstore/Howard Lowery auction in 1978, re-creating his cover to *Crime SuspenStories* #23. This was done in India ink and watercolor as well.

George Evans cover re-creation: no resales reported

CHAPTER FiFTEEN

Foreign EC Reprints

EC comics have been reprinted in a number of countries and in several formats. The first to appear were issued by Superior Comics in Canada during the 1950s. The printing was generally poor. Contrary to previous reports, the negative asbestos matrices used in printing the American ECs were sent to Canada by EC's printer. Once in Canada, a new set of rotary plates was made for the Canadian editions. Gaines guessed that the poor reproduction was due more to shoddy printing than re-using the asbestos mats. According to the *Overstreet Price Guide*, Pre-Trend and New Trend reprints exist, but no New Direction titles have been seen, nor any reprints after January 1954.

The most interesting Canadian reprint is the title *Weird SuspenStories*, which juxtaposes logos from *Weird Fantasy* and *Crime SuspenStories*. The hybrid lasted three issues. The Canadian ECs had print runs of about 30,000. U.S. print runs were between 250,000-450,000.

Canadian EC comics (1950s): price about half of U. S. editions, see *Overstreet Price Guide*

According to the 1984 book *A Haunt of Fears* by Martin Barker (a study of the British anti-comics movement in the 1950s), one issue each of *Tales from the Crypt*, *The Haunt of Fear*, and possibly *The Vault of Horror* were published in Britain by Arnold in 1954; these books are extremely rare.

Arnold EC reprints (1954): no reported sales

L. Miller and Co., an English firm, reprinted some EC New Trend stories in the late 1950s in black and white 68 page comics, under the titles *Mystic*, *Black Magic*, and *Zombie*. L. Miller also reprinted some EC New Direction stories around 1960 under the titles *Spellbound* and *Mystic*.

L. Miller and Co. comics with EC stories: $5-$10

After the demise of EC, the metal plates of all the New Trend comics were sold to Una Revista Publications in Mesones, Mexico for $2,000. Mexican reprints began to appear around 1957 under the titles *Historietas* and *Cuentos de Abuelito*. As recently as 1972, EC stories appeared in Mexican comic books; the issue of *Aventuras* shown has a Frank Frazetta "art swipe" cover (from *Famous Funnies*), and reprints Wood's "My World." An issue of the title *Episodios* from the same time period reprints the Jack Davis story "Witch Witch's Witch" from *The Vault of Horror* #36.

Mexican EC reprint comics: $15

A series of six hardcover reprint volumes was issued in France between 1983 and 1985 by Xanadu under the titles *Les Meillures Histoires de Science Fiction*, *Les Meillures Histoires de Terreur*, *Les Meillures Histoires de Horreur*, *Les Meillures Histoires de Suspence*, *Les Meillures Histoires de Guerre Corree*, and *Les Meillures Histoires de Aventures*. These volumes appear to have been shot from Cochran's *Complete EC Library*, with translated text. Material from *Squa Tront* also appears.

Xanadu French EC reprint hardcovers: $35 each

Another French publisher, Albin Michel, produced two hardcovers of EC Ray Bradbury adaptations in 1984 and 1985, under the titles *Planete Rouge* and *Monsieur Sourire*. In 1975 Albin Michel published a history of American comics, *Comics U.S.A.*, including a 13-page chapter on EC, with panel reproductions.

Planete Rouge: $35

Monsieur Sourire: $35

Comics U.S.A.: $15-$20

Monsieur Sourire was released as a trade paperback in Brazil (in smaller size and fewer stories) as *O Papa-defuntos* in 1990, with Portuguese text. A companion volume with the remaining stories was issued in 1991 as *O Pequeno Assassino*.

O Papa-defuntos: $20

O Pequeno Assassino: $20

CHAPTER FiFTEEN

Norbert Hethke Verlag, a German publisher, began issuing a series of reprints under the name *Phantastische Geschichten* in 1986. Volumes one through four are black and white hardbounds with color covers; from volume five they are color softbound books. Seven issues have appeared as of this writing.

Phantastische Geschichten: #1-4 $35 each, #5-7 $20 each

Also from Germany, this 1973 8 1/2" x 11" trade paperback, *Der Beste Horror Aller Zeiten*, contains material shot from the Nostalgia Press *EC Horror Library*.

Der Beste Horror Aller Zeiten: $35

Material from the Nostalgia Press *EC Horror Library* was released in 1973 in four Scandanavian countries as *Den Store Skraek Bog, Nacht der Vampiers, Jatti Kauhu Kirja,* and *Stora Skrack Boken*; all four softcover books had similar covers and formats, with translated text.

Den Store Skraek Bog, Nacht der Vampiers, Jatti Kauhu Kirja, and *Stora Skrack Boken*: $35 each

Framed poster from *Iskalde Gross* (from issue #3 of 1988)

A series of Norwegian comic book-size reprints was begun in 1987 titled *Iskalde Gross (Ice Cold Shivers)*. These 66-page books appear eight times a year and have color covers with black and white interiors. Numbering starts over at #1 each year. Two magazine-size paperbound *Iskalde Gross* albums have appeared, with color interior pages.

Iskalde Gross: $4-$5 each

Iskalde Gross album #1 and 2: $10-$20 each

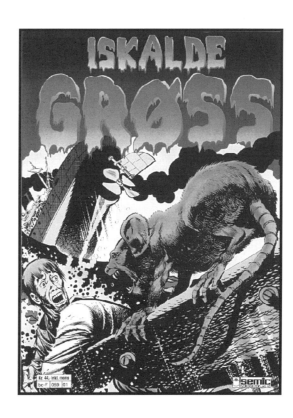

Also from Norway, the black and white comic book *Fantomet (The Phantom)* has reprinted stories from *Piracy* under the heading "Pirater!" These stories began appearing in 1990.

Fantomet, reprints from *Piracy*: $3 each

Swedish reprints, titled *Kalla Karar*, had a four issue run in 1990. The books are 52-page comic books, with color covers and black and white interiors. They were published for the Swedish market by a former publisher of the Norwegian *Mad*; the publisher's death ended the series.

Kalla Karar #1-4: $4-$5 each

From Spain, this issue of *Historia de los Comics* is devoted to EC, and features many reprints in full color.

Historia de los Comics, EC issue: $10-$20

Brazilian EC reprints were begun in 1991 under the title *Cripta do Terror*. These magazine-size books have black and white interiors with color covers and were produced by the publisher of the Brazilian *Mad*. Seven issues were released.

Cripto do Terror: $4-$5

Opiumdroom, a softcover collection of some of Bernard Krigstein's EC work, was published in the Netherlands in 1990.

Opiumdroom: $10-$20

An Italian edition titled *Il Popolo Dell'Autunno/ Domani A Mezzanotte*, containing translations of *The Autumn People* and *Tomorrow Midnight* was published by Oscar Mondadori in 1972.

Il Popolo Dell'Autunno/Domani A Mezzanotte: $20

The Italian fanzine *Exploit Comics* has done two issues devoted to EC, both with complete stories. Issue #27 appeared in November, 1982 and #43 appeared in March 1988. Both are oversize publications with color covers and black and white interiors.

Exploit Comics #27 and #43 (EC issues): $10-$20 each

In 1991 a series of magazine-size Italian EC reprints began under the titles *I Racconti del Terror* and *Fantascienza*; these 48-page books had color covers and black and white interiors. The series failed after nine and seven issues, respectively. Another reprint series, *Frontline Combat*, was in squarebound format and also were 48 pages; the series ended after seven issues.

I Racconti del Terror: $4-$5

Fantascienza: $4-$5

Frontline Combat (Italian): $4-$5

Gladstone EC Reprints

In 1990 Gladstone Publishing began a series of color comic book-size reprints; each issue reprinted two EC comics. The first titles were *Tales from the Crypt, The Vault of Horror,* and *Weird Science.* After four issues, the *Weird Science* title was moved to a backup position and was replaced with *The Haunt of Fear*, which lasted two issues. The line debuted at $1.95 and moved to $2.00 after several issues. Some of the stories were altered slightly in an effort to "modernize" them, which resulted in an outcry from the purists. Gladstone, a partnership between Bruce Hamilton and Cochran, had been successfully issuing Disney reprint comics for a number of years; when its license with Disney expired the company decided to keep its production machine running via the EC reprints. After 18 issues (about a year's time), Cochran persuaded Gaines to revoke Gladstone's license, citing "editorial differences" with Hamilton. Rights to future EC reprints were awarded to Cochran (see *Extra-Large Comics* and "Russ Cochran EC reprint comics").

Gladstone EC reprints: $3-$4 each

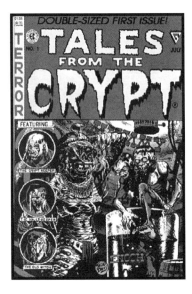
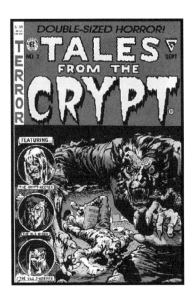
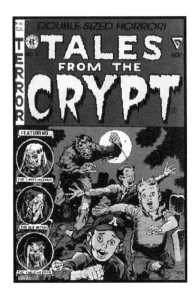
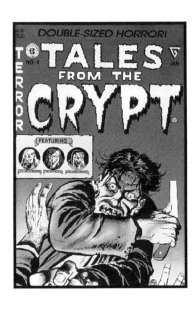

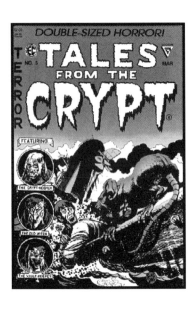
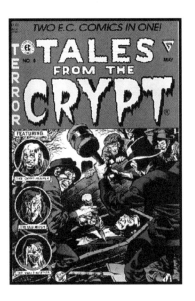

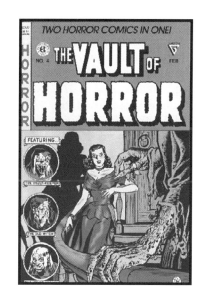

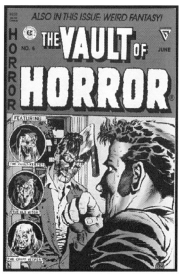

Extra-Large Comics and Russ Cochran EC reprint comics

After Gaines pulled the plug on the Gladstone reprints, Cochran announced a new series called *Extra-Large Comics*. The intention was to proportion the line of color oversize comics (10 1/4" x 13 1/4") to the size of the person reading them. Retailer and consumer resistance killed the series after one issue, *Tales from the Crypt* #1 (July 1991, $3.95). The book is impressive, and Cochran has stated that like many EC beings, the *Extra-Large* EC comics may rise again.

Extra-Large Comics/Tales from the Crypt #1: $5

Cochran returned to the standard comic book size with new first issues of *Tales from the Crypt*, *The Vault of Horror* and *The Haunt of Fear*, all cover dated September 1991 (This *Tales From the Crypt* #1 contains the same material as the *Extra-Large Tales from the Crypt* #1.) These books reprint two comics and sell for $2.00 each. The comics were disseminated via direct distribution and to newsstands. Newsstand copies have a UPC symbol on the front cover. The books did well in comic shops but not at newsstands, so after 17 issues Cochran abandoned the format, and announced yet another line of reprints.

Russ Cochran EC reprint comics: all issues, $2-$3 each

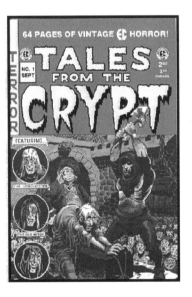 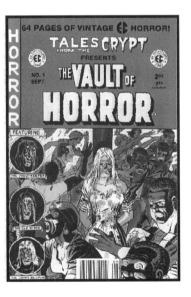 

The new Cochran EC reprint comics (begun in 1992) are distributed via direct distribution only, and the plan is to reprint all the EC titles as originally issued, in chronological order. *Tales from the Crypt, Weird Science,* and *Shock SuspenStories* were the first titles to appear; the books are issued on a quarterly schedule. The price for each thirty-two page issue is $2.00 (the first few issues were priced at $1.50), and five issue sets re-bound in softcover sell for $8.95. Cochran sold his business to Steve Geppi's Gemstone Publishing in 1994; under the terms of the agreement, Russ will stay on as publisher.

Russ Cochran EC reprint comics: all issues, $2-$3 each

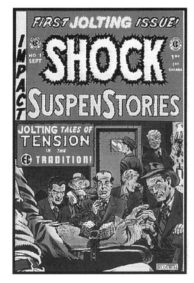

8" x 36" promo poster for
Cochran EC reprint comics

Tales from the Crypt paperback adaptations

In 1991 Random House released a set of three *Tales from the Crypt* paperback books adapting stories to prose (for younger readers), written by Eleanor Fremont and Richard Wenk. New covers by Jack Davis and illustrations taken from the original comics complement the text. The books retail for $2.99. Three more volumes in the series were released in 1992: volumes four and five of *Tales from the Crypt* and *Jokes from the Crypt*, again with covers by Davis. Two different point-of-purchase display stands were created for the 1992 volumes, along with a *Tales from the Crypt* promotional sticker.

Tales from the Crypt paperback adaptations (Random House): $3 each

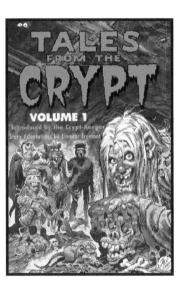
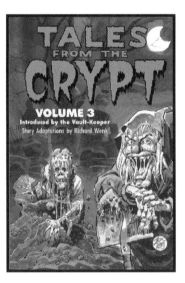
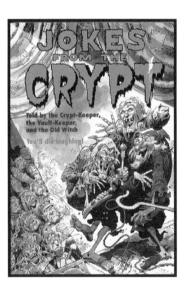

Tales from the Crypt 16 month calendar

Released by Sterling Calendars of Novato, California, the calendar features 13 photos of the Crypt Keeper taken from the HBO *Tales from the Crypt* series. The calendar ran from September 1991 through December 1992 and cost $10.95.

Tales from the Crypt 16 month calendar: $10.95

CHAPTER SEVENTEEN

The Gaines EC File Copies

In 1968, it became known (via *Squa Tront* #2) that Gaines saved 12 copies of every EC New Trend comic. In August 1989, Cochran and Robert Overstreet (publisher of the *Overstreet Price Guide*) met at Gaines's apartment to open the boxes and prepare the comics for sale. The books were in mint condition, even retaining the smell of fresh ink. Some of the packets had been depleted over the years, containing between seven and eleven copies. In the case of *The Vault of Horror* #12 (the first issue), there was only one. Cochran began selling single issues on October 15, 1990, and in the first week over $100,000 worth were sold, at roughly three times *Guide*. Complete runs were offered for sale in April 1991, with set prices roughly four times *Guide*. A Certificate of Authenticity, initialed by Gaines, Cochran, and Overstreet is issued with every file copy sold; a pair of film editor's gloves are also provided. Archival cases for storing the comics are also available

Gaines EC File Copies: single issues, roughly two to three times *Overstreet Price Guide*; sets, four times

Five Gaines File Copy ECs, with initialed certificates and film editor's gloves.

Other items of interest:

"The Boogeyman" by Stephen King

The short story "The Boogeyman" from the March, 1973, *Cavalier*, collected in King's 1978 anthology *Night Shift*, contains the following EC-related passage (found on page 102 of the hardcover edition):
"I had a dream," Billings said. "I was in a dark room and there was something I couldn't...couldn't quite see, in the closet. It made a noise...a squishy noise. It reminded me of a comic book I read when I was a kid. Tales from the Crypt, you remember that? Christ! They had a guy named Graham Ingles [sic]; he could draw every god-awful thing in the world–and some out of it."

Books with sections on EC Comics

Books with sections on EC Comics: various, average price $20

A Haunt of Fears, Martin Barker, Pluto Press, London, 1984, study of British anti-comics drive, EC covered

All in Color for a Dime, Don Thompson and Dick Lupoff, Arlington House, 1970, chapter on comics pioneer M.C. Gaines

Art of Al Williamson, The, by James Van Hise, 1983, Blue Dolphin Enterprises, Gaines interviewed, EC art repros

Art of Jack Davis, The, by Hank Harrison, Stabur Press, 1987, lists Davis's EC work with some art repros

Comic Book Book, The, Don Thompson and Dick Lupoff, Arlington House, 1973, chapter on EC with several cover repros

Comic Book in America, The by Mike Benton, Taylor Publishing, 1989, section on and cover repros from EC comics

Comic Book Makers, The, by Joe Simon, Crestwood/II Publications, 1990, Gaines's 1954 Senate subcommittee testimony covered

Comic Books as History by Joseph Witek, University Press of Mississippi, 1989, EC discussed

Comix, The, by Les Daniels, Outerbridge and Dienstfrey, E.P. Dutton, 1971, chapter on EC and many art repros

Crawford's Encyclopedia of Comics by Hubert H. Crawford, Jonathan David Publishers, 1978, many art repros but full of factual errors

Crime Comics: The Illustrated History, by Mike Benton, Taylor Publishing, 1992, chapter on EC with repros

Danse Macabre by Stephen King, Everest House, 1981, book length analysis of horror, EC discussed

Fish Whistle by Daniel Pinkwater, 1989, short chapter on author's experiences with *Mad* comics

From ARRGH to ZAP!, A Visual History of Comics by H. Kurtzman, Prentice Hall Press, 1991, EC and *Mad* reprints

Great Comic Book Artists, The, Vol. 1, by Ron Goulart, St. Martin's Press, 1986, bios and art repros of various EC artists

Great Comic Book Artists, The, Vol. 2, by Ron Goulart, St. Martin's Press, 1989, bios and art repros of various EC artists

Great Comics Game, The, Price/Stern/Sloan, 1966, quiz book, EC "GhouLunatics" pictured

Great History of Comic Books by Ron Goulart, 1986, EC covered

Hey Look! by Harvey Kurtzman, Kitchen Sink Press, 1992, shows cover of *Two Fisted Tales* #30 on back cover

Horror Comics: The Illustrated History, by Mike Benton, Taylor Publishing, 1991, chapter on EC with repros

International Book of Comics, The, by Denis Gifford, Crescent Books, 1984, sections on and repros from EC comics

Marvel: Five Fabulous Decades..., by Les Daniels, Abrams, 1991, section on EC's influence on Atlas (Marvel)

Masters of Comic Book Art, by P.R. Garriock, Images Graphiques, 1978, EC art repros

My Life As a Cartoonist, by Harvey Kurtzman, 1988, autobiography, reprints from EC and *Mad*

New Comics, The, Gary Groth and Robert Fiore, eds., Berkley, 1988, interview with Harvey Kurtzman

Over 50 Years of American Comic Books, by Ron Goulart, Publications International, Ltd., 1991, section on EC, with color repros

Overstreet Comic Book Price Guide #9, Harmony Books, 1979, EC tribute issue, Wood cover, many EC cover repros

Photo Journal Guide to Comic Books, vols. 1 & 2, by E. Gerber, Gerber, 1990, pictures cover of every EC comic

Pow! Zap! Wham! Comic Book Trivia Quiz, The, by Michael Uslan and Bruce Solomon, William Morrow and Co., 1977, EC related questions

Ray Bradbury Chronicles 1-6, 1992-93, NBM/Bantam, each contains reprinted EC Bradbury adaptation in color

Science Fiction Comics: The Illustrated History, by Mike Benton, Taylor Publishing, 1992, section on EC with color art repros

Smithsonian Book of Comic Book Comics, A, Smithsonian-Abrams, 1981, color reprints from EC comics

Sotheby's Comic Books and Comic Art Catalog, Sotheby's, 1991, EC covers, art, and oil paintings pictured

Sotheby's Comic Books and Comic Art Catalog, Sotheby's, 1992, EC covers, art, and oil paintings pictured

Sotheby's Comic Books and Comic Art Catalog, Sotheby's, 1993, EC covers, art, and oil paintings pictured

Teenaged Dope Slaves and Reform School Girls, Eclipse, 1989, *Lucky Fights It Through* reprint

Examples of books with sections on EC comics:

from The Great Comics Game

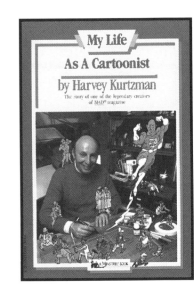

My Life as a Cartoonist

Overstreet Price Guide #9

A Haunt of Fears

Unauthorized EC reprints

Incredible Science Fiction #33 cover, circa late 1960s, produced in association with underground comix publisher Gary Arlington to advertise an unauthorized "EC Reprint Club." These full color slicks were shot from the original comic and sold for 10¢ each; a cease and desist order from Gaines's lawyers stopped them. The slicks have blank backs, and compared to the original comic, the reproduction is somewhat cloudy.

Incredible Science Fiction #33 unauthorized cover slick: $5

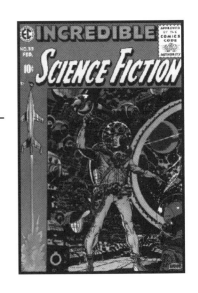

Nickel Library, early 1970s, Gary Arlington series published one binder-style sheet at a time; "new" EC comic covers were done by various underground artists without permission, and later stopped by Gaines. *Nickel Library* #4, 33-37, 42, 43 (there are two #43s in the series), 47-49, 51, 52, 54-60 are confirmed as having EC-style covers, but there may be several others. Also shown are a *Picture Stories from the Bible* #4 cover and a *Crime SuspenStories* #29 cover intended for the series, but never published (art by Roger Brand).

Nickel Library sheets with unauthorized
EC covers: $3 each

 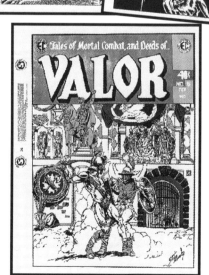

Strange Planets #1 (IW), circa 1963, reprints *Incredible Science Fiction* #30 (with letters page) but with different cover and ads.

Strange Planets #1 (IW reprint): $30

"Spooky Lite Up Pin," circa 1960s, middle pinback button on bottom row is art swipe of EC's Old Witch; third button on top row is a Jack Davis-style Frankenstein art swipe (probably from *Tales from the Crypt* #34). The eyes of each pin light up.

"Spooky Lite Up Pin": no reported sales

"EC Lives" sticker, unauthorized, art from the cover of the 1972 "EC Fan-Addict Convention" program book; notice reads "© 1990 William M. Gaines, Agent"

"EC Lives" sticker: $3

EC Pin, origin and date unknown, brass and black enamel stud pin, 3/4" in diameter.

EC Pin: $35

EC alternate printings

Crime SuspenStories #1

Two versions of *Crime SuspenStories* #1 exist, identical except for the indicia on the inside front cover. *Crime SuspenStories* was to have replaced *Vault of Horror* with the 15th issue (the first issue of *Vault of Horror* was #12). The original printing reads "*Crime SuspenStories*, Oct.-Nov. 1950, Vol. 1, No. 15 (Formerly *Vault of Horror*)"; when the decision was made not to drop *Vault of Horror* this was blacked out with "Vol. 1, No. 1" inserted above it. A second run of covers had the revised indicia. The first printing version is harder to find, though not rare.

Crime SuspenStories #1 (#15, blacked out indicia): $600 (nm-mint copy)

Crime SuspenStories #1 (Vol. 1, No. 1): $500 (nm-mint copy)

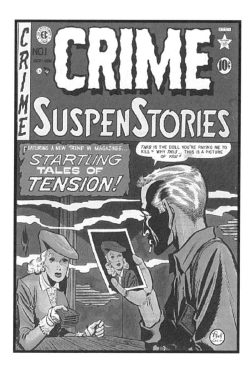

Impact #1

Two printings of *Impact* #1 exist; the cover on the first printing is much darker and the *Impact* logo is white as opposed to yellow on the second printing. Gaines said the book was originally printed by Charlton Press, which did such a poor job that it was reprinted by EC's regular printer. Gaines ordered the entire first printing to be destroyed, but copies of it were distributed.

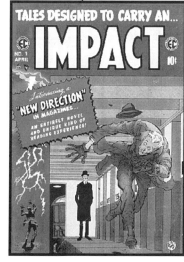

Impact #1 rejected printing: $100 (nm-mint copy)

Impact #1 second printing: $75 (nm-mint copy)

EC-related "cameos" and parodies

EC-related "cameos" and parodies: various prices, average $25 for older material, less for newer

3D Alien Worlds #1 (Eclipse), 1986, reprints the EC parody "The Wishing World" by Mark Evanier and John Pound from Bill Spicer's fanzine *Graphic Story Magazine* #16, with 3D effect by Ray Zone

Baffling Mysteries #10, 1952, Crypt Keeper art swipe on cover

Beware #6, 1953, EC art swipe on cover

Big Apple Comix, 1975, contains "My Word" by Wallace Wood, parody of "My World" from *Weird Science* #22

Bruce Gentry #1, 1948, EC emblem appears on stationery drawn in story

Cracked #250, 1989, HBO *Tales from the Crypt* parody, Gaines pictured

Cracked #252, 1990, Gaines cameo

Cycletoons, June 1973, EC tribute issue, Wm. Stout art

Death Rattle #18, Oct. 1988, EC homage story "Small Acts of Revenge," *Crypt* #37 cover appears

Donald Duck Adventures #11, 1991, cover is a delightful parody of the cover to *Mad* #1, by Todd Kurosawa and Scott Shaw!

Get Lost #2, 1954, EC parody story with the "Sewer Keeper"

Get Lost , vol.2, #2, 1987, black and white reprint of "Sewer Keeper" story from *Get Lost* #2 (1954)

Horrific #8, 1953, EC parody featuring "The Teller"

Mysterious Adventures #14, 1953, EC Old Witch art swipe

National Lampoon #29, Aug. 1972, "Tales from the South" EC parody

National Lampoon, vol. 2 #46, May 1982, "Tales from the Tombs" EC cover parody by Howard Nostrand

Not Brand Ecch #9 (Marvel), 1968, "Three Ghoulunatics" cameo in "Arch and the Teen Stalk" story

Outsiders, The, #22 (DC), 1987, EC parody stories

Saturday Evening Post, The, Jan. 20, 1951, this cover was parodied on the cover of EC's *Panic* #3

Spoof! #2 (Marvel), Nov. 1972, "Tarz an' the Apes" homage to Kurtzman by John and Marie Severin, "Tales from the Creep" parody

Strange Suspense Stories #18, 1954, EC art swipe from *Haunt of Fear* #7

Strange Suspense Stories #34, 1956, character "Wm. B. Gaines" in story of ruthless businessman

Very Large Book of Comical Funnies (National Lampoon), 1975, parody "history of comics" with panels and covers from the supposed "lost" EC comics

Weird Chills #3, 1954, EC art swipe on cover

Weird Trips #2, 1977, Wm. Stout cover pictures face of the Old Witch

What The—? #16, Jan. 1992, EC parody back cover ("The Vault of What The?!") and story

Worse Than Slime no. 1, 1989, Beat Brothers Recordings, CD with EC homage cover by Steve Stiles

X-Terminators #1 (Marvel), 1988, Gaines appears

Donald Duck Adventures #1

from *X-Terminators* #1

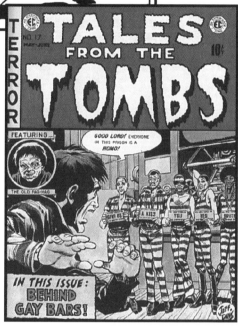

"Tales from the Tombs," from *National Lampoon*,
May 1982

from "My Word," *Big Apple Comix* #1

from *Not Brand Ecch* #9

Saturday Evening Post (Jan. 20, 1951) and *Panic* #3
(June-July 1954)

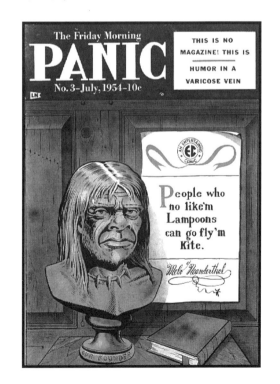

EC "Educational" Comic Books

Although published by EC, these 16-page educational comics pamphlets were actually produced by David Gaines, Bill Gaines's uncle. These books are more of a curiosity to collectors. One, *Lucky Fights It Through* (an anti-VD book) contains the first work done by Harvey Kurtzman for EC. *Lucky Fights It Through* is rare, and two of the others (*The K.O. Punch* and *Out of the Past a Clue to the Future*) are nearly impossible to find.

EC "Educational" Comic Books: refer to *Overstreet Price Guide*

K.O. Punch, The, 1948, Al Feldstein-penciled splash page, interior art by George Roussos (?)
Lucky Fights It Through, 1949, Harvey Kurtzman art
Out of the Past a Clue to the Future, 1946 (?)
Reddy Kilowatt (1946, reprinted 1958), #2 (**Edison**, 1947), Comic Book #2 (**Lights Diamond Jubilee,** 1954; **Wizard of Light,** 1958), Comic Book #3 (**The Space Kite,** 1956 and 1960)
Reddy Made Magic #1 (1956, 1958), reprint of **Reddy Kilowatt** with splash panel change
Story of Edison, The, 1956, reprint of **Reddy Kilowatt** #2 (1947) with different splash page

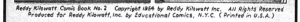

113

EC Watch

Two EC watches were made by the author; one to keep and one for Bill Gaines. The watch was presented to Gaines on the occasion of the interview done for this book (July 17, 1990).

EC Watch: no reported sales

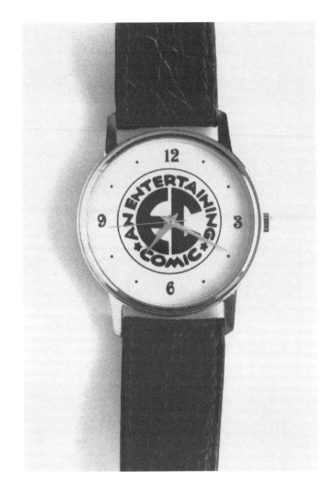

In cooperation with **William M. Gaines**, *Micro Chromatics* is recording all the E.C. comic books onto colored film. Present plans are to make available **35mm** full frame slides of covers and **16mm** colored microfilm of complete issues, although other film formats are also being considered. To recieve detailed information and get on our mailing list, write:

Micro Chromatics, Box 27, MIT Br., Cambridge, Ma. 02139

Micro Chromatics has on colored film comic material ranging from **Winsor McCay** and **R.F. Outcault** to **Vaughn Bode, Jeff Jones,** and **Berni Wrightson**.

Full color slides of EC covers

Micro Chromatics of Cambridge, Mass., made arrangements with Gaines in 1973 to offer 35 mm. full frame color slides of EC comic book covers and 16 mm. color slides of complete EC issues; an ad for the products appeared in the 1973 third edition of the *Comic Book Price Guide*. Not much came of the plan, but Gaines recalled that a set of 15 or 20 slides of various covers was made available.

Full color slides of EC covers: no reported sales

Recent or forthcoming EC-related products:

The New Two-Fisted Tales

From Dark Horse Comics and Byron Preiss, *The New Two-Fisted Tales* was planned as a six-issue series edited by Harvey Kurtzman. Each comic was to contain four new stories and one reprint from *Two-Fisted Tales* or *Frontline Combat*. One issue appeared in 1993, with a re-vamped new series due out in 1994.

Tales from the Crypt pinball machine

Tied in to the HBO series of the same name, this is a full size arcade-style machine, made by Data East of Chicago.

Tales from the Crypt Trading Cards

Cardz has released a set of *Tales from the Crypt* trading cards, with scenes from the HBO series. A full color illustrated binder for displaying the cards was also available.

Tales from the Crypt Halloween costumes

Collegeville/Imagineering has released several costumes based on the HBO version of the Crypt Keeper, geared to both adults and children.

Statuettes of the *Three GhouLunatics*

Graphitti Designs is issuing full figure statuettes of the Three GhouLunatics, based on designs by William Stout. The statuettes were sculpted by Bowen Designs and sell for $195 each. Each statuette has a limitation of 2,500 made. Also available is a full color signed-and-limited edition poster (750 copies) of the Three GhouLunatics by William Stout, priced at $39.95.

Signed, limited poster: "The Gang's All Here" by William Stout

Crypt Keeper statue

Vault Keeper statue

Tales from the Crypt model kit

Screamin' Products, Inc. released in 1993 a "museum-quality scale model kit" of the HBO version of the Crypt Keeper, priced at $54.95.

EC lithographs

Phantomb Publishing Co. of San Francisco is releasing a series of fine art lithographs of EC-related oil paintings. All lithos are signed and numbered by the artists, which include Johnny Craig, Al Feldstein, Jack Kamen, and Kelly Freas. Prices range from $300-$1,000 for the "Gold Casket Series" (with a small sketch) and from $200-$500 for the "Silver Casket Series." The EC seal appears at the bottom of each lithograph.

Tales from the Cryptkeeper animated cartoon series

The *Tales from the Cryptkeeper* animated series debuted in 1993. Airing Saturday mornings on ABC, the series was produced by Nelvana of Canada. The show is not based upon actual EC stories, but rather features toned-down morality plays for the younger audience. Merchandising tie-ins for the show have included Cadaver Putty, Googely Eyes, Ghoul Guts, and a set of eight Action Figures. A talking 12" doll also bears the *Tales from the Cryptkeeper* logo, but is based on the HBO Crypt Keeper.

Tales from the Crypt feature films, and other *Crypt* items

1995 and beyond are shaping up to be banner years for the *Tales from the Crypt* property. In the works are three feature films, with the first, "Demon Knight," to appear in January 1995. More *Crypt* merchandising is due, including Halloween candy, a coffee table book on the history of *Tales from the Crypt*, and a Christmas album (featuring such titles as "Deck the Halls with Parts of Charlie"). An article on the *Crypt* phenomenon appeared in the New York Times on Sunday, September 4, 1994.

Everywhere You Look, 'Crypt' and More 'Crypt'

By ANN HORNADAY

WILLIAM M. GAINES MUST be spinning in his grave, albeit happily. Mr. Gaines, who published the macabre comic-book series "Tales From the Crypt" in the early 1950's, would probably never have predicted that those slightly schlocky-schlocky cartoons featuring the creepy Crypt Keeper as host would someday become a billion-dollar industry. But that is precisely what may happen over the next two years as a sixth season of HBO's "Tales From the Crypt" hits the market along with three feature films based on the series, an adventure-game show called "Secrets of the Crypt Keeper's Haunted House" and a line of "Crypt" merchandise.

From the lurid comic-book gore usually consumed by boys in flashlight under-the-blanket fashion, "Tales From the Crypt" has become a slick ratings hit for HBO, a successful series of reruns on Fox and a Saturday-morning cartoon, "Tales From the Crypt Keeper," on ABC. The thread these vehicles share is the Crypt Keeper, the morbid and skeletal host of the HBO series who has become a star in his own right, even jamming with the band on "The Tonight Show With Jay Leno."

"I've been in the franchise business for 19 years, but I've never seen a phenomenon like this," says Toper Taylor, the senior vice president for United States operations at Nelvana Communications, which produces the ABC cartoon and is overseeing the "Tales" licensing program. "Usually networks are extremely territorial about their programming. The fact that you have three different networks promoting the same character, I think, speaks to the fact that the Crypt Keeper has transcended being a puppet and has become an actor. He's become the skeletal Groucho Marx, who goes from 'A Night at the Opera' to 'What's My Line?'"

To what might the series owe its phenomenal appeal, mainly to a 12- to 14-year-old audience? It may lie in the perennial fascination of youngsters and adults alike with the macabre. But perhaps it's the shows' finales, in which the selfish, duplicitous and just plain mean come to gruesomely fitting ends, that explain their cult popularity.

In one episode, for example, Joe Pesci

A gruesomely fitting end: schlocky cartoons with a skeletal Groucho Marx as host turn into an industry.

plays a man who cuts twin sisters into bed his comeuppance occurs in the form of their Solomonic decision literally to split him. In another episode two lovers caught entwined by the woman's mad-scientist husband are surgically conjoined forever.

"We're in an age of true lies," says Frederick Elkind, president of Trend/Consult, a strategic-marketing planning firm for broadcast and print media. "People have a certain degree of bitterness, the feeling that there's no justice in the world. Lorena Bobbitt, the Menendez brothers, O. J. Simpson. Nobody is responsible for anything. Or they can buy their way out. 'Tales From the Crypt' provides a kind of black justice."

Joel Silver, an executive producer of the series who is best known for action films like "Die Hard" and "Lethal Weapon," says he wasn't necessarily a "Crypt" fan when he was young. "But at camp, if one of the kids had their older brother's 'Tales From the Crypt,' it was covered."

In 1983, Mr. Silver recalls, when he was working on "Streets of Fire" with Walter Hill, a co-executive producer of the HBO series, "we were talking about some episodic movie that had come out — 'Twilight Zone' or 'Creepshow,' I don't remember which. And he said to me, 'Remember that comic book "Tales From the Crypt"?' And I said, 'Yeah, yeah, yeah!' And he said, 'We should do that.'"

Soon after, Mr. Silver optioned the rights to the comics and tried to sell studios on the idea of a feature package of three short films, but it never got off the ground. In 1986, when Mr. Silver was producing "Lethal Weapon," he mentioned the "Crypt" project to Richard Donner, the film's director. "He said, 'I love

The Crypt Keeper—A star so big he jams with the "Tonight Show" band.

that thing!'" Mr. Silver laughs. "Everybody had the same reaction: 'I love that thing! I want to do that!'"

Mr. Donner signed on with Mr. Silver and Mr. Hill, and in 1988 they approached HBO. "They said if we could get three giant directors to do something like this, they'd be interested," says Mr. Silver.

While working on "Who Framed Roger Rabbit," Mr. Silver mentioned the project to the film's director, Robert Zemeckis. Mr. Zemeckis, too, loved the idea, recalls Mr. Silver. With Mr. Zemeckis as the third director, the HBO deal was on.

The first three episodes of "Tales From the Crypt," which had its premiere in 1989, set the shows' signatures: stylish looks, cynical humor and an unbridled approach to sex, violence and strong language. "What was exciting to me was that it was perfect alternative television," says Mr. Zemeckis. "It's what cable television should be doing. A 30-minute piece without commercial breaks or censorship of any kind was very liberating and exhilarating."

Fans have seen 65 episodes of "Tales From the Crypt" so far. The new season, fittingly, starts on Halloween night, with 13 new shows.

From the outset, says Mr. Silver, it was crucial that production values and special effects be sophisticated enough to attract HBO's movie audience as well as the big-name stars who would lend the series allure. The strategy worked. "Tales From the Crypt" was an instant ratings hit for HBO. It has provided actors like Arnold Schwarzenegger and Tom Hanks with their directorial debuts. It has also attracted stars like Kirk Douglas and Whoopi Goldberg.

The Crypt Keeper will introduce each of the three feature films in the works for 1995 and possibly into 1996. "Demon Knight" is expected in theaters in January, the second film, tentatively called "Fat Tuesday," is planned for next October. An opening date and title for the third film are yet to be announced. "Unlike the television show, where we basically shoot him from the waist up and have six puppeteers running him, he'll walk and talk, and we'll convince you that he directed the movie," says Gil Adler of the Crypt Keeper, Mr. Adler, with Alan Katz,

Continued on Next Page

New York Times, **Sunday, September 4, 1994**

Demon Knight promo button

12" Talking Doll

Halloween candy

SECTION 2: MAD COLLECTIBLES

CHAPTER ONE

Pre-*Mad* "What–Me Worry?" items

It surprises people to learn that the face of the "What–Me Worry?" kid, who later became Alfred E. Neuman in *Mad* magazine, pre-dates its appearance in *Mad* by as much as sixty years. The earliest known version of the face dates to the 1890s, in an advertisement for a "painless dentist." The face appears with the slogan "It Didn't Hurt a Bit." In later incarnations and on different items, the slogan became "Me Worry?" and finally "What–Me Worry?" This face and slogan have appeared on many different items in several countries, including political buttons, castings, post cards, soft drink ads, lithographs, etc., which pre-date their use in *Mad*. *Mad* was in fact sued in the early 1960s by a woman who held a 1914 copyright on the face; *Mad*'s lawyers found examples that pre-dated the copyright and argued successfully that the copyright was invalid because it was applied to a creation already in the public domain. Furthermore, because the face had become so identified with *Mad*, *Mad* won the right to use the likeness exclusively as a trademark.

Following are examples of pinback buttons using the face; they are also highly sought after by collectors of political and advertising memorabilia:

January 25, 1952

Circa early 1900s

Circa 1930s

1941

1940s

Pinback button, "Comfort Soap": $500-$600

Pinback button, "Malmberg's": $300

Pinback button, "I'm a Simp": $350

Pinback button, "Me Worry? Superior, 1941": $350

Pinback button, "I'm Daft for Taft": $525

The two small postcards express an anti-President Franklin Roosevelt sentiment. On the bottom is an anti-Roosevelt envelope; these pieces all date from 1944. The ink blotter, "Guys Like Me Will Vote For Guys Like Him For A Fourth Term," is from 1943. Also shown is an anti-Wendell Wilkie card which, according to legend, so angered the anti-Roosevelt forces that they developed their own series of campaign items using the "Me Worry?" face.

Postcard, anti-Roosevelt: $15-$25

Envelope, anti-Roosevelt: $25

Blotter, 1943, "Guys Like Me Will Vote For Guys Like Him For A Fourth Term": $25

Postcard, anti-Wilkie: $15-$25

Sure - I'm for Roosevelt

"Sure! I'm for the 4th Term"

Guys like me will vote for guys like him for a fourth term.

Copyright applied for

Sure I'm a New Dealer
for "just the two of us" are indispensible

MY GUIDING STAR

From the "WINDY WILKY" BOYHOOD ALBUM —

Postcards

This "imitation bronze" three-dimensional casting bears a copyright date of 1928, and was manufactured by the A.E. Mitchell Art Company in Los Angeles.

Casting, imitation bronze
(A.E. Mitchell, 1928): $100-$150

1908 "Antikamnia" calendar, 8" x 10". A Spanish version also exists:

Calendar, "Antikamnia," 1908: $300

A "Me Worry?" arcade card (arcade cards were sold in vending machines, usually in vacation settings), circa 1940s or '50s. Arcade cards are about the size of postcards but have blank backs.

Arcade card, "Me Worry?": $10-$20

Me ----------- Worry ?

Me–Worry?

ME WORRY?

WHAT–ME WORRY?

LIKE MAN–ME WORRY?

ME WORRY?

DA-A-H...ME WORRY?

ME WORRY? HECK NO! I WORK FOR THE GUV'MINT

"ME WORRY?"

C-103

Greetings

What - me worry?

ME WORRY? Not in Hollywood

WHY WORRY?

THERE ARE ONLY TWO THINGS TO WORRY ABOUT:
EITHER YOU ARE WELL OR YOU ARE SICK.
IF YOU ARE WELL THERE IS NOTHING TO WORRY ABOUT.
IF YOU ARE SICK THERE ARE TWO THINGS TO WORRY ABOUT.
EITHER YOU WILL GET WELL, OR YOU WILL DIE.
IF YOU GET WELL, THERE IS NOTHING TO WORRY ABOUT
IF YOU DIE THERE ARE ONLY TWO THINGS TO WORRY ABOUT
EITHER YOU GO TO HEAVEN OR HELL,
IF YOU GO TO HEAVEN THERE IS NOTHING TO WORRY ABOUT
BUT IF YOU GO TO HELL, YOU WILL BE SO DARN BUSY
SHAKING HANDS WITH YOUR FRIENDS;
YOU WON'T HAVE TIME TO WORRY.

The most numerous pre-*Mad* "What–Me Worry?" items are postcards, which appeared from the early 1900s until well into the 1960s, when *Mad* secured use of the face as a trademark. It is not known how many different postcard variations exist.

Postcards, various, pre-*Mad*: average $3-$25, more for examples pre-1940

"Get well" card, circa 1930s or '40s.

"Get well" card, circa 1930s or '40s: $35

Front

Inside

The face on this 6 1/2" x 10 1/2" card is literally four-eyed, circa 1940s or 1950s.

Card, four-eyed "Me Worry?" face: $20-$25

This Valentine's Day card dates from the 1900s.

Valentine's Day card, early 1900s: $35

Placard, 7" x 11", circa 1940s or 1950s.

Placard, 7" x 11", circa 1940s or 1950s: $45

In this set of twelve metal *Sillie-Willie Crazy Coasters* are two of interest to *Mad* collectors: "Me Worry?" and "Son of Me Worry?" The other ten coasters have silly or misspelled slogans. From the late 1940s or early '50s.

Sillie-Willie Crazy Coasters: full set in box, $35-$50

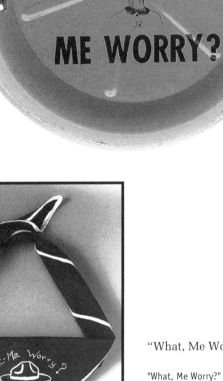

"Me Worry?" ceramic ashtray, souvenir of Chester, West Virginia, circa 1940s or '50s.

Ashtray, "Me Worry?": $50

"What, Me Worry?" scarf

"What, Me Worry?" scarf: $75-$100

Male and female versions of the "Me Worry?" face appear on these World War II-era envelopes to advertise War Bonds.

Envelopes, War Bonds: $25-$50

This plaster-of-Paris "Me Worry?" bust was made by Moseley Products in Miami, Florida circa 1940s or '50s. Moseley also made at least one other bust (a "Me Worry?" sailor), and an 8 1/2" x 11" black and white "Me Worry?" picture.

Bust, "Me Worry?", Moseley Products: $150-$200

Picture, "Me Worry?": $35

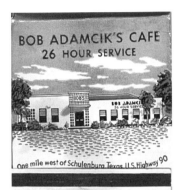

A book of matches, circa 1950s, promoting Bob Adamcik's Cafe in Schulenberg, Texas. Adamcik also used the image on at least two postcard designs.

Matchbook, Bob Adamcik's Cafe: $15-$20

America for Peace card.

***America for Peace card**: $20*

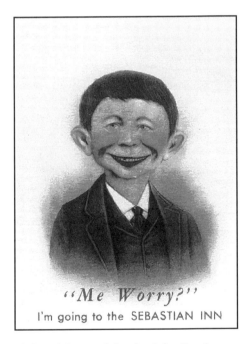

Advertising card for the Sebastian Inn ("midway between Jacksonville and Miami, Florida on the main U.S. No. 1 highway").

Advertising card, Sebastian Inn: $15-$20

Match book covers with "Me Worry?" face.

Match book covers with "Me Worry?" face: $10-$20

These examples (of unknown origin) are printed on cardboard and measure 8 1/2" x 11," circa 1950s.

Another print, also 8 1/2" x 11," but on thin stock.

Pictures with "What, Me Worry?" face: $25

Ink blotter advertising auto insurance.

Blotter, auto insurance ad: $25

"Me Worry?" picture and thermometer advertising George A. Cox and Company Insurance and Bonds, vintage unknown.

"Me Worry?" picture and thermometer, George A. Cox and Company Insurance: $50-$75

Pacific Dental card, 1910.

Pacific Dental card, early 1900s: $25-$50

"Me Worry?" statue in Kansas City, Missouri; similar statues are reported in Dallas, Texas and Burlington County, New Jersey (at Tom's Diner on Route 130).

Extremely rare sport shirt with "Me Worry?" image, circa 1940s.

Shirt, with "Me Worry?" face, 1940s: $450

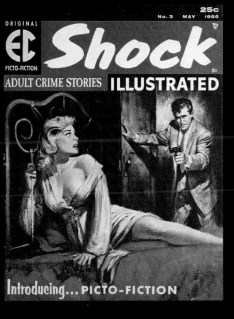

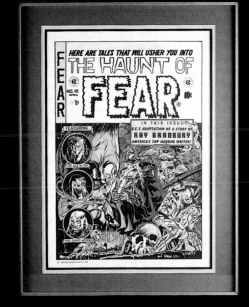

One of the "crowning touches" of EC collections, the very rare *Shock Illustrated* #3. Only one or two hundred copies (accounts vary) were made; few were distributed.

Marie Severin hand colored print of *Haunt of Fear* #18 (one of only ten issued, 1971).

The first high quality collection of EC material, *The EC Horror Library* hardback book (Nostalgia Press, 1971).

Mint condition Gaines EC File Copies, with initialed certificates and film editors gloves (to wear when handling the comics).

The original EC Fan-Addict Club kit, with bulletins (1953).

Sheet of EC stationery
(with Jack Davis art),
circa 1954.

*Les Meilleures Histories De
Terreur, Horreur, Guerre,
Aventures, Suspense,* and
Science-Fiction, a six-
volume series of French
EC hardbacks, 1983-1985.

EC Classics on illustrated
display stand (magazine-
sized Russ Cochran EC
reprint series, 1985-
1989).

Grouping of various EC
paperback books.

Various foreign EC reprint
publications.

Harvey Kurtzman's
original cover rough
of the cover to *Mad* #10
(April 1954).

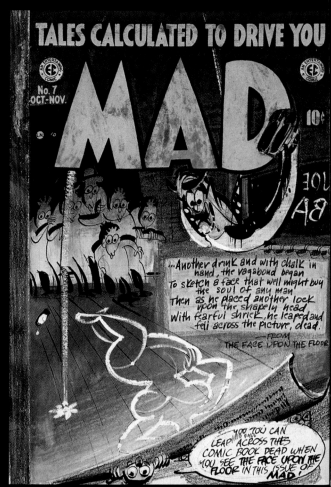

EC fanzines from various eras (1950s-present).

The classic EC fanzine, *Squa Tront* (1967-1983).

Original Johnny Craig oil painting of the Three Ghoulunatics and Drusilla, entitled *Group Portrait* (1991).

The *EC Portfolios*, a series of six black and white oversize volumes of classic EC stories, shot from the original art (Russ Cochran, 1971-1977).

1908 Antikamnia calendar with an early version of the "What, Me Worry?" face.

Pre-*Mad* "Me Worry?" postcards, greeting cards, and advertising material.

The two rarest and most sought-after items of *Mad* clothing, the *Mad* Straight Jacket (1959) and the 1958 *Mad* T-shirt.

The 1960 and 1964 "Alfred E. Neuman for President" kits. Bill Gaines described the mail-order only sales of these kits as a "disaster."

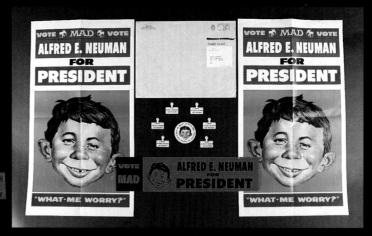

In the back row are the "China Bisque Busts" of Alfred E. Neuman sold through *Mad* in the 1960s (the middle bust is Swedish). In the front are various unauthorized or pre-*Mad* busts.

The *Mad* record albums: *Musically Mad* (1959), *Mad Twists Rock 'n' Roll* (1962), *Fink Along With Mad* (1963), *The Mad Show* (1966) and the soundtrack *Up the Academy* (1980).

Alfred E. Neuman Sings "What, Me Worry?" 45 (promo and standard issues, 1959); the picture sleeve is much rarer than the record itself.

Alfred E. Neuman Halloween costumes (Collegeville, 1960). The "conventional" costume and mask (right) is easier to find than the large "Mardi Gras Walk Along," which is quite rare.

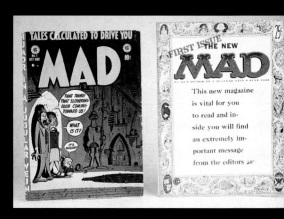

Foreign *Mad* collections from Japan, England, France, Sweden, and Norway.

Swedish "casting" of Alfred E. Neuman; this formidable-looking object is actually made out of thin plastic.

Mad #1 (a 10¢ comic book, Oct.-Nov. 1952) and #24 (the first issue as a 25¢ magazine, July 1955).

The first issue of the British edition of *Mad*, 1960.

First printing copies of the five Ballantine Books *Mad* paperbacks (mid-1950s): *The Mad Reader*, *Mad Strikes Back*, *Inside Mad*, *Utterly Mad*, and *The Brothers Mad*.

Mad hardcover books: *Mad for Keeps* (Crown, 1958), *Mad Forever* (Crown, 1959), *A Golden Trashery of Mad* (Crown, 1960), and *The Ridiculously Expensive Mad* (World, 1969).

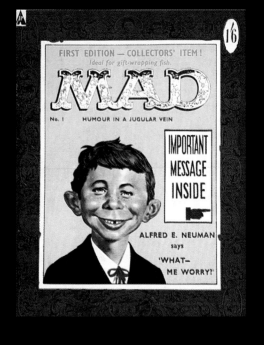

The *Mad*/Alfred E. Neuman model kit made by Aurora in 1965; the kit is sought after not only by *Mad* collectors but by model kit collectors as well.

A beautifully sculpted statue of Alfred E. Neuman, done by Kent Melton for the unreleased Hanna-Barbera *Mad* TV special.

"What, Me Worry?" doll made by the Baby Barry doll company in 1961. A doll with virtually the same face exists that dates back to the late 1920s or early 1930s.

"What, Me Worry?" hand puppet, 1960. The puppet has "What, Me Worry?" and "Crestline Enterprises" stamped at the base of the head.

"What, Me Worry?" poster, late 1960s or early 1970s. The copyright notice reads "© Stuff and Wilson"; it was Harry Stuff's widow who sued *Mad* (and lost) over copyright infringement in the early 1960s.

Display poster and promotional tile pot holder for *The Mad Show* (1966).

Grouping of various *Mad* and pre-*Mad* pinback buttons.

Screwball, the Mad Mad Mad Game was released in 1960 by Transogram. After Bill Gaines threatened legal action, the box top was modified to the version shown at the bottom.

"What, Me Worry?" decals, circa early 1960s.

Grouping of various *Mad* items from the "New Collectibles" era (1987-present).

Norman Mingo's original cover art to *Mad* #97, along with the issue as published (Sept. 1965). *Mad* original art is done at twice the size it will appear in the magazine.

Robert Grossman original cover art to *Utterly Mad,* one of five such covers Grossman did for a 1975 re-issue of the Ballantine paperbacks. Bill Gaines hated these covers, and because they were done without his approval they were withdrawn after less than a year.

Color cover rough by Jack Rickard for the *Mad Weirdo Watcher's Guide* paperback (1982). Although the final art has a smoother look, the rough is equally effective.

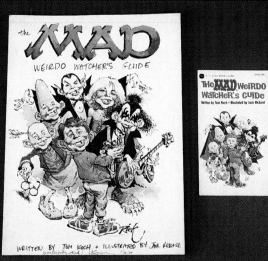

The face was used to advertise Cherry Sparkle, a brand
of soda pop, circa 1920s. The item below is a cardboard
advertisement designed to slip around a bottle neck.
The metal sign at the bottom is an original (roughly
4" x 12"); the sign to the right was made in about 1989
by the Desperate Sign Co. (11" x 15"):

"Cherry Sparkle" paper advertisement, fits on bottle: $250-$300

"Cherry Sparkle" tin sign, circa 1920s: $400

"Cherry Sparkle" reproduction tin sign, 1989: $35

Pictures of Alfred E. Neuman

Shortly after *Mad* began using "the face," the magazine offered a 5" x 7" black and white print for 15 cents. The offer appeared in issue #27 (April 1956). The portrait, by Will Elder, was discontinued after issue #29, which not so coincidentally was the first issue edited by Al Feldstein (Harvey Kurtzman edited issues #1-28). Gaines recollected that perhaps 10,000 of the prints were sold. Few are available, so perhaps purchasers took the editorial advice and used them to "patch the hole in your wallpaper."

Beginning with issue #30 (Dec. 1956), the face of the "What–Me Worry?" kid and the name "Alfred E. Neuman" were cemented for all time. Feldstein wanted the face to be more "real," so advertising artist Norman Mingo was hired to create a cover that became the archetypal Alfred E. Neuman face. Also in issue #30, *Mad* offered for 25 cents a full color portrait of Alfred, taken from #30's cover art. This print was captioned "'What–Me Worry?' (I read *Mad*!)". The print was available in every issue through the mid-1980s. On the first printing the background is a shade of turquoise and the scrolled border is pink. On later printings the background is sky blue and the scrolled border is a light purple. Hundreds of thousands of the prints have been sold. Al Feldstein recalls that Norman Rockwell originally agreed to do the portrait but later declined because he couldn't work from a live model.

"What--me worry?"

Picture of Alfred E. Neuman,
black and white (1956): $50-$100

Picture of Alfred E. Neuman, color:
1st printing (1956) $25-$50,
later printings $5

"What--me worry?"
(I read MAD!)

Mad cufflinks and tie tack

Mad jewelry

On the inside front cover of *Mad* #33 (June 1957) appeared an ad for one of the two items *Mad* collectors lust after the most: the five styles of *Mad* jewelry. Molded in "stunning satin silver plate" by the now-defunct Astrahan Co. of N.Y., the pieces include a lapel/scatter pin, tie tack, cufflinks, key chain, and charm bracelet. All pieces sold for $2.00 each, except the cufflinks at $3.00 a pair. Gaines reported that 1,000-2,000 pieces were sold, making *Mad* jewelry extremely rare today. As far as can be determined, no single collector has all five styles. The jewelry ceased to be offered by issue #41.

Jewelry (1957), cufflinks, lapel pin, charm bracelet, tie tac, key chain: $150-$200 each

Original ad for Mad *jewelry*

CHAPTER TWO

Another kind of jewelry was offered in *Mad* #45 (March 1959), the "goldbrick cufflinks." Designed by actor Wally Cox and made to order by his company, Gauche Jewelry, the cufflinks were 14-karat gold and sold for $66 a pair. Gaines bought a set for himself, and only one other pair was ordered, which Gaines ended up giving as a gift to the lone buyer. The whereabouts of this set is unknown.

Goldbrick cufflinks, 1959: no reported sales

"Goldbrick cufflinks," and the ad from Mad #45

Two styles of 14-karat gold lapel pins were ordered by Gaines as presents for staff and regular contributors. The first (with block style letters) was made in the late 1950s. The second, with the actual *Mad* logo, was given prior to the trip to the Virgin Islands in 1962. This pin has been made in several versions, including "shiny" finish, florentine finish, and with a hook to enable women to wear it on a chain. A silver version was also made on the occasion of a publisher's convention in Munich to give to the foreign *Mad* editors and other staff people. Few of these pins have found their way into private collections. The pins are mentioned on page 164 of the hardback edition of *The Mad World of William M. Gaines.*

Lapel pin for staff, block letters (late 1950s): $100

Lapel pin for staff, *Mad* logo(1962): no reported sales

Staff pin, block letters

Staff pin, Mad logo

Early *Mad* trip group photo: several "*Mad* logo" pins can be seen. Gaines is kneeling in front with his daughter, Cathy.

Mad Pin Collection

These *Spy vs Spy* and "*Mad* logo" pins were created in 1991 as bonuses for subscribers. All three were given away for a 40-issue subscription ($53.75). The "*Mad* logo" pin was offered with a 24-issue subscription ($33.75). (200 alternate pins with a yellow logo on a blue background were ordered by Gaines, the version he actually preferred. These pins were given to staff and contributors. Also, the first run of the "White Spy" pins had a much lower skyline; these were not officially released.)

A *Mad* ruler was made by the company that produced the pins. The three pins are affixed to a 6" gold color metal ruler; about ten of these were made and given to the *Mad* staff.

Four new pins were created in 1994: the Alfred pin was sent as a gift to the 50,000 or so people who responded to the reader survey in *Mad* #326. The other pins are the new bonus for subscribers. The "*Mad* Zeppelin" pin will go to three-year subscribers, the set of all three will go to five year subscribers, and Anne Gaines reports that one-year subscribers "get to look at someone else's pins."

Alternate logo pin

Mad Pin Collection (1991): *Mad* logo $15-$20

Spy vs Spy pins $15-$20 each, set of all three $50-$60

1994 pins: no reported sales

Mad Pin Collection, alternate *Mad* logo pin, yellow on blue (1991): $25

Mad Pin Collection, unreleased *Spy vs Spy* pin (1991): $25

Mad Pin Collection gold ruler, for staff (1991): $50

This self-portrait cloisonné pin of Al Jaffee was made in 1990 for private release; it sold for $3.00.

Al Jaffee lapel pin: $5-$10

Graphitti Designs made this Sergio Aragonés self-portrait cloisonné pin as a special giveaway.

Sergio Aragonés lapel pin: no reported sales

1994 Mad Pins:

Mad T-shirt

Mad Straight Jacket

Unused photo for T-shirt ad (Feldstein, De Fuccio, Meglin).

For the First time in your life...feel really MAD!
Get that MAD Glow...from Head to Toe...in a...

MAD STRAIGHT JACKET

Be the first in your "gang" to wear MAD's own genuine simulated straight jacket. Looks exactly like the real thing, but has the added advantage that you can get your hands loose to fight them off when they come to take you away. Just the thing for busting up Olympic Drinking Team warm-ups, and other such sporting events. Doubles as an autograph, beach, or lounging jacket. Has deep outside pockets roomy enough to carry a whole salami, a bottle of beer, a loaf of bread, a hatchet, a clarinet, a sub-machine gun, etc. (Not all at once, though—but one at a time!) Also handy in case you break both your arms, as outside criss-crossed pockets cradle arms comfortably—no sling needed. Printed on back in four permanent colors. Trompe l'oeil (phony) belt is secured by genuine padlock, which you'll love till you sit in a hard-backed chair. Made for Small, Medium, and Large lunatics. Only $4.95 postpaid.

- - - - use coupon or duplicate - - - -

MAD STRAIGHT JACKETS
225 Lafayette Street
New York City 12, N.Y.

I want to feel really MAD. Rush my MAD Straight Jacket(s). I enclose $4.95 for each jacket, and I have indicated my size(s) — S, M, or L. Hey, y'know I'm beginning to feel MAD already, falling for this ad!

NAME_____
ADDRESS_____
CITY_____
NO. OF JACKETS_____ ZONE____ STATE____
AMOUNT ENCLOSED AT $4.95 each_____ SIZE(S)◄ (S) small (M) medium (L) large

Original ad for the Straight Jacket

Straight Jacket (1959): one example sold at auction in March 1992 for $2,500; another sold in June 1994 for $3,440

T-shirt (1958, sold through Mad): one sold in January 1992 for $450

Mad T-shirt and Straight Jacket

Shortly after introducing the jewelry, *Mad* offered its first T-shirt. The first shirt ad appeared on the inside back cover of issue #39 (May 1958; Al Feldstein, Nick Meglin and Jerry De Fuccio appear in the photo). The shirts were manufactured by the sister-in-law of EC artist Johnny Craig, sold for $1.25, and came in men's and boy's sizes. Alfred's face is silkscreened in five colors and the captions "What—Me Worry?" and "I Read *Mad*" are screened in red and blue, respectively. Three or four thousand were sold, but few are in the hands of collectors.

The *Mad* Straight Jacket, as with the jewelry, is discussed in hushed and reverential tones among longtime collectors, because so few are known to exist. The first ad for the jacket appeared in issue #46 (April 1959) and it ceased to be offered after issue #53 (March 1960). The jacket is designed to look like a real straightjacket, but there are deep pockets in the front to allow the wearer to pull his or her arms in and out. The image of Alfred and the caption "What—Me Worry? I'm wearing my *Mad* Straight Jacket" are silkscreened in a similar fashion to the *Mad* T-shirt, and there was a working padlock on the back. Gaines reported sales of about 1,500. The Straight Jacket is one of the rarest and most *Mad*dening collectibles to find.

CHAPTER THREE

Mad Records

Musically Mad

In 1959 RCA Victor released the long playing album *Musically Mad* ("mis-led by Bernie Green with the Stereo *Mad-Men*"), with narration on several cuts by comedian Henry Morgan. Morgan was a contributor to *Mad*, and Green was Morgan's longtime musical collaborator. Liner notes were provided by Al Feldstein, and for the back cover Wallace Wood drew thirteen b&w illustrations, one for each track. The front cover used a detail from Norman Mingo's classic cover to *Mad* #30. Green's style was not unlike Spike Jones's, and the record's highlights (lowlights?) include an anvil chorus, dog barks, and a man who plays melodies on his hands (Joseph Julian). *Musically Mad* was issued in both monaural and "Living Stereo," which is harder to find. Promotional (disk jockey) copies also exist. RCA Victor was quite a powerful record company at the time (being the home of Elvis Presley) and the album enjoyed good distribution; *Musically Mad* is therefore not difficult to find in record collecting circles. A house ad plugging the album appeared in *Mad* #46 (April 1959), but the album's concept was probably lost on the majority of the *Mad* readership, as it was neither satirical enough nor wacky enough to capture the spirit of *Mad*.

Musically Mad LP (1959): mono $35/stereo $50/promo $50

Two of Wallace Wood's drawings for the liner notes to Musically Mad.

Alfred E. Neuman Sings 'What–Me Worry?' 45 rpm single

Toward the end of 1959, ABC-Paramount released a 45 rpm record (with picture sleeve) credited to "Alfred E. Neuman and his Furshlugginer Five" entitled "What–Me Worry?", backed with "Potrzebie." "What–Me Worry?" is a silly, catchy tune about Alfred E. Neuman done in typical late-50s rock 'n' roll style; "Potrzebie" is an uninspired 12-bar blues instrumental based on the riff to "Night Train." The picture sleeve has a rear view portrait of Alfred by Norman Mingo, taken from the back cover to *Mad* #30, along with six Don Martin drawings taken from various features (both sides of the sleeve bear the art). White label promo copies of the record exist, and Canadian pressings are reported as well. As with most 45s, the sleeve is more difficult to find than the record itself, and is considered rare.

Alfred E. Neuman Sings 'What–Me Worry?' single (1959): with picture sleeve
$75-$100, record only $20

Alfred E. Neuman Sings 'What–Me Worry?' single, promo: with picture sleeve
$100-$125, record only $25

CHAPTER THREE

Mad Twists Rock 'n' Roll

Released in 1962, the LP *Mad Twists Rock 'n' Roll* captured both the spirit of *Mad* and the early 1960s Brill Building songwriting style it was parodying. Included are such titles as "Please, Betty Jane, Shave Your Legs," "When My Pimples Turned to Dimples," and the now-classic "She Got a Nose Job." Written and produced by Norm Blagman and Sam Bobrick, the record featured performances by Jeanne Hayes, Mike Russo, and The Dellwoods. The label, Big Top Records, had rather weak distribution and while not rare, *Mad Twists Rock 'n' Roll* is somewhat difficult to find. A one-sided paper flexi-record of "She Got a Nose Job" appeared in the 5th annual edition of *The Worst From Mad*.

Two songs that appear on *Mad Twists Rock 'n' Roll* were released earlier on RCA Records, credited to the "Sweet Sick-Teens," as a 45 rpm single (RCA #47-7940) and as a 33 1/3 rpm single (RCA #37-7940). RCA declined to release the rest of the material, and it was put out under *Mad*'s aegis.

Mad Twists Rock 'n' Roll (1962): $35-$50, promo copy $45-$60

"Sweet Sick-Teens" single, RCA: 45 rpm version $25, 33 1/3 rpm version $40

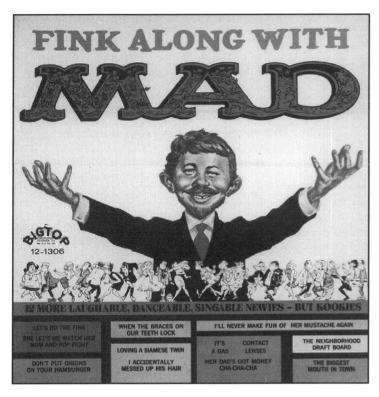

Fink Along With Mad

Fink Along With Mad was released by Big Top Records in 1963 and continued the formula of the first album, with such titles as "When the Braces On Our Teeth Lock," "Loving A Siamese Twin," and "She Lets Me Watch Her Mom and Pop Fight." A paper flexi-record of "She Lets Me Watch Her Mom and Pop Fight" was included in the 6th annual edition of *The Worst From Mad.* A 45 rpm single of "Don't Put Onions On Your Hamburger" b/w "Her Moustache" (Big Top #3137) was also issued, credited to the Dellwoods, and a white label promo copy was released to radio stations. Several of the people who worked on the record went on to greater heights: arranger Claus Ogerman worked with George Benson and released several acclaimed orchestral/jazz albums of his own, and recording engineer Phil Ramone produced some of the most successful records by Simon and Garfunkel, Billy Joel, and Julian Lennon. Unfortunately this particular record fared only marginally well in the marketplace, and like its predecessor is somewhat difficult to find.

Fink Along With Mad LP (1963): $35-$50, promo copy $45-$60

"Don't Put Onions on Your Hamburger" b/w "Her Moustache" 45 RPM single (by The Dellwoods, promo): $25

Note: also see *Up the Academy, Mad Annuals, The Mad Show* and *Foreign Items* for other *Mad* records.

CHAPTER FOUR

Mad hardcover books:

Mad for Keeps, Mad Forever, A Golden Trashery of Mad, and *The Ridiculously Expensive Mad*

The first of three hardcover collections from Crown Publishers, *Mad for Keeps,* appeared in 1958. The second, *Mad Forever,* in 1959, and the third, *A Golden Trashery of Mad*, in 1960. The books sported full color dust jackets, were printed on white paper stock, had saddle-sewn bindings, and measured about 8 1/4" x 10 3/4". All three were sold in bookstores and via ads in *Mad* magazine. Priced at $2.95, all included bonus color sections of various features and articles. Amusing introductions were offered by Ernie Kovacs, Steve Allen, and Sid Caesar respectively. The collections remained in print for a respectable length of time; *Mad for Keeps* went through at least six printings. The books are now somewhat difficult to find, particularly with dust jackets intact.

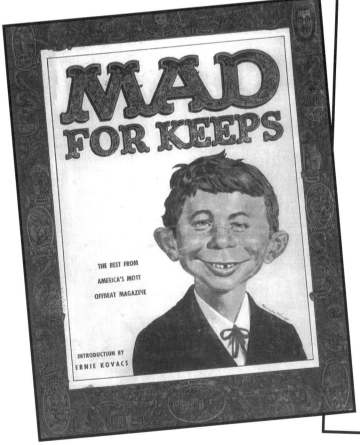

Mad for Keeps:
1st printing with dust jacket $150-$200

A few well-chosen words to introduce *Mad for Keeps.*

WHEN THE little posh clique of degenerates who comprise the editorial staff of this literary hoax, yclept MAD, happily informed me that a collection of their "humor in a jugular vein" was to be put into a hardback edition by Crown, I knew at once that the owners of this once-respected publishing establishment had certainly flipped their marbles, and that the world of literature had generally gone to hell.

MAD has held a tender place in my heart since its inception. How well I remember its very first issue, and its very first funny drawing. It was of a little carrot-topped boy and a large giant eating. Or, perhaps it was of a little giant eating carrots and a large boy. Well, that's of small consequence. Come to think of it, that picture appeared in another magazine, which, though I cannot recall the title, was superior to MAD in many ways!

Anyway, MAD first appeared in August of 1952.

The steady retrogression of this magazine since then has been most encouraging. The nation's readers should soon be blessed by a posted bankruptcy in a not-too-distant issue of an obscure backwoods newspaper.

I, for one, look forward to this thundering decline in the public's acceptance of MAD, and to the happy prospect of seeing a long, ragged line consisting of the editorial staff waiting for handouts of thin soup somewhere on New York's Bowery.

Added to my personal feelings about the MAD staff is my humiliation at witnessing their blatant piracy of my material, surreptitiously changing a comma here and there to disguise the theft. I have watched, with *una furtiva lagrima* coursing its melancholy way down my cheek, the abject desecration of my creation, the eminent Cowznofski.* I have seen this hallowed Pole's name captioned beneath that ridiculously freckled face of the publisher's mother-in-law.

I am quietly waiting for the day when my own magazines will replace MAD. These, owing to their mass appeal, will make me a millionaire many times over. Mark my words! You will eventually be seeing them on the market:

The All-Girl Orchestra's Digest, The Zoo Keeper's Monthly, Young Interne's Love Story Magazine, and *The Two-Headed Calf Owner's Guide....*

Until then, I say..."So-long!"

ERNIE KOVACS

*Corrupted from "Cowznowski."

Foreword

IT IS always gratifying to be able to boast of early familiarity with a person or institution that eventually achieves greatness.

Several years ago a group of angry young men, united only in their feeling that the satirical ramparts had been abandoned, determined to make available to American readers a publication that would be at once amusing, disrespectful, and original. The first issue of their publication came to my attention, received my encouragement, and benefited from my counsel.

The periodical to which I refer, of course, is *The Daily Worker*. Who these idiots are with this MAD thing I have no idea.

Be that as it may, however, (and how seldom it is) it behooves me. As a matter of fact I feel I would be remiss. Which reminds me of a story. I imagine most of you know it; it's called *Huckleberry Finn*.

But I doubt if there is a man alive today and I suppose a great many men think the same of me. All solemnity aside though, there is one thing I would like to drive home and that's a '59 Mercedes-McCambridge.

We must, however, give the devil his due. I have always said that if a man wants to do a thing badly enough he will do it. For several years the editors of MAD wanted to put out a magazine very badly, and that is just how they are doing it.

But the magazine is undeniably a success. The men who struggled to create it have gone from Nedick's to Twenty-one, from franks-and-beans to *Belgian Hares in Flagrante Delicto*, from Brooklyn to Westport, from Natchez to Mobile, wherever the four winds blo-o-o-www.

Of course, all this success has not been accomplished without sacrifice. There have been dark times, such as that shattering morning on which it was learned that the magazine's esteemed editor had been arrested for impairing the morals of a nation. And there was the day

Mad Forever: 1st printing with dust jacket $150-$200

I was forced to institute suit against the publication for plagiarism of my comedy material, a suit I lost on the ridiculous technicality that publication had taken place several days before the jokes involved had actually occurred to me.

But if MAD is prepared to let bygones be bygones, so am I. No grudge-holder I. A romantic guy I.

Live and let live, say I. Backwards talk I.

In closing, I would like to admit publicly what a number of MAD readers have already guessed from seeing a recently published picture of me taken at the age of two. My picture is on the left below. The picture on the right is that of the character customarily identified as Alfred E. Newman.

The secret is out: *I* am Alfred E. Newman.

STEVE ALLEN

A Golden Trashery of Mad:
1st printing with dust jacket $150-$200

Foreword

IT IS always painful when someone or something you love disappoints you. Like when your favorite lighter doesn't work, or your dog bites you, or your son decides not to be a doctor.

In that way MAD has been painful to me. I once loved MAD because I had such high hopes for it as a publication that fought injustice, debunked the fake, deflated the pompous and crusaded for a better life. But MAD disappointed me.

For instance, the new big-circulation MAD has yet to bring up the issue of postal rates in Kenya. That may not seem terribly important until you realize there are people walking the streets of Nairobi with unmailed letters in their hands because they haven't been able to save up enough money to buy a stamp.

Another thing. This is supposedly a sampling of MAD's best. Is there an article on pipes? No.

However, if MAD had the courage to print an article telling us how to break in a pipe, it would prevent the burning of many tongues and gums, and even suits. MAD, that once-great believer in humanity, doesn't care to print the very best and thereby prevent burned tongues. To say nothing of taste buds that are dulled for three or four days.

These may seem like minor complaints, but what about a few of the other things that MAD has overlooked, like the overpricing of fly repellent in India, or warning the public of the danger of being hit by a meteor, or an asteroid, or another man walking down the street.

Yet, the editors represent themselves as men of vision. If they're such men of vision how come they haven't been able to see that new carpeting gives you a shock of electricity when you touch a doorknob? Who are they covering up for? The implication is that the Carpet Lobby and the Doorknob Lobby have been up to some hanky-panky in MAD's lobby.

No, MAD doesn't dare offend the carpeting and doorknob people. Nor do they dare offend the womanhood of America who every year squeeze more and more toothpaste tubes *at the top,* making it impossible for men to brush their teeth properly, leading to decadence in the teeth and other high places.

It may seem that I'm carping, but while these *oversights,* in themselves, don't mean anything, they are symptomatic. The MAD magazine that I loved would not have allowed these trickles of nastiness to pass unnoticed.

The old MAD would not have suppressed the up-to-now unknown fact that clothing manufacturers breed millions of moths yearly. This is a fact which should be investigated.

And what has MAD said about the shortage of plankton which has reached such a frightening degree that millions of salmon and tuna-fish die every year before they reach the cannery?

Also, what about those men in parking lots who would have been a prime target for the MAD I loved? I'm talking about those men in grease-stained pants who put dents in cars and then look at you with innocent disbelief in their eyes and say those famous words: "You drove it in that way, Mac!"

And why did MAD refuse to print my exposé telling of shoelaces that break in the middle of tying a shoe, and telling how hard it is to tie the ends? Why did MAD suppress that?

Have they once called on me to help them expose the *real* problems in the world today? No. The new MAD is too busy attacking silly things like **conformity, misleading advertising, togetherness, mediocre TV programs and insipid motion pictures** to be concerned with the real issues of the day like burned tongues, dented fenders and broken shoelaces.

Is MAD afraid to tackle these subjects? Is MAD a mag or a mouse?

The question is academic. What is important, however, is that we do not blame the publication. Remember, there is no such thing as a bad magazine; there are only rotten editors.

Sid Caesar

In 1969, the World Publishing Company produced *The Ridiculously Expensive Mad,* priced at $9.95 (which was a small fortune at the time). A smorgasbord of articles, front and back cover reprints, records, stickers, stencils, and other bonus items, the book represented 17 years of *Mad*ness. Because of all the bonuses it is quite difficult to find intact and in nice condition. To make matters worse, the dust jacket was printed on delicate stock and was easily torn. Tipped into the front of each copy were directions on assembling the "*Mad* Mobile" which were omitted in the body of the book. The book sold out its run of 25,000 copies, but because of the expense, World did not choose to reprint.

A NOTE TO HELP YOU ENJOY THIS BOOK

In order to encourage you to participate in the fun, we have deliberately omitted the Instructions for assembling the "MAD Mobile" at the bottom of page 208. So here they are. Cut them out and paste them there yourself! See?! You're busy enjoying this book already!!

INSTRUCTIONS FOR ASSEMBLING THIS RIDICULOUS MESS

Okay, Gang, here we go! Follow these simple instructions, and you'll be the proud owner of this colorful, artistic and amusing dust-catcher. The first and most important step is to obtain the materials needed to connect the various units of the Mobile together. These consist of a package of "King Size Plastic Straws," a spool of thread, a needle, and a pair of scissors. Take your scissors and carefully cut out the individual MAD Mobile units on their dotted lines. After all the parts are cut out, lay them out in the approximate position shown in the diagram above. Then, measure and cut the plastic straws to the sizes indicated, and place them in their correct positions. Now comes the hard part: Thread a needle! As soon as your eyes come back into focus, attach slightly more than the indicated length of thread to each Mobile unit by piercing it with the threaded needle at the point indicated by the white dot, and tying a firm knot. The other end of the thread is then attached to the end of the straw in the same manner, piercing the straw about ⅛" from the end. However, where the threads are attached to the centers of straws, DO NOT PIERCE! Wrap thread around middle of straw twice and tie a knot! This will enable you to slide the straw back and forth to balance it after Mobile is completely assembled. When all Mobile units and straws are connected as per diagram, hang the Mobile from the top thread and adjust the wrapped threads at the centers of the straws until they (and their hanging units) balance horizontally, and everything falls apart, you tear all your hair out, and you swear never to buy MAD Magazine again . . .

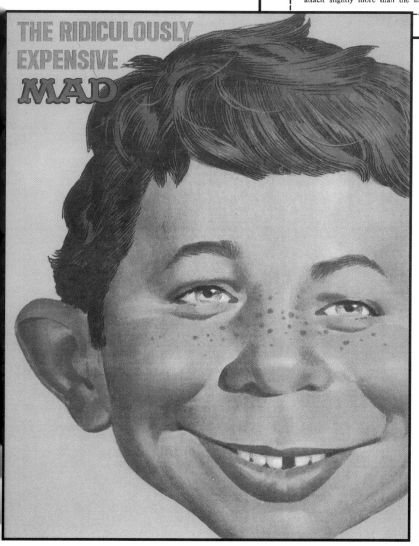

This classic Royal Copenhagen ceramic, circa 1950s, has absolutely nothing to do with this book. HOOHAH!

The Ridiculously Expensive Mad: with dust jacket $150–$200

CHAPTER FIVE

Alfred E. Neuman Halloween Costumes

In 1960 Collegeville Costumes issued two versions of costumes bearing the likeness of Alfred E. Neuman; a photo of the costumes appeared in the letters column of *Mad* #59. In a 1989 letter Gaines reported "very poor sales" of the costumes, and indeed these items are seldom encountered today. Of the two, the larger "Mardi Gras walk along" is much more rare than the "conventional costume and mask." No example of the box for the "Mardi Gras" version could be found for inclusion in this book, but the "conventional" costume came in a generic box with "*Mad*-(What–Me Worry?)" stamped on the side, along with the costume size and an EC Publications copyright.

(See "The New Collectibles" [section two, chapter twelve] for the "Alfred E. Neuman Disguise Kit" and "Alfred Ears.")

Halloween costumes (1960): conventional, in box $350-$400

Mardi Gras walk-along $375-$425, add $50 for box

Conventional

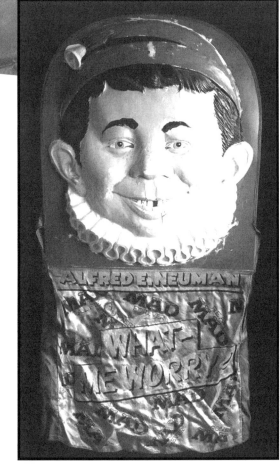

The Mad-men pose in Alfred E. Neuman masks on an early Mad trip; each mask today would be worth $50-$100. Gaines is standing second from left.

Mardi Gras walk along

"Alfred E. Neuman for President" kits

Mad's candidate for President in 1960 was supported by a five-piece kit, available for $1.00 by mail order; a full page ad appears on the inside back cover of *Mad* #55. Included was a full color 2 1/2" pinback button, campaign cap, door sign, 17" x 22" 2-color poster, and a Day-Glo bumper sticker. Also included in some kits was a business card size "Alfred E. Neuman Fan Club Member" card. Kits were also sent to radio and television stations to promote *Mad* and Alfred's campaign, along with an extremely rare cover letter on *Mad* stationery. Complete kits are rarely encountered, but individual pieces do turn up, particularly the pin back button.

In 1964, with issue #89 *Mad* offered a new version of the kit, which included two color posters, 2 1/2" pinback button, six lapel tabs, and a day-glo bumper sticker. Complete 1964 kits are more frequently encountered than the 1960 version; when individual pieces are found they tend to be the pinback button, tab pins, and bumper sticker.

For the 1968 election, *Mad* recycled the 1964 kit (with one less tab pin) and offered them in a few low-key ads in the letter columns. There is one difference between the 1964 and 1968 kits: The return address on the manila envelope bears the 485 MADison Avenue address, not the 850 Third Avenue address on the 1964 kit. Gaines described the sales of all three kits as "a disaster."

"Alfred E. Neuman for President" kit (1960): A complete kit (in envelope) with the rare cover letter sold at auction in June 1994 for $1,192

"Alfred E. Neuman for President" kit (1964): full kit (in envelope) $250, button $40, tab pin $20, poster $25, bumper sticker $20

"Alfred E. Neuman for President" kit (1968): full kit (in envelope) $225-$250, button $40, tab pin $20, poster $25, bumper sticker $20

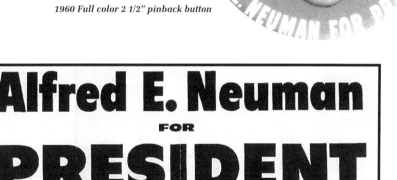

1960 Full color 2 1/2" pinback button

1960 Campaign cap

Alfred E. Neuman
FOR
PRESIDENT
CAMPAIGN HEADQUARTERS

1960 Door sign

1960 Day-Glo bumper sticker

1960 Poster

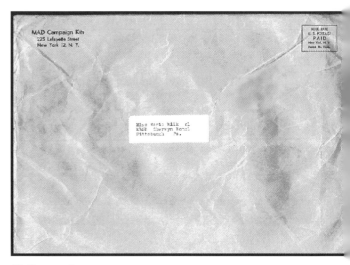

Mailing envelope

OFFICIAL
ALFRED E. NEUMAN
FAN CLUB MEMBER

When money talks, nobody criticizes an accent.
Sometimes the best scheme for doubling your money is to fold it in half and stuff it back into your wallet.

1960 Fan Club Member card

MAD

225 LAFAYETTE STREET • NEW YORK 12, NEW YORK • CAnal 6-1994

Dear Fellow Communicator:-

This issue of MAD triggers the opening gun in Alfred E. Neuman's campaign for the Presidency. (The Presidency of what, we're not too sure, but we're willing to go along with a gag...and we assume you are, too!) So, we are including, along with your regular issue of the magazine, one of our "Alfred E. Neuman for President" kits.

We'd like to thank you for your support of MAD in the past, and for the kind words you've said about us over the air. (If you haven't said anything, we'd like to thank you for that, too. Because you could have said some awful things, so we're still ahead!)

As in the past, we invite you to cite (a nice word for "swipe") from our pages to help you fill your air time, asking only for an occasional credit in return (which is only smart, since you wouldn't want to be blamed for the stuff, anyway!) And, if you like the idea, help support Alfred E. Neuman for President. As you can see by the cover of this issue, you'll be in good company.

MAD-ly

Al Feldstein
Editor

Rare promotional cover letter

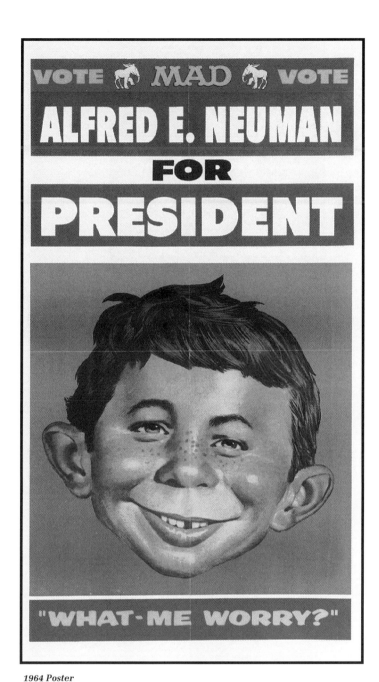

1964 Poster

1964 Lapel tabs

1964 2 1/2" Pinback button

1964 Day-Glo bumper sticker

Other "Alfred E. Neuman for President" Items:

"Alfred E. Neuman for President" Poster (1980)
This full color poster was made for sale during the 1980 Presidential campaign. The manufacturer is unknown, but the poster was likely a licensed product.

"Alfred E. Neuman for President" poster (1980): $20-$25

1984 "Alfred E. Neuman for President" T-shirts

A company calling itself "Alfred for President" issued T-shirts coinciding with the 1984 Presidential election. A licensed product, the shirts were sold in retail stores nationwide. A full page ad appears on the inside front cover of *Mad* #251. The shirts sold at $10 for an adult size and $8 for a "kid" shirt, and came with a "write-in ballot" card that entitled one to a bumper sticker.

"Alfred E. Neuman for President" T-shirt (1984): $25-$35

Ballot card $15

Bumper sticker $15

Shirt and write-in ballot

Bumper sticker

Busts of Alfred E. Neuman (china bisque)

In issue #53 (March 1960) *Mad* began offering two sizes of china bisque busts of Alfred E. Neuman, probably as a play on the small bisque busts of composers like Mozart and Beethoven popular at the time. Two sizes were offered, a 5 1/2" piece for $2.00 and a 3 3/4" size for $1.00. The model for the head was sculpted by Kelly Freas and the busts were manufactured by Contemporary Ceramics of Chatham, New Jersey. Prices for the busts have escalated sharply in recent years. The large version is more difficult to find. Reportedly, of the largest size (7" tall) prototypes that were made, Feldstein preferred the fully glazed version while Gaines preferred the unglazed version, so a compromise was reached with the base glazed and the head unglazed on the production models. In all probability, only a few thousand of these were sold as they were available only through ads in *Mad*. Counterfeit busts appeared in the Pacific Northwest around 1992. These are slightly smaller than the large bust, are lighter in weight, and have red felt bottoms.

Busts, china bisque (1960): 5 1/2" size $350-$400

3 3/4" size $275-$325

7" prototype bust, no reported sales

Counterfeit bust $50

Mad Busts

Fully-glazed prototype

Aurora Alfred E. Neuman model kit

In 1965 Aurora, maker of plastic model kits, issued an Alfred E. Neuman kit for $1.49. The model came complete with four different signs ("Down with TV, school, etc.," "Listen to the Voice of Experience," "Love thy Neighbor," and "Honesty is the Best Policy") and four sets of arms. Norman Mingo provided the full color Alfred portrait for the box, but the likeness on the model itself leaves something to be desired. The kit is sought both by *Mad* and plastic model kit collectors. A premium is put on kits that are "mint in box," meaning unopened and wrapped in the original cellophane. Also desirable is the fully-painted factory production model used for display purposes in hobby shops; this version is quite hard to find. A version of the model with bi-lingual packaging (in English and French) was made for sale in Canada. The 1965 Aurora catalog is called "Alfred E. Neuman presents Aurora" and features Alfred on the cover.

Model kit, Aurora (1965): kit in sealed box $225-$275, nice "built up" $75-$90

factory-made demo $275-$325, 1965 Aurora catalog with Alfred on cover $100

"Who Needs You?" *Mad* poster

Issued in 1969 at the height of the '60s poster craze, the "Who Needs You?" slogan and the Uncle Sam image of Alfred E. Neuman were right at home next to psychedelic posters of John Lennon and Mr. Spock. Licensed by Pandora Productions of Wayzata, MN, the full color poster measured 29" x 23" and sold for $1.98. The Norman Mingo artwork was taken from the cover of *Mad* #126. The poster is rare. A similar "Who Needs You?" poster was made in 1991 by *Mad* for promotional purposes.

Richard Nixon against a flag

"Who Needs You"

He Kept Our Boys Out Of Northern Ireland

While not a technically a *Mad* product, Pandora Productions released an interesting poster in 1971, a collaboration between *Mad* artist Jack Rickard and staffer Jerry De Fuccio, showing Richard Nixon against a flag. The poster measured about 17" x 22" and was in full color; it sold for $1.00.

Western Graphics Corporation of Eugene, Oregon, released two *Mad* posters in the late 1970s, both with Don Martin artwork. The posters each bore the legend "Another *Mad* Poster" and carried catalog numbers of #446 and #447. Poster #446 lists a copyright of 1977 and #447 lists a date of 1974, but these are likely the dates of EC Publications' original copyrights on the artwork, and not the actual date of release.
(See section on "The New Collectibles" [section two, chapter 12] for other *Mad* posters.)

Poster, "Who Needs You?," rare (1969): $100

Poster, "Richard Nixon against flag" (1971): $20

Posters, "Another Mad poster" (Western Graphics #446 and 447, late 1970s): $15-$20 each

"Another Mad Poster"

CHAPTER SiX

Mad Stationery

Mad has been published from three different offices over the years and has used several types of unique and desirable stationery, all of which is difficult to come by. The first example was used when *Mad* graduated to a 25¢ magazine (mid-1955). Note the use of the original magazine logo. The second example (with envelope) probably dates from 1956 or '57, after Al Feldstein took over editorship. The third (with envelope) dates from the early 1960s after *Mad* moved to 850 Third Ave. The fourth (with envelope) was used from the late '60s through the 1970s and bears the 485 MADison Ave. address; the letterhead reveals a watermark of Alfred E. Neuman when held up to the light. Because of cost, *Mad* opted for the version shown in example five, the most recent version at this writing.

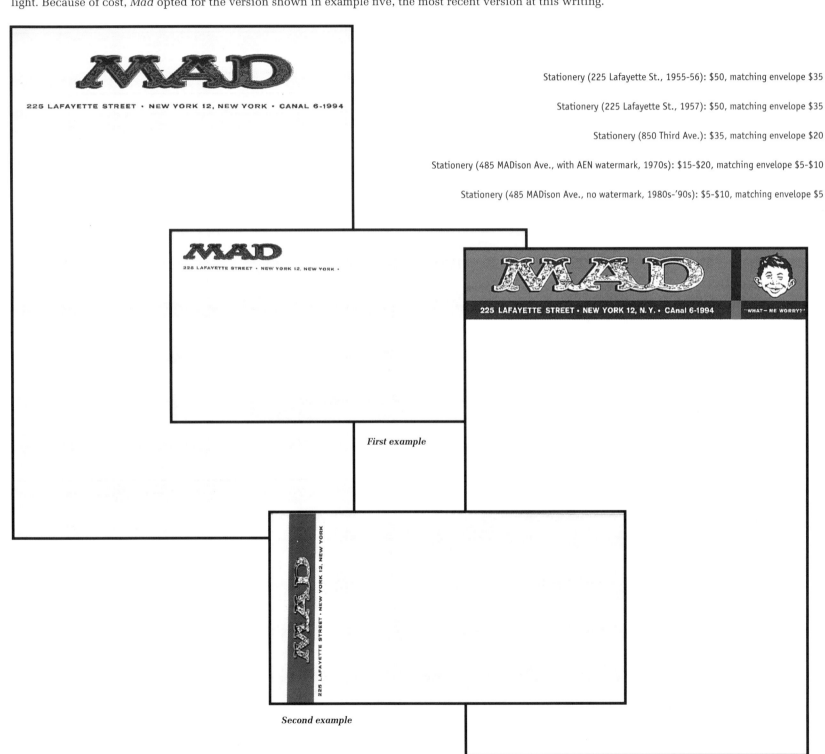

Stationery (225 Lafayette St., 1955-56): $50, matching envelope $35

Stationery (225 Lafayette St., 1957): $50, matching envelope $35

Stationery (850 Third Ave.): $35, matching envelope $20

Stationery (485 MADison Ave., with AEN watermark, 1970s): $15-$20, matching envelope $5-$10

Stationery (485 MADison Ave., no watermark, 1980s-'90s): $5-$10, matching envelope $5

First example

Second example

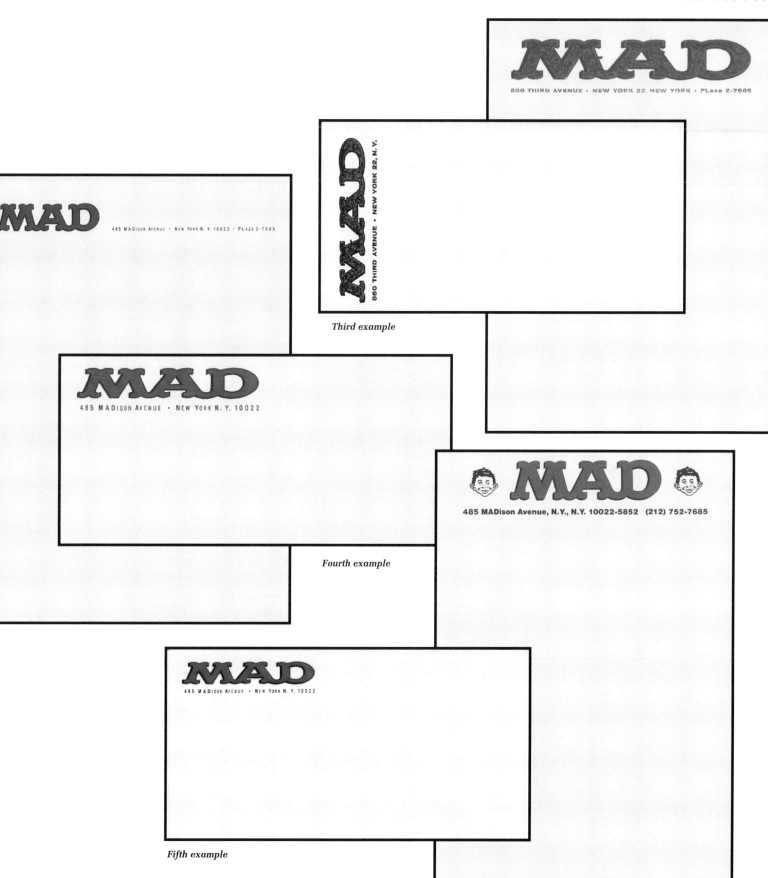

Third example

Fourth example

Fifth example

This mailing envelope (12" x 9") dates from shortly after *Mad* became a magazine:

Mailing envelope (225 Lafayette St., 1956, 12" x 9"): $40

Mad Change of Address Cards

When *Mad* moved its offices in 1961 from 225 Lafayette St. to 850 Third Ave., this 7 1/4" x 3 3/4" card was sent; the card is on white stock with red ink. The Don Martin art was taken from "The Children's Hour" in *Mad* #36.

A different card was sent in 1966 when the office changed again to the current address of 485 MADison Ave.; this card was also on white stock with red ink. Art director John Putnam provided the artwork for this mailing piece.

Change of address cards: 850 Third Ave., $25-$50; 485 MADison Ave., $25-$50

Mad rejection slips:

Rejection slips (circa 1971): $25-$50

Rejection slips (current): $5

Dear Contributor:-

Sorry, but we've got bad news!

You've been rejected!

Don't take this personally, though. All of us feel rejected at one time or another. At least, that's what our group therapist tells us here at MAD. He says we shouldn't worry about it.

So that should be your attitude: "What-Me worry?"

Besides - although you've been rejected, things could have been a lot worse. Your material might have been ACCEPTED!

Then where would you be?

MAD-ly

Al Feldstein

Al Feldstein
Editor

P.S. Our group therapist also mentioned that many people are so rejected by a rejection that they don't try again. And we wouldn't want THAT! We really WOULD like you to keep sending us your article ideas and scripts. . .so we can keep sending you these idiotic rejection slips!

Rejection slip, circa 1971. These bear the signature "Al Feldstein," but these letters were usually signed by assistant editors Nick Meglin and Jerry De Fuccio. The example shown was signed by De Fuccio.

485 MADison Avenue, N.Y., N.Y. 10022-5852 (212) 752-7685

Dear Friend,

Unlike many cold, callous Editors, we at Mad believe that anyone taking the time and trouble to submit material deserves a warm, personal note rather than an indifferent form letter. So please consider this to be a warm, personal note rather than the indifferent form letter it really is!

Obviously, since no check fell out of the envelope, we didn't find your material acceptable. Sorry about that! We herewith return it to you as positive proof of our stupidity and poor judgement. Perhaps some of the statements listed below will offer more in the way of an explanation. Then again, perhaps not. In any case, let us assure you that all submissions are read by at least one Editor and not by some part-time High School English major!

Unfortunately, we cannot guarantee that one Editor has as much intelligence, taste, or capability as some part-time High School English major, so proceed at your own risk!

MAD-ly yours,
The Editors

☐ We did it.

☐ We're doing it!

☐ Material not in the MAD vein or it just didn't tickle our funny bone.

☐ Always include a stamped, self-addressed envelope with submission.

☐ We're not interested in comic strips, cartoons, "characters," book manuscripts, poetry, song parodies, TV or movie satires, riddles, articles about Alfred E. Neuman, classifieds, advice columns, articles like "you know you're really a _____ when," or rehashes of what we've already done.

☐ The enormous amount of submissions and special requests have made individual criticism, sketches, caricatures, biographical data, and other professional advice from MAD artists, writers, and editors impossible.

☐ We cannot use very timely material as we are often planning issues as far as six months in advance.

☐ We're not interested in prose, text, or first/second/third person narratives—even though you're sure "one of our great artists can do wonders with it!"

☐ Submit a premise with 3 or 4 examples of how you intend to carry it through, describing the action and visual content of each example. Rough sketches are welcomed, but not necessary.

☐ With hundreds of weekly submissions, it is impossible to recall each one individually. All material is read, considered, and returned within three to four weeks if not accepted, provided it was submitted with a stamped, self-addressed envelope. If after that time it hasn't been returned, it must be assumed it never arrived here, or, if it did, it was mailed back to you and never arrived there! Check your post office!

☐ Since all MAD art and script is bought freelance, there are no staff writing or drawing positions available.

Rejection slip, circa 1991

"Cheap Crummy Souvenir of My Visit to *Mad*"

As a gesture to fans who stop by, *Mad* has produced several giveaway posters. The first version (fig. 1), used throughout the 1960s, measures about 17" x 8 1/2" and is printed on beige stock; the same art was used with a grey background and a green background, at a size of 15 3/4" x 7 1/2." The second version (fig. 2) is from the mid-'70s and measures 11 1/2" x 15." An 8" x 10 1/4" flyer with the same art (fig. 3) was sent to people who wrote letters to *Mad*, bearing the legend "Our Cheap Crummy Answer to Your Letter to *Mad*." The third version (fig. 4) is the 1980s giveaway, with the legend "State of the *Mad* Art;" the poster measures 15 1/2" x 12." The back has biographies of the *Mad* artists who are depicted on the front. The Don Martin flyer (fig. 5) dates from the 1970s.

fig. 2

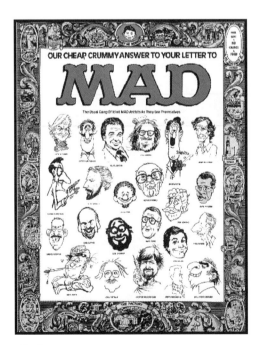

fig. 3

A CHEAP, CRUMMY SOUVENIR OF MY VISIT TO MAD MAGAZINE

The Usual Gang Of Idiot MAD Artists As They See Themselves

fig. 1

The Fake Don Martin

The Real Don Martin

DON MARTIN was born in Passaic, New Jersey, grew up in Brookside, New Jersey, and attended public school in Morristown, New Jersey. It is interesting that all 3 towns deny any and all of this information.

After graduating from high school, Don attended the Newark School of Fine and Industrial Art for 3 years, then completed a 4th year of art education at the Pennsylvania Academy of Art in Philadelphia. It is interesting that both schools deny any and all of this information.

Seeking "his place in the sun," Don figured the best place for things like that was Miami Beach, where indeed he found sun, but very little else. He worked as a shipping clerk, window trimmer, and parking lot attendant before he discovered what he "was born to do with his life"—unemployment! But since that field had better opportunity in the New York City area, Don moved himself and some of his humorous sketches back north and found freelance work designing studio cards, record album covers, and advertising spots. When he felt that what was left of his art talent had been thoroughly spent, he tried MAD Magazine, known for its high level of low taste! Don's work was so bad he was given freelance assignments immediately. That was in MAD's Issue #29 (1956) and he hasn't missed an issue since!

Don's first MAD Paperback Book appeared in 1962 and to date has sold over one million copies. His subsequent paperbacks are selling at about the same rate of speed, and have been translated into 8 languages, none of which are understandable.

Don is married and has one son. It is interesting that both his wife and child deny any and all of this information!

fig. 5

"Cheap Crummy Souvenir" posters (1960s; beige, grey or green): $25-$40

"Cheap Crummy Answer to Your Letter to *Mad*" flyer (1970s): $20-$25, poster $25

"State of the *Mad* Art" poster (1980s): $5-$10

Don Martin flyer (1970s): $15-$25

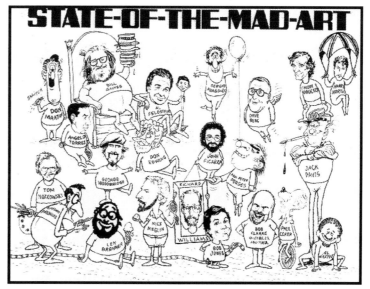

fig. 4

161

CHAPTER SEVEN

The Mad Show items

The Mad Show premiered January 9, 1966 at the New Theatre off-Broadway in New York. The show enjoyed good reviews and had quite a healthy life, adding companies in Chicago and in Pittsburgh, and touring companies in Boston, Los Angeles, Detroit, and San Francisco. A number of items related to the show exist, not the least of which is the *Original Cast Album* on Columbia Records. Sporting art by Jack Davis, the LP jacket featured humorous liner notes by Nick Meglin detailing the show's development. The album can be found in monaural and stereo versions.

The Mad Show LP (1966): stereo $50, mono $35

The March 11, 1966 *Life* magazine had a two-page photo spread on *The Mad Show* that gives a good indication of what the show looked like (the "Batman" tv show cover makes this issue much more expensive than it would normally be).

Life magazine, March 11, 1966 (*Mad Show* photos): $25

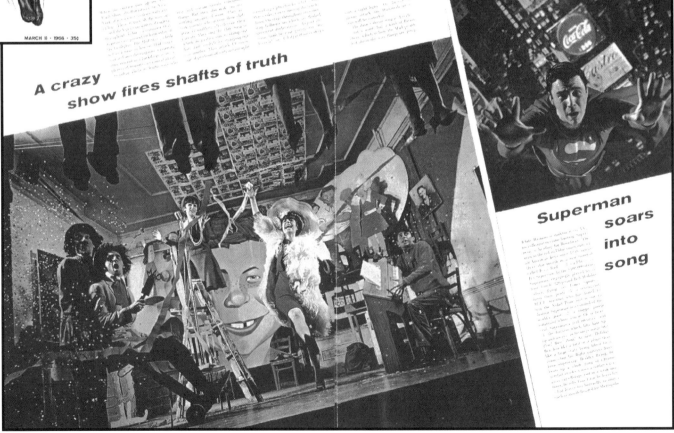

The "Showcard" program was given to the audience and features bios of the actors and show creators; on the back cover is an ad for the album. Also shown: program from the Pittsburgh, Pa. production.

The Mad Show Showcard (program): $35

Chicago, Pittsburgh or other cities $20

These two tab pins were given to the audience in the early part of the show's run, and both are difficult to find. The button reading "HAPPY Medium" is from the Chicago company, and the other is from the New York production ("Happy Medium" was the name of the Chicago theatre staging the show).

The Mad Show tab pins (two different): $35 each

A *Mad Show* sweatshirt was made for cast members, and is extremely rare. Unfortunately, one of these shirts, owned by Nick Meglin, was lost in the mail on its way to appear in this book. More fortunate in its fate is this rare *Mad Show* tile potholder (courtesy of Meglin) that was made for members of the cast and staff, from Designed Tiles of New York.

The Mad Show sweatshirt: no reported sales

The Mad Show tile potholder: $150

Mayor Lindsay congratulates Capt. Stan Hart of "The MAD Show Team" on its win.

Mad writer Stan Hart in a *Mad Show* sweatshirt, with New York Mayor John Lindsay (from *Mad* #109).

Mad Show tile potholder

This 22" x 14" Day-Glo poster for display outside the theatre is scarce; in 1991 a Long Island nostalgia dealer found a small cache in mint condition.

The Mad Show display poster: $75

Ticket stub

Mad logo slide projection for The Mad Show.

Theatrical publisher Samuel French got the right to sell the show package for use in regional productions. For a licensing fee, one could get everything needed to produce the piece, including music, slides and script. For those interested in simply reading the script, a small size paperback is available from French, as are a set of 34 color slides for use in mounting the show. Collectors must affirm that a production is not being planned, and that the slides are for collecting purposes only. The ticket stub shown is from one such regional production.

The Mad Show script (Samuel French): $5.50

The Mad Show color slides (for staging play): $12

Script

Slide projections for The Mad Show.

Report obscene mail to your postmaster. He loves it.

SUPPORT AIR POLLUTION

The Mad World of William M. Gaines

Published as a hardcover in late 1972, *The Mad World of William M. Gaines* is a "must read" for EC and *Mad* collectors. Published by Lyle Stuart, a somewhat renegade publisher and one of Gaines's closest friends, the book was written by Frank Jacobs, one of *Mad*'s most venerable and best contributors. Though some of the material is now dated, it is packed with anecdotes and other information and makes for quite an enjoyable read.

Bantam Books published a paperback version in 1973 which contains a 16-page color section of artwork given to Gaines by various *Mad* artists to commemorate *Mad* trips. The paperback omits the black and white photos that appear in the hardback; completists will want both editions. A "Paperback Book Club" edition has also been reported.

The Mad World of William M. Gaines:
hardback with dust jacket $25-$50

Paperback $5-$10

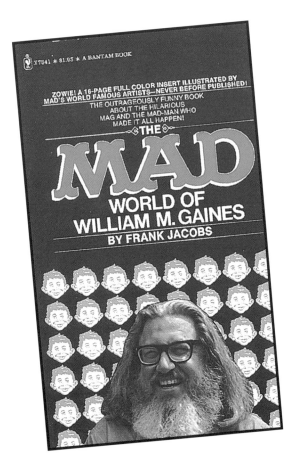

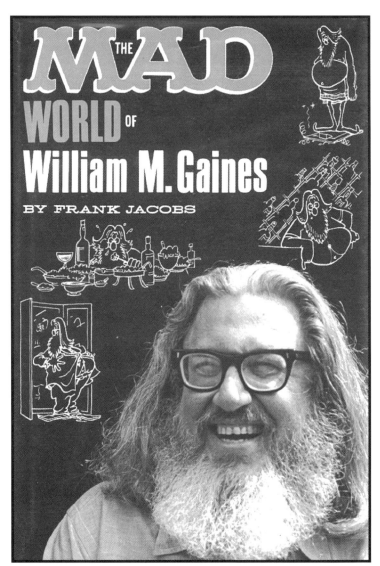

The Mad Morality

Written by Vernard Eller, a Professor of Religion, *The Mad Morality* was published in 1970 by Abingdon Press, publisher of religious books. The book is illustrated with reprints of various *Mad* articles to illustrate Eller's point that *Mad*'s viewpoint is more moral than many people give it credit for. The book was issued as an 8 1/2" x 11" trade paperback for $2.79; a hardback with dust jacket has also been seen, probably manufactured for sale to libraries. The book had its origins in an article Eller wrote for the December 1967 issue of the *Christian Century*, an ecumenical weekly printed on pulp paper. No *Mad* artwork appears in this article.

A paperback was issued by Signet in January 1972, for 95¢. The book used the same cover artwork as the full size version.

A 1 1/2" two color (red and black) pinback button with Alfred E. Neuman's face and the slogan "What, Me Moral?" was made to promote the book. While it is not clear whether Abingdon Press or Signet made the button (but probably Signet), what is clear is that Gaines was greatly offended by the slogan and forced the publisher to destroy the buttons. Few got out.

The Mad Morality: hardback with dust jacket $50-$100
Trade paperback $25-$35, paperback $5

Christian Century, Dec. 1967 (*Mad Morality* article): $10

Pinback button, "What, Me Moral?": no reported sales

Completely Mad

Completely Mad

Writer Maria Reidelbach's *Completely Mad* was published by Little, Brown and Co. in 1991. Designed as a 10" x 10" "coffee table" hardcover, the book contains a *Mad* cover gallery and numerous reprints, as well as a history stretching back into the EC era and before. The book was priced at $39.95. A paperbound pre-release version of *Completely Mad* containing eight pages of excerpts from the book was made for solicitation purposes, and a 2 1/2" pinback button was given out at the 1991 American Bookseller's Association convention in New York. The 3,000 buttons were given out in about three hours. For the 1992 American Bookseller's Association convention in Anaheim, California, a promotional Shriner-style red felt fez was created. These also quickly disappeared. The book received widespread attention in print and on television, with Reidelbach and Gaines and the *Mad* staff granting interviews. Apparently catching Little, Brown by surprise, *Completely Mad* completely sold out of its first printing of 30,000 copies well before Christmas of 1991. A second printing was issued in the middle of 1992, at $50. A trade paperback edition was published in September, 1992, at $24.95, and a Quality Paperback Book Club edition was issued at $16.95.

Fez

Pinback button

Completely Mad (1991), first printing hardback with dust jacket: $40

Paperback: $25

Quality Paperback Book Club (no UPC symbol or price on cover): $16.95

Pinback button, *Completely Mad*: no reported sales

Fez, *Completely Mad*: $65

Good Days and Mad

Dick DeBartolo's memoirs of life at *Mad* in general and of Bill Gaines in particular, entitled *Good Days and Mad*, was released in November 1994. The 8 3/4" by 9 1/2" hardcover book (in dust jacket) was published by Thunder's Mouth Press and retails for $29.95. In typical *Mad* fashion, the book includes thirteen different forwards by the likes of Annie Gaines, Nick Meglin, John Ficarra, Lenny Brenner, Al Jaffee, Charlie Kadau and Joe Raiola, George Woodbridge, and Mort Drucker. Among other revelations, DeBartolo recounts a clandestine climb up into the arm of the Statue of Liberty (with Gaines getting stuck in the narrow stairwell near the top) and a conversation with Bill Gaines from beyond the grave.

Good Days and Mad (1994), first printing hardback with dust jacket: $29.95

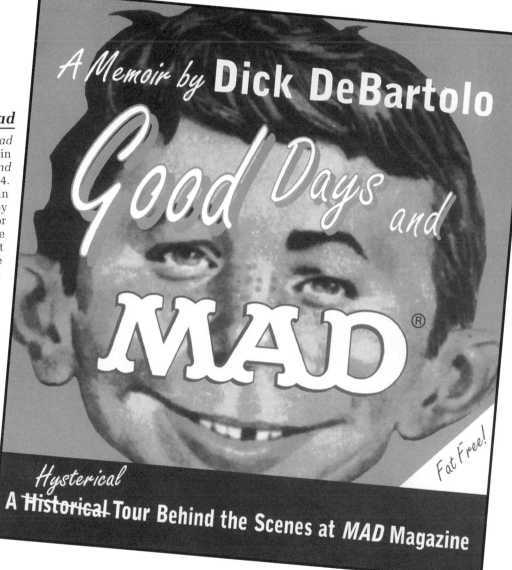

A Memoir by **Dick DeBartolo**

Good Days and **MAD**®

Fat Free!

~~Historical~~ Hysterical
A ~~Historical~~ Tour Behind the Scenes at *MAD* Magazine

The Mad Magazine Game

In 1979 Parker Brothers released a board game inspired by *Mad*, entitled *The Mad Magazine Game*. Artwork on the box lid was by Jack Davis. A popular game upon introduction, it even outsold *Monopoly* for a time; the objective, however, was to lose all your money. The game was unavailable by the mid 1980s, and in 1988 a new edition in a slightly larger box was brought out, as the *What–Me Worry?* game; the *Mad* logo appears prominently on the box. Foreign versions exist; the example shown is a Canadian product that was exported for sale in Japan (with a tipped-in instruction sheet in Japanese).

Mad Magazine Game (1979): $25

"What-Me Worry?" Game (1988): $15

foreign versions: $35

Mad Magazine Card Game

Parker Brothers released a companion to *The Mad Magazine Game* in 1980, entitled *The Mad Magazine Card Game*. Artwork on the playing cards and box was again by Davis; the objective was to lose all your cards. Unlike its companion game, the *Mad Magazine Card Game* has been unavailable for a number of years. Foreign versions of the game exist; the example shown was made for sale in Japan.

Mad Magazine Card Game (1980): $20

foreign versions: $30

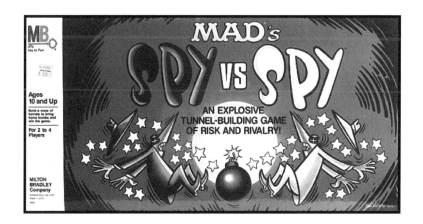

Mad's Spy vs Spy board and computer games

Milton Bradley released in 1986 a board game based on the *Mad* feature *Spy vs Spy*; the object is to steal the most bombs.

Spy vs Spy board game (1986): $15

In 1984 First Star Software released the first volume of the *Spy vs Spy* computer game, for use on Commodore 64, Apple II, and Atari home computers. (A Nintendo version of Volume one was issued in 1988 by Kemco). Volume two, "The Island Caper," was released by First Star in 1985. Advantage, under license from First Star, later released both volumes in the same box as "Spy vs Spy Vol. I and II". "Arctic Antics" (*Spy vs Spy* vol. III) was released in 1989 by EPYX. A Nintendo Game Boy version of *Spy vs Spy* was issued in 1992.

Spy vs Spy video game (Nintendo version, 1988): $10

Spy vs Spy computer game (1984): $15-$20

Spy vs Spy III, Arctic Antics (1987): $10

Spy vs Spy, the Island Caper computer game (1985): $15-$20

Spy vs Spy, Vol. I and II" computer game: $10

Spy vs Spy Game Boy (Nintendo) video game (1992): retail $29.99

CHAPTER TEN

Mad Calendars

From 1976-1981 Warner Books issued an attractive series of *Mad* calendars, designed by Thomas Nozkowski. The 1978 version is noteworthy, as its center section features postage stamp-size reproductions of every cover published to that time.

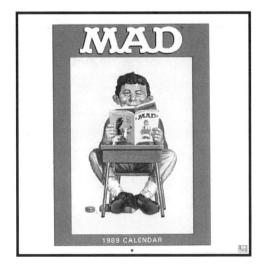

Landmark Calendars issued two calendars in 1989 and 1990; their version reproduces classic covers shot from the original art with no type or logos.

For 1993, Character Imprints of Boulder Colorado released the *Mad 1993 Prehysterical Calendar*, at $9.95. Plans for a *Mad Sports Calendar* in 1994 were abandoned.

Calendars, 1976-1981: $10-$15 each

Calendars, 1989, 1990: $8-$10 each

Calendar, 1993: $9.95

Fleer Goes Mad stickers

In 1983 the Fleer company issued a series of stickers called *Fleer Goes Mad*. The stickers came in an illustrated wax paper wrapper ("wax pack") with a slab of bubble gum; there are 128 numbered stickers and another 64 un-numbered stickers in the complete set. Complete sets are difficult to put together, with many card dealers unable to complete even one, after opening several boxes; many dealers gave up and refused to offer complete sets at all. A "*Mad* Sticker Album" was also issued. As with all bubble gum cards, the wrappers and the display boxes are collectible. A promotional banner, 4 3/4" x 17," was issued to dealers and is also desirable.

Fleer Goes Mad stickers (1983): complete set $50-$75,

singles 35¢, album $5-$10, empty box $20, banner $15,

wrapper $10, unopened pack $5

Fleer released a *Mad* parody card as part of its *Crazy Magazine Covers* set (circa 1972); the magazine is called "Bad". The card is reproduced on the box, and the backs of the nine checklist cards to the set are puzzle pieces that make up a large version of the "Bad" cover.

Crazy Magazine Covers, Bad card (1977): card $1.00
display box (shows Bad card) $5

Fleer released a *Best of Cracked Magazine* set, and card #11 shows the cover to *Cracked* #107 which pictures a voodoo doll that casts a familiar shadow.

Best of Cracked Magazine cards, card #11 (AEN shadow): $1.00

Another *Mad* parody card, issued by Topps in 1980, is found on card #145 of the *Wacky Packages* set, entitled "Mud, the humor magazine for pigs."

Wacky Packages #145 ("Mud" card): $1.00

Active Marketing International released a "Bad" parody card in 1993 as part of their "Defective Comics" card set. The back of the card has a parody of *Mad*'s origins and creators (Bill Gainsweight and Hardly Kurtzy).

Defective Comics "Bad" card: 50¢

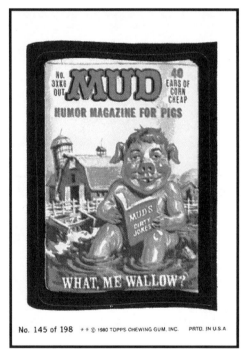

Mad Magazine Trading Cards

Lime Rock International released their *Mad Magazine Trading Cards* in 1992. This 55-card set includes special Alfred E. Neuman holograms (20,000 made), and 2,000 uncut sheet instant winners, all randomly inserted in the packs. A set of six promo cards were issued to dealers. A second series was released in late 1992, again with 55 cards. A four card promo set was released to dealers (numbered 7-10). Two holograms were randomly inserted: a gold double-sided "Vote *Mad*" hologram (with Bush and Clinton) and a silver *Spy vs Spy* hologram. A special gold *Spy vs Spy* hologram was also made for Lime Rock Insider Trading Club members. A numbered Commemorative Set, containing both series (and four *Spy vs Spy* promo cards) in a plastic binder, was offered at $25. A *Spy vs Spy* set (55 cards and two holograms) was issued in 1993. Available to Lime Rock Insider Trading Club members were numbered uncut sheets of each set ($50), uncut promo card sheets ($10), and Gold Bush/Clinton holograms signed by James Warhola ($25). A third series was released in 1994, but collector interest had begun to fade; prices for the third series are about the same as for the second series.

Mad Magazine Trading Cards, series one (1992): unopened box $25, unopened pack $1, hologram $20-$25, promo cards $2.50 each, uncut sheet $50, uncut promo sheets $10, set $6-$10

Mad Magazine Trading Cards, series two (1992): unopened box $25, unopened pack $1, holograms $5-$10, promo cards $2.50 each, uncut sheet $50, uncut promo sheets $10, set $6-$10

Mad Magazine Trading Cards Commemorative Set, in binder: $25

Spy vs Spy Trading Cards (1993): unopened box $25, unopened pack $1, holograms $5-$10, promo cards $2.50 each, uncut sheet $50, uncut promo sheets $10, set $6-$10

Hologram, Bush/Clinton signed by James Warhola: $25

CHAPTER ELEVEN

Up the Academy items

Although the 1980 feature film *Up the Academy* was not all it could (or should) have been, it has generated some interesting collectibles. The "one sheet" has artwork by Jack Rickard done for the film, and a pre-release poster features a closeup of the "Alfred E. Neuman" statue that serves as the film's mascot.

Pre-release poster

"One sheet"

Soundtrack album, Warner Bros. Records

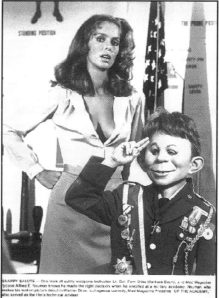

Various lobby cards and stills featured Alfred E. Neuman

Video tape and poster with no references to Mad or Alfred E. Neuman

Two different pinback buttons were issued as giveaways. The small button measures about 1 1/4"; the larger 3 3/4".

Up the Academy lobby cards: $2-$3 each

Up the Academy one sheet (1980): $15, quarter sheet $10

Up the Academy pinback buttons: 3 3/4" $25; 1 1/4" $25

Up the Academy poster, home video (no AEN or *Mad* mention): $3

Up the Academy pre-release poster: $10

Up the Academy shooting script: $25

Up the Academy soundtrack album: $20, cassette $20

Up the Academy stills: $1.50 each

Because Gaines hated the movie, he paid $30,000 to remove all references to *Mad* and Alfred E. Neuman from the film in its television and home video versions. The video box has no references to *Mad* or Alfred, but the tape itself has the *Mad* logo in the main title credits, and Alfred appears at the beginning and end. Gaines's $30,000 was eventually refunded when it became clear that prints and videos without the required cuts had been distributed worldwide. Actor Ron Leibman also demanded that his name not be used in connection with the film.

The New Collectibles (1987-present)

In 1987 *Mad* embarked on a concerted effort to license its name and the "Alfred E. Neuman" character. This was both a blessing and a curse for collectors, for while some attractive items were made, most of them were poorly distributed.

One of the first products to appear (c. 1987) was a series of wristwatches made by Concepts Plus, available in three styles. The nicest version was the *Mad* "limited edition collectible," available in gold or chrome finish for $49.95. Next was a quartz analog watch for $34.95 and a mechanical analog for $24.95. Evidently these watches had trouble keeping accurate time and the return factor was unusually high. Announced but never marketed were a large wall clock and an alarm clock. With regard to the wall clock, the cardboard display insert cards were prematurely printed, and a few prototype wall clocks were completed and given to members of the *Mad* staff.

Watch, analog (1987, in package): $25-$35

Watch, "limited edition" (gold or silver, 1987): $50-$100

Watch, quartz (1987, in package): $35-$50

Wall clock, promo only: no reported sales

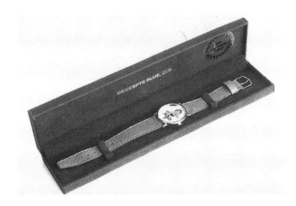

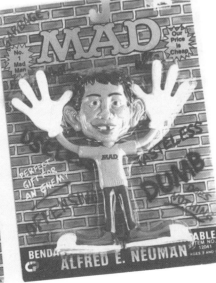

Concepts Plus also made a bendable Alfred E. Neuman figure, modeled after a sketch by Nick Meglin, which sold for about $4.95. This product enjoyed wider distribution than the watches. Two versions of packaging are known, with different placement of slogans on the front, and one version shows photos of the doll in different positions on the reverse.

Bendable Alfred E. Neuman figure, Concepts Plus, 1988: $15-$25

Applause, a large manufacturer of licensed products, took over the remaining stock of *Mad* wristwatches from Concepts Plus, which they packaged in slim cardboard display boxes (1988). Also offered were a set of six *Mad* "Classic Cover" coffee mugs (in illustrated boxes, 1988) and *Spy vs. Spy* and "Alfred E. Neuman" pens (1988).

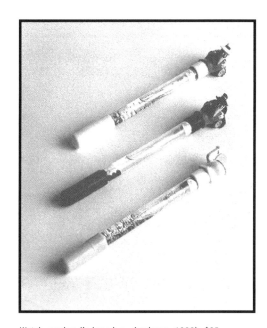

Watch, analog (in long box, Applause, 1988): $25

Coffee mugs (*Mad* "Classic Cover" mugs): single mug, in box $20-$25, set of six, in boxes $125-$150

Pen, AEN in toilet (Applause, 1988): $10, full display box $200

Pen, *Spy vs Spy* (Applause, 1988): $10 (black or white), full display box $200

Imagineering, a maker of Halloween products, released *Mad* "Squirt Toys" (a set of eight, 1987), an "Alfred E. Neuman Disguise Kit" (1987), and four "Nosey Shades" (1989). Leftover ears from the "Disguise Kit" were issued separately as "Alfred Ears" (1988).

Squirt Toys: set of eight, $175
single $20, empty display stand $50-$100

Disguise Kit: $5-$10
full display box $100

Nosey Shades: $20-$25 each

Alfred Ears: $5-$10

Disguise kit display

Squirt toys display

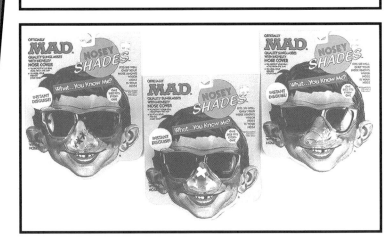

Nash, a skateboard manufacturer, made *Mad* skateboards in two sizes, both c. 1987. Variations in logo placement and color on the skateboards are reported.

Skateboards: large $35-$50, small $30-$45

Bi-Rite Posters

Bi-Rite made four large posters, c. 1987 and 1988, and a set of 24 full color pinback buttons. It is difficult to obtain the complete set of 24, but *Mad* has used some of the buttons as giveaways to new subscribers.

Posters (Bi-Rite, '87-'88):
"Surf's Up," "1988 Calendar,"
"What—Me Worry?,"
"AEN for Pres." $10 each

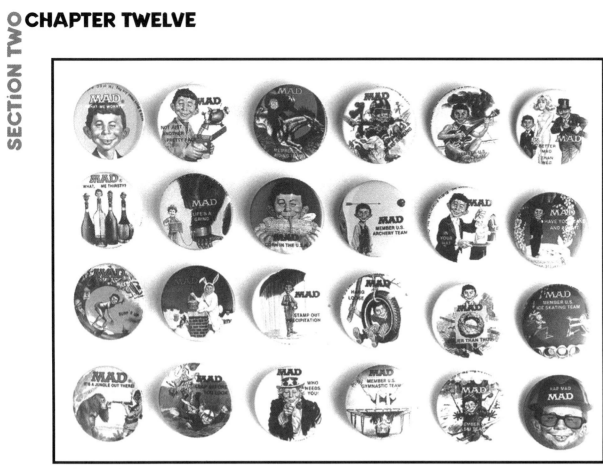

Bi-Rite Button Set

Pinback button set, Bi-Rite:
single button $5-$6, set of 24 $120

O.S.P. Publishing released two *Mad* posters in 1992: "Alfred E. Neuman for President" (#2151) and "Who Needs You?" (#2152). The "Alfred E. Neuman for President" poster was similar to the Bi-Rite poster of the same name, and the "Who Needs You?" poster was similar to the Pandora Productions poster of the same name (see section two, chapter five). Both posters had a retail price of $7.00.

Posters, "Alfred E. Neuman for President" and "Who Needs You?" (O.S.P. Publishing, 1992): $7.00 retail

CIA released a number of *Mad* T-shirts and sweatshirts, as did Sun and American Marketing Works. The Sun shirts were available nationally in chain stores like K-Mart, but the other shirts had much spottier distribution. The shirts have copyright dates between 1987 and 1989. A Canadian T-shirt was also made in 1988 by Watson's.

T-shirts, CIA: $10-$20 each

T-shirts, Sun: $10-$20 each

T-shirts, American Marketing Works: $10-$20 each

T-shirt, Watson's: $20

CIA T-shirts

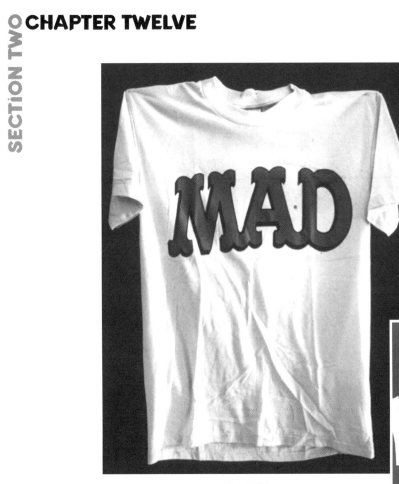

Sun T-shirts

Sun T-shirts and sweatshirts

Sun T-shirts and sweatshirts

Sun sweatshirt

Watson's T-shirt

American Marketing Works T-shirts

Two additional T-shirts were made in 1990 for limited sale direct through the *Mad* office, referred to as the "Three Faces of *Mad*" and "*Mad* logo"; the shirts cost $8.00 each, or two for $15.00.

T-shirts (sold through *Mad* office, 1990): "Three Faces of *Mad*" $15, "*Mad* logo" $15

Stanley Desantis of North Hollywood released in 1992 an attractive line of T-shirts, sweatshirts, and caps. The shirts retail for $15, and are silk-screened. A silk-screened cap was released at $11 (an embroidered version was announced but never made). The shirt with just the logo is an unapproved prototype. The sweatshirts have the same designs as the T-shirts; suggested retail $30.

T-shirts, Stanley Desantis: $15

Caps, Stanley Desantis: silk-screened $11

Sweatshirts, Stanley Desantis: $30

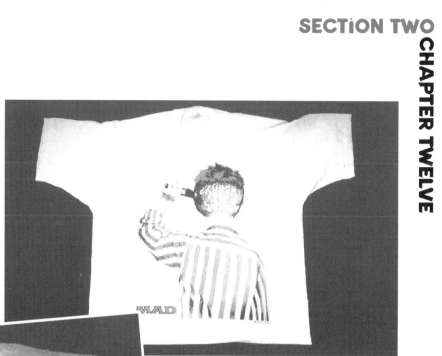

Stanley Desantis shirts

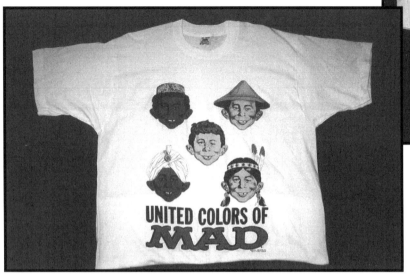

Stanley Desantis shirts and sport cap

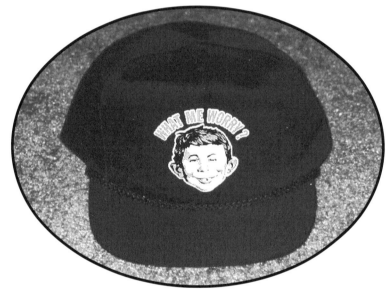

Other *Mad* T-shirts were licensed prior to the "New Collectibles" era. This "Alfred E. Neuman Original" T-shirt (Kedsco, circa 1981) was offered in several styles (long sleeve, short sleeve, and with a pocket) and sold at Sears.

(See section two, chapter five for the 1980 "Alfred E. Neuman for President" T-shirt.)

T-shirt, "Alfred E. Neuman Original": $25

Watson Brothers released a full line of *Mad* neckties, boxer shorts, and socks in late 1992. The garments were sold in Canada exclusively at Eaton's Department Store; the neckties were later offered in the United States at Sears. The neckties were available in at least ten different *Mad* designs and four *Spy vs Spy* designs. The boxer shorts came in two *Mad* designs and two *Spy vs Spy* designs. The socks were offered in three *Mad* designs and one *Spy vs Spy* design. The items were all available in several different colors as well.

Neckties: retail $35 (Canadian)

Boxer shorts: retail $19 (Canadian)

Socks: retail $12.50 (Canadian)

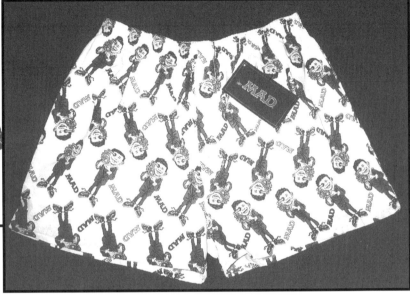

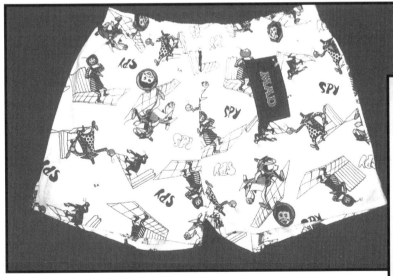

Mad beach towels were manufactured by a company called "a la carte/sayde" in 1988 and 1989. The towel from 1988 had limited distribution, but the 1989 towel was widely available.

Beach towels: 1988 $25-$50/1989 $25-$35

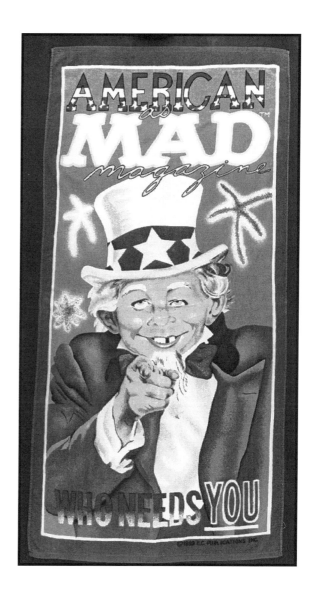

Hardee's fast food restaurants produced a set of six small "Hardee's Special Edition" *Mad* magazines as giveaways in 1989; each book has eight pages.

Hardee's Special Edition *Mad* magazines: set of six $140/single issues $20-$25

Hallmark Cards released this *Mad* greeting card (from the cover of *Mad* #31) in 1991 as part of its "Union Hill Paperworks" series; the card sold for $1.50 and is blank on the inside.

Also from Hallmark (in the Ambassador Cards series), this 1991 card uses the cover art from *Mad* #77. The salutation reads "Happle Birthday!"

Greeting card, Union Hill/Hallmark (1991): $5

Greeting card, Ambassador/Hallmark ("Happle

Birthday"), 1991: $5

CHAPTER TWELVE

Character Imprints created 10 or 12 *Mad* birthday cards in 1992; these were test-market items and not widely distributed.

Greeting cards, Character Imprints (1992): test-marketed $1.75 at point of sale; no reported sales on collectors' market

CHAPTER THiRTEEN

Foreign *Mad* items

The first foreign *Mad* publication was the British edition, 1959, and soon publishers in other countries followed suit. Some of these editions, including the British, Swedish, and German versions, have been continually published since their inception, but many of the others have struggled and died in their marketplace (the Swedish and British editions have just recently suspended publication). Yet other editions have had several publishers. Most countries have published their own versions of *Mad* paperback books and other annual editions. The following is a gallery of foreign first issues:

Foreign *Mad* editions: single issues any country $2-$5 each, early '60s first issues $100

Denmark, 1962

Britain, 1959

Sweden, 1960

Holland, 1964

Second Danish edition, 1979

France, 1965

Germany, 1967

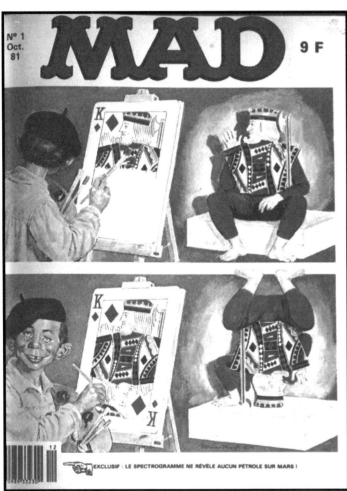

Second French edition, 1981

Finland, 1970

Second Finnish edition, 1982

Second Norwegian edition, 1981

Norway, 1971

Italy, 1971

Third Italian edition, 1991

Second Italian edition, 1985

Brazil, 1974

Spain, 1974

Second Brazilian edition, 1984

Second Spanish edition, 1975

Mexico, 1978

Argentina, 1977

Second Mexican edition, 1985

Puerto Rico, 1979

Greece, 1979

Australia, 1980

South Africa, 1985

China, 1990

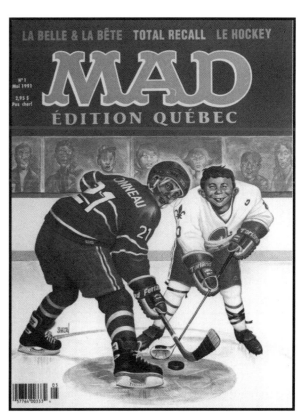

French Canada, 1991

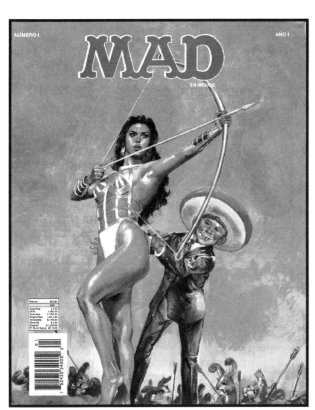

Third Mexican edition, 1993

Israel, 1994

Australian reprint of *Mad* #24
(first magazine issue), 1988.

Mad #24, Australian reprint: $20

Australian series of 7" x 10 1/4"
paperbound reprint books.

Paperback books, Australian (7" x 10 1/4"):
$10 each

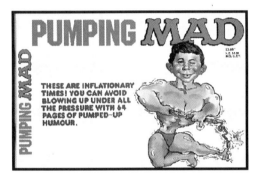

Two oversize "quality paperback"
Mad books (with dust jackets) were
published in Japan by ITS
Information in 1979. They are full
of color cover repros, various *Mad*
article reprints, and other features.
Though the books are lavishly
produced, *Mad*'s anti-authoritarian
stance did not fare well with the
Japanese and the series was
cancelled. About 5,000 copies of
each issue were printed.

Japanese *Mad* "quality paperbacks"
(1979 and 1980): $35-$50 each

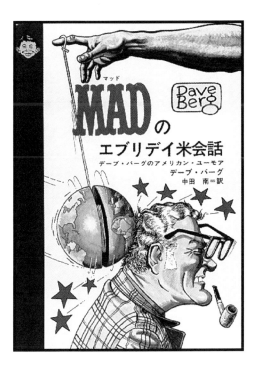

This Japanese Dave Berg/*Mad* book was published in 1986 to help Japanese students of English learn American speech patterns; the material originally appeared in various issues of *Mad* as "The Lighter Side of..."

Japanese Dave Berg book (1986): no reported sales

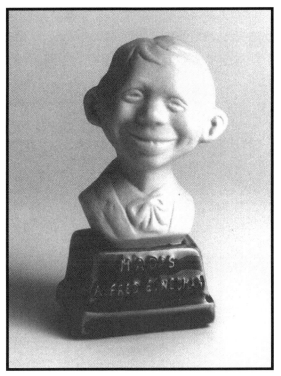

Swedish *Mad* bust (4 1/2" tall)

Bust, Swedish: $300-$400

Some of the foreign publishers have issued their own premiums, with Sweden producing some particularly outstanding items:

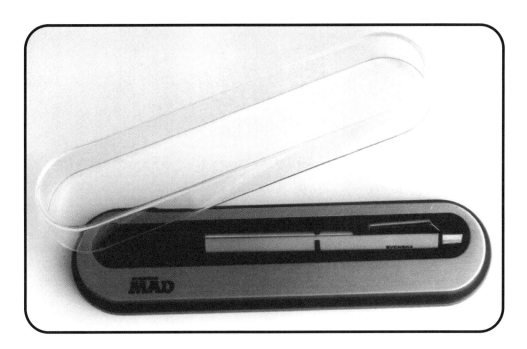

Swedish *Mad* pen set

Pen set, Swedish: $50-$75

CHAPTER THiRTEEN

Swedish *Mad* binder for back issues.

Binder, Swedish: no reported sales

Swedish sport cap

Sport cap, Swedish: no reported sales

Swedish *Mad* tie tac and belt, given as gifts by the publisher.

Tie tac and belt, Swedish: no reported sales

Swedish imitation bronze casting, 11 1/2" x 17 1/2"

Bronze (imitation, plastic) casting of AEN, Swedish: $300-$350

Swedish Alfred E. Neuman stickers.

Stickers, AEN, Swedish: no reported sales

Ad for "AEN Fan Club" metal stick pin, a giveaway with Swedish subscriptions in 1968.

Stick pin, "AEN Fan Club", 1968: no reported sales

Swedish *Mad* banner.

Banner, AEN, Swedish: no reported sales

Swedish *Mad* TV Banner, to be placed at bottom of TV for "theatre" effect.

Swedish *Mad* TV Banner: no reported sales

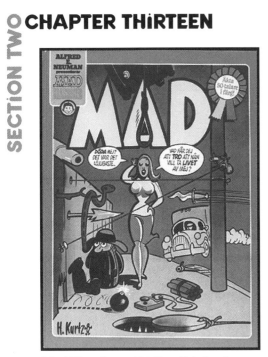

Mad Klassiker, 1989 Swedish hardcover with full color reprints from *Mad* comics.

Mad Klassiker, 1989, Swedish: $35

British *Mad* T-shirt, given with subscriptions.

T-shirt, British: $35

Many foreign publishers offer complete years of *Mad* back issues in paperbound volumes; shown are British, Brazilian, German, and Swedish bound volumes.

Foreign bound volumes of *Mad* (softcover): $20-$30 each

British *Mad* binder, to hold back issues.

Binder, British: $25

ALFRED E. NEUMAN

This full color poster of Alfred in Elizabethan garb was offered in Britain and some Scandanavian countries in the early 1970s.

Poster, AEN in Elizabethan garb:
no reported sales

25 Years of British Mad (1985), *30 Years of British Mad* (1990) softcover volumes.

25 Years of British Mad (1985): $25

30 Years of British Mad (1990): $25

Reencuentro Con el Pais de las Hipotesis, Mexican Sergio Aragonés 8" x 10 1/2" softcover, 1988 (reprints from *Viva Mad, Mad About Mad,* and *Mad-ly Yours*).

Reencuentro Con el Pais de las Hipotesis: $10

Les Singes Rient (1988) and *Les Chauves Sourient* (1989), French Don Martin hardcover compilations, published by Comics USA.

Les Singes Rient (1988): $20

Les Chauves Sourient (1989): $20

Chinese *Mad* poster.

Chinese *Mad* poster: $20

Wie Es Tont & Stohnt, German LP, released in 1981.

Wie Es Tont & Stohnt, German LP, 1981: $20-$30

This *Mad* "Bic" lighter was made by one of the foreign *Mad* publishers, and given to *Mad* co-editor Nick Meglin.

Lighter, *Mad* Bic, foreign: $35

Finnish 1990-91 *Mad* Calendar.

Calendar, Finnish (1990-1991): $10-$20

German *Mad* T-shirt.

T-shirt, German: $35

German *Mad* Sticker.

Sticker, German *Mad*: $5

The Italian fanzine *Funnies* #1 is devoted to *Mad*, with many cover repros and full stories translated to Italian. Included are bios of Wally Wood, Jack Davis, Harvey Kurtzman and Will Elder. This oversized volume appeared in 1983.

Funnies #1, Italian fanzine: $10

Mad Klassiske Latterligheter vol. 1 and 2 (1989 and 1990), Norwegian hardcover reprints from *Mad* comics in black and white (shown is vol. 2).

Mad Klassiske Latterligheter vol. 1 and 2 (1989 and 1990): $25 each

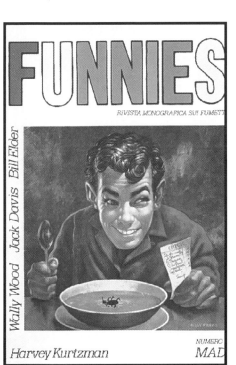

Gold-colored German *Mad* bust, awarded to politicians and public figures for particularly idiotic acts. The bust stands almost 10" tall.

Bust, German presentation item: no reported sales

Five hardcover editions of material from *Mad* comics were released in France under the titles *Les Annees Folles de Mad* (1983), *Mad se Paie Une Toile* (1984), *Les Bandes Desinees de Mad* (1985), *Un Max de Mad* (1986), and *La Fin de Mad* (1987). All have color covers and black and white interiors. *Les Annees Folles de Mad* had been previously released in 1978 as a trade paperback.

Les Annees Folles de Mad : softcover (1978) $25, hardcover (1983) $35

Mad se Paie Une Toile (1984): $35

Les Bandes Desinees de Mad (1985): $35

Un Max de Mad (1986): $35

La Fin de Mad (1987): $35

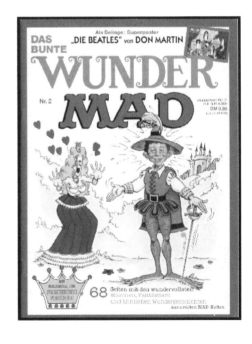

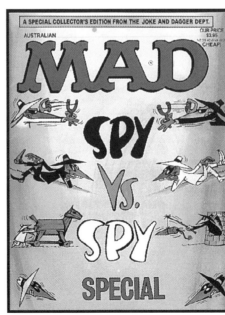

A sampling of foreign *Mad* paperbacks and special editions:

Foreign *Mad* paperbacks: various, average $2-$5 each

CHAPTER FOURTEEN

Non-licensed items

A number of items featuring the image of Alfred E. Neuman have appeared, even after *Mad* won the copyright suit over use of the image. Some of these were probably honest mistakes carried over from a time when the "Me Worry?" face was fair game, but most were red-blooded attempts to cash in on *Mad*'s name and audience recognition. *Mad*'s lawyers have taken a dim view of this and have been (and remain) quick to respond.

This Plaster of Paris bust was made in Japan, circa early 1960s, and is hand painted. A card attached to the bust reads, "Your official worrying mascot...Let him do your worrying"; the bust came in a plain cardboard box. Examples have been seen with yellow painted hair, and with green fuzzy hair.

Bust, "Worrying Mascot" with fuzzy hair, Japan: $150

Another bust, this one ceramic and more delicately hand painted, origin unknown.

Bust, hand painted ceramic: $150-$200

This "What–Me Worry?" doll was released in 1961 by the "Baby Barry" doll company; the face is based on earlier versions of the "Me Worry" face. The rubber bank, maker unknown, was apparently modeled after the head of the "What–Me Worry?" doll; the coin slot is in the top of the head.

Doll, "What, Me Worry?" (Baby Barry 1961): one example sold at auction in May 1993 for $1,400, and another auctioned in November 1993 for $2,500

Bank, "Me Worry?" head, mid-1960s: $50

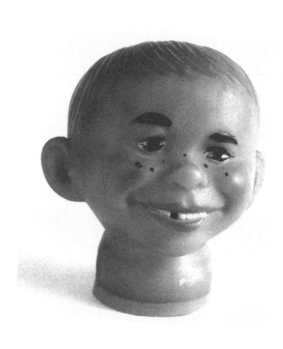

This "Happy Boy" doll's face was likely inspired by the "Me Worry" face. The doll was made in 1960 by Effanbee, and can be found in three different sets of clothing.

Doll, "Happy Boy" (Effanbee 1960): $85

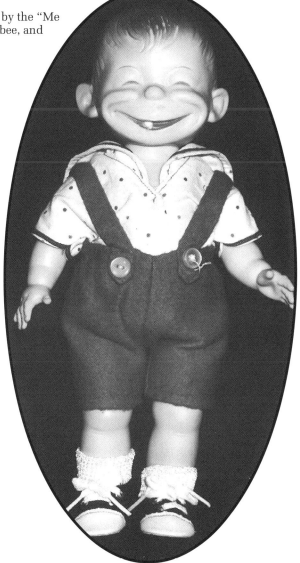

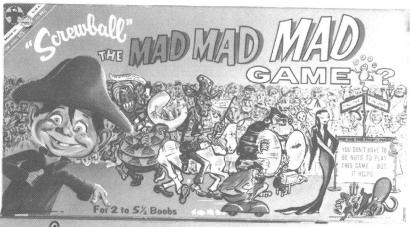

Transogram released two versions of *Screwball, the Mad Mad Mad Game* in 1960. The first version is shown at left, with three large *Mad* logos and an AEN lookalike. The second was released after Mad objected; note the "Screwball" logo is much larger, there is one less *"Mad,"* and the Alfred face has a microphone in front of his mouth.

Screwball, the Mad Mad Mad Game: first version $35-$50

altered version $45-$60

Doll, "Happy Chap" (Japan, early '60s): $50

Another variation (made in Japan, early 1960s), the "Happy Chap."

Several masks with the "Me Worry?" face have appeared. Below is an ad that appeared in early issues of *Famous Monsters* (around 1960). Other such masks are reported, including one released in 1981 by Cesar (with "life-like" hair), one made by Don Post in 1977, and a plastic "half head" style mask, circa late 1970s.

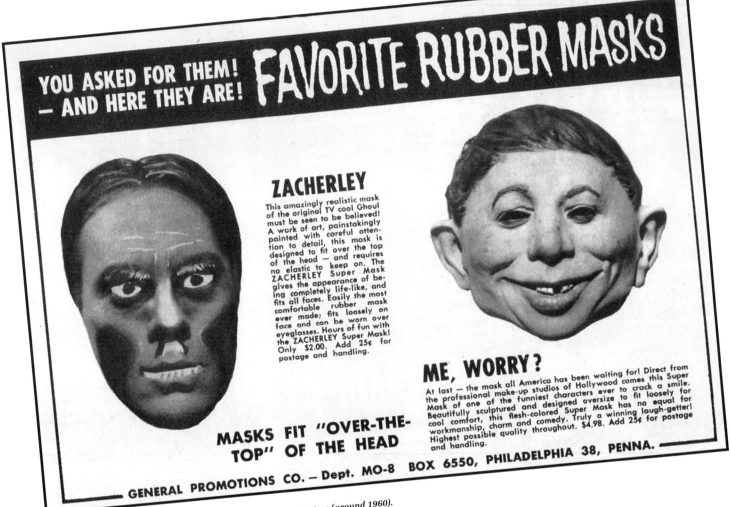

Advertisement that appeared in early issues of Famous Monsters (around 1960).

Mask, "Me Worry?" face, circa 1960: no reported sales

Mask, "Me Worry?" face, Cesar (1981): $35

Mask, "Me Worry?" face, Don Post (1977): $25

Mask, "Me Worry?" face, half head (circa late 1970s): $35

In 1967 Family Dog Productions, a San Francisco-based concert promoter, used a disguised Alfred face on a poster and handbill.

Poster, Family Dog with unauthorized AEN (1967): $25

handbill $5

"The Best of Kermit Schafer, For Those Who Have Everything" LP (Jubilee KS-1, Volume 1) with "Me Worry?" portrait on cover, circa late 1950s or early '60s.

"The Best of Kermit Schafer, *For Those Who Have Everything*" LP (Jubilee KS-1, Volume 1): $25

CHAPTER FOURTEEN

This "What–Me Worry" poster appeared in the late 1960s or early 1970s, manufactured by AA Sales of Seattle, Washington. The black areas are flocked, and when viewed under a black light, the poster is mind-blowingly psychedelic. A copyright notice reading "© Stuff and Wilson" appears; it was Harry Stuff's widow who sued *Mad* (and lost) over copyright infringement in the early 1960s.

Poster, "What, Me Worry," flocked: $35

These two brass "Alfred on a bomb" pins, with a *Dr. Strangelove* motif, probably date from 1964. The maker is unknown, but they are not "one of a kind."

Pin, "Alfred on a bomb": pin $100, pendant $100

"What, Me Worry?" brass charm bracelet, circa 1960s, image of "the face" with "What-Me Worry?" on reverse.

Charm bracelet, "What-Me Worry?", brass: $50

A "*Mad* Money" slot machine was made by Sega in the early 1960s. Made for foreign distribution, the machine took English pennies. The likeness of Alfred on the glass top and wheel strips is a "swipe" of Kelly Freas's art style. Two other Sega machines with the Alfred face were released in 1966, the "Continental" and the "Aztec." A "Mills High Top" slot machine has also been reported with the "Me Worry?" face on the wheel strips and glass insert; the "Mills High Top" machine is more highly regarded by slot machine collectors and is worth more.

Slot machine, "*Mad* Money," Sega, early '60s: machine $1,000-$1,500, glass top only $75

Slot machine, Sega "Aztec" or "Continental", 1966: $1,000

Slot machine, Mills High Top with "Me Worry?" face: $2,200, glass insert only $75

Alternate glass top (8 1/2" x 13") and inset panel (3 1/4" x 5 1/4")

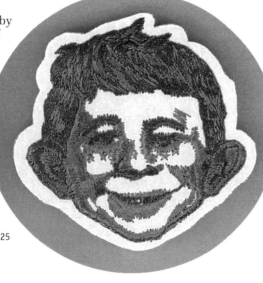

This cloth patch, made by Gandalf Products Co. of New York, appeared around 1975. Gandalf made other comic character patches as well, and their full page ads can be found in comics of the era. The second patch (in full color) measures 8 1/2" in diameter, origin unknown.

Patch (Gandalf Products Co.): $25

Patch, "What, Me Worry?": $35

Pinback buttons and gum machine prize:

Pinback button, "What, Me Worry?," b & w on purple background: $25

Pinback button, b & w face: $20

Gum machine prize, plastic (1960s): $50-$80

Pinback buttons using the "What, Me Worry?" slogan in an atypical way.

Pinback buttons, "What, Me Worry?" (no AEN face): $10-$20

The Marlboro Smoke Shop of Marlboro, Massachusetts, used an Alfred face taken from *Mad* as a mascot until *Mad*'s attorneys objected. Shown are a bumper sticker and plastic pocket protector.

Bumper sticker, Marlboro Smoke Shop: $7.50

Pocket protector, Marlboro Smoke Shop: $10

CHAPTER FOURTEEN

"What–Me Worry?" decals were produced in the early to mid-1960s by Imprint Art Products, Inc. of Hackensack NJ ("decals for trains, planes, boats, bikes, and windshields"). At least four designs were produced, all in color.

Decals, "What, Me Worry?": $25

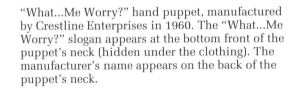

"What...Me Worry?" hand puppet, manufactured by Crestline Enterprises in 1960. The "What...Me Worry?" slogan appears at the bottom front of the puppet's neck (hidden under the clothing). The manufacturer's name appears on the back of the puppet's neck.

Puppet, "What, Me Worry?", 1960: $150-$175

Security Awareness Poster," made in 1991 by NSA, a "watchdog" agency. The company apparently got permission to do the poster but forgot to include the necessary copyright information.

Poster, "Security Awareness," 1991: $10

Birthday card, circa 1958-'59:

Birthday card, circa 1958-'59: $20-$25

Gro-Grass Greeting card, Pico Novelty, 1969:

Gro-Grass card, 1969: $20-$25

Ross Perot pinback button, 1992. This same image also appeared on a T-shirt and coffee mug.

Button: $3

Coffee mug: $7

T-shirt: $13

These 3-D plastic postcards were issued in 1958 and 1959 in four different colors:

Postcards, 3D plastic, 1958 and 1959: $25-$35 each

"What, Me Worry?" coin, found in both silver and bronze, circa late 1980s.

"What, Me Worry?" coin: $20

This tin "*Mad* Money" bank was made in 1976 by Chelsea Marketing Group; no other information appears.

Bank, "*Mad* Money," unauthorized, 1976 (Chelsea Marketing Group): $15

"*Mad* Office" Sticker, art by Sergio Aragonés (taken from the cover to T*he Complete Mad Checklist* #3). The origin of this unauthorized sticker is unknown, but a notice of "© 1990 William M. Gaines, Agent" appears.

Sticker, "*Mad Office*," unauthorized: $3-$5

A three-ring binder with the word *Mad* and an Alfred E. Neuman likeness appeared in the early 1960s. The art was not by a *Mad* artist. The binder with the Alfred likeness is believed to depict a campfire scene; no example of this version could be located for inclusion. Companion binders, including *Mad Astronaut* and *Mad College Pin Ups* do not have a recognizable Alfred E. Neuman face and are of marginal interest to *Mad* collectors. *The Mad College Pin Ups* version is shown for reference.

Binder, early 1960s, with *Mad* and AEN likeness, unauthorized: $45

CHAPTER FiFTEEN

Mad paperback books

The potential collector of *Mad* paperback books faces a mind-boggling assortment of reprintings, cover changes, publisher changes, variations in logo and background colors, and other minutiae, and in this writer's opinion to try and collect them all lies *Mad*ness. I recommend adopting the book collector's rule of first printings only, except in the case of major changes in cover artwork.

The first *Mad* paperback book, The *Mad Reader* (Ballantine Books #93) was issued in early 1955 just as *Mad* was changing from a comic book to a magazine. It was followed by *Mad Strikes Back* (Ballantine #106), *Inside Mad* (#124), *Utterly Mad* (#178) and *The Brothers Mad* (#267). These books remained in print through the mid-1970s, and were issued with several different sets of cover artwork.

Ballantine paperbacks, first printings: $15 $25 cach

First printing Ballantine paperbacks

The first major change in cover art on these books was a set of "Pop Art" style covers that appeared in the late 1960s. These were followed in 1975 by a set of airbrushed covers by sometime *National Lampoon* contributor Robert Grossman. Gaines so detested the art that he persuaded publisher Ian Ballantine to issue another set with art by Norman Mingo (released in 1976, these were the last versions before the books went out of print).

"Pop Art" style covers: $2-$3 each

"Pop Art" style covers

Robert Grossman covers

Robert Grossman covers: $2-$3 each

Norman Mingo covers: $2-$3 each

Norman Mingo covers

In 1959 Signet (New American Library) took over the *Mad* paperback line with the release of *The Bedside Mad*. New titles were added at the rate of two or three a year. Due to the acrimony surrounding Harvey Kurtzman's departure from *Mad*, the first four titles from Signet (and the last two from Ballantine) had William M. Gaines's name above the book title, although these books contained material reprinted from the Kurtzman written and edited *Mad* comics.

Signet first printings: $5-$10

The Bedside Mad

Noteworthy is *The Mad Frontier*, released in February 1962. The cover depicted AEN in a rocking chair as a spoof on John F. Kennedy's "New Frontier" (Kennedy was reportedly a *Mad* fan). After Kennedy's assasination the cover was quickly pulled and replaced with the covered wagon version.

The Mad Frontier, Kennedy parody cover (1962): 1st printing $10-$20, revised cover $2-$3

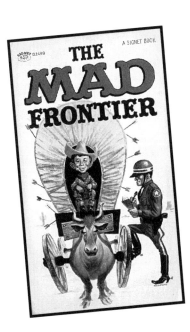

233

Signet display rack for *Mad* paperbacks, 1963.

Signet display rack for *Mad* paperbacks, 1963: no reported sales

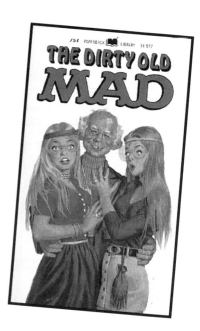

In April, 1971, Paperback Library (later Warner Paperback Library and finally Warner Books) took over the line with *The Dirty Old Mad*. The *Mad* paperbacks have been published by Warner ever since; the earlier Signet titles were gradually re-released by Warner with new cover art.

Paperback Library, Warner Paperback Library and Warner Books first printings: $1-$3

Mad paperback gift sets

A number of *Mad* boxed paperback gift sets have been issued over the years by several publishers. The first sets to appear were *Completely Mad* and *The Mad Scene*, both from Signet. The sets cost $4.00 and contained eight books each; both appeared in the late 1960s. Also from Signet were *An Insanely Mad Collection* and *It's A Mad World*, each containing four books for $5.00. Warner Paperback Library released two sets: *The World is Going Mad* (five books, $3.75) and a set called *Mad* (six books, $4.50).

Completely Mad

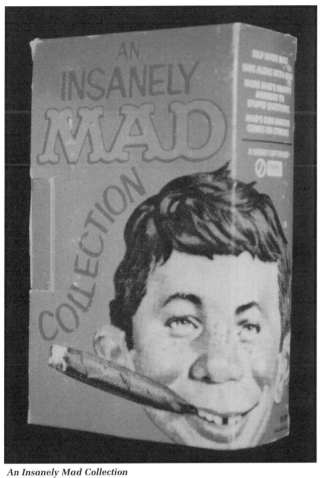

An Insanely Mad Collection

It's A Mad World

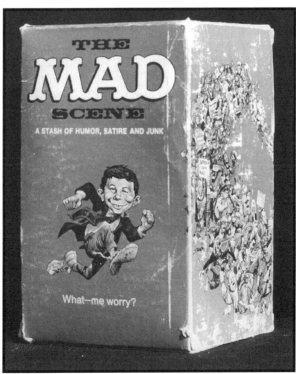

The Mad Scene

CHAPTER FIFTEEN

In the 1970s, Warner Books issued *The Mad Sampler Box* (four books, $5.00), *A Certifiably Mad Collection* (available in lime green, blue, or gold boxes, five books, $7.50), *The Whole "Don" Set* (five books, $7.50), and *Don Martin Carries On (*four books, $5.00). A *Spy vs Spy* collection was released with the subtitle "The Certifiably *Mad* Prohias." Warner then produced pairs of *Mad* Bookends, shrink-wrapped together with five *Mad* paperbacks. The bookends can be found in gold plastic with blue printing, and in red plastic with gold printing.

The Mad Sampler Box

A Certifiably Mad Collection

Don Martin Carries On

Mad Bookends

Classically Mad

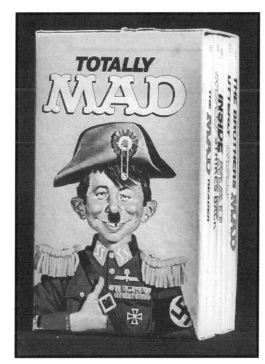

Totally Mad

Ballantine Books jumped on the boxed set bandwagon with *Classically Mad*, a collection of the five Ballantine titles (this also appeared as *Totally Mad* with different artwork). The versions with Mingo art were used on this set, which appeared in the 1970s.

Mad paperback gift sets: $15-$35 each

Bookends, red or gold: $25-$50 a pair

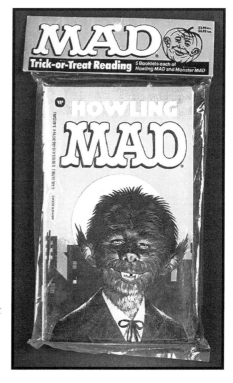

For Halloween, Warner issued sets of paperback booklets for "trick-or-treaters," entitled *Mad Trick or Treat Reading*. The booklets, released in 1987, contained 16 pages.

Mad Trick or Treat Reading packs, with booklets (1987): $15-$25

⬤CHAPTER FiFTEEN

Checklist of all *Mad* paperbacks, in order of publication (first edition publisher listed first, followed by reprint publisher, if any):

Note: every Signet title was reissued by Warner (or affiliates) with new cover art; these later books are considered new editions, and all had information to indicate a "first printing".

The Mad Reader, Dec. 1954, Ballantine/ "pop art" cover/ R. Grossman cover/ Mingo cover
Mad Strikes Back, May 1955, B/ "pop art" cover/ R. Grossman cover/ Mingo cover
Inside Mad, Nov. 1955, B/ "pop art" cover/ R. Grossman cover/ Mingo cover
Utterly Mad, Oct. 1956, B/ "pop art" cover/ R. Grossman cover/ Mingo cover
The Brothers Mad, Oct. 1958, B/ "pop art" cover/ R. Grossman cover/ Mingo cover
The Bedside Mad, April 1959, Signet, Warner Paperback Library
Son of Mad, Nov. 1959, S, WPL
The Organization Mad, April 1960, S, WPL
Like, Mad, Sept. 1960, S, WPL
The Ides of Mad, March 1961, S, WPL
Fighting Mad, August 1961, S, WPL
The Mad Frontier, Feb. 1962, S, W
Mad in Orbit, Aug. 1962, S, W
The Voodoo Mad, March 1963, S, W
Greasy Mad Stuff, Oct. 1963, S, W (reissued as *The Greasy Mad*)
Three Ring Mad, April 1964, S, W
The Self Made Mad, Dec. 1964, S, W
The Mad Sampler, April 1965, S, WPL
It's a World, World, World, World, Mad, Oct. 1965, S, WPL
Raving Mad, April 1966, S, WPL
Boiling Mad, Oct. 1966, S, WPL
The Questionable Mad, April 1967, S, WPL
Howling Mad, Oct. 1967, S, WPL
The Indigestible Mad, March 1968, S, WPL
Burning Mad, Oct. 1968, S, W
Good 'n' Mad, April 1969, S, W
Hopping Mad, Oct. 1969, S, W
The Portable Mad, April 1970, S, W
Mad Power, Oct. 1970, S, W
The Dirty Old Mad, April 1971, Paperback Library
Polyunsaturated Mad, Oct. 1971, PL
Recycled Mad, April 1972, PL
The Non-Violent Mad, Oct. 1972, WPL
The Rip Off Mad, April 1973, WPL
The Token Mad, Oct. 1973, WPL
The Pocket Mad, April 1974, WPL
The Invisible Mad, Oct. 1974, WPL
Dr. Jekyll and Mr. Mad, April 1975, WPL
Steaming Mad, June 1975, WPL
Mad at You, Oct. 1975, W
The Vintage Mad, Feb. 1976, W
Hooked on Mad, June 1976, W
The Cuckoo Mad, Oct. 1976, W
The Medicine Mad, Feb. 1977, W
A Mad Scramble, June 1977, W
Swinging Mad, Oct. 1977, W
Mad Overboard, Feb. 1978, W
Mad Clowns Around, June 1978, W
A Mad Treasure Chest, Oct. 1978, W
Mad Sucks, Feb 1979, W
Super Mad, June 1979, W
The Abominable Snow Mad, Oct. 1979, W
Mad About the Buoy, Feb. 1980, W

Like, Mad

Son of Mad

Greasy Mad Stuff

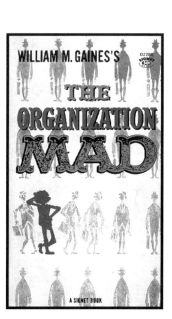

Organization Mad

Mad for Kicks, June 1980, W
The Uncensored Mad, Oct. 1980, W
Pumping Mad, Feb. 1981, W
Mad Horses Around, June 1981, W
The Eggs-rated Mad, Nov. 1981, W
A Carnival Mad, Feb. 1982, W
The Explosive Mad, June 1982, W
Mad Barfs, Oct. 1982, W
Eternally Mad, Feb. 1983, W
Mad About Town, June 1983, W
Big Mad on Campus, Oct. 1983, W
The Endangered Mad, Feb. 1984, W
Stamp Out Mad, June 1984, W
Forbidden Mad, Oct. 1984, W
Monster Mad, Feb. 1985, W
The Plaid Mad, June 1985, W
Son of Mad Sucks, Oct. 1985, W
The Qwerty Mad, Feb. 1986, W
Monu-mentally Mad, June 1986, W
Big Hairy Mad, Oct. 1986, W
The Wet and Wisdom of Mad, Feb. 1987, W
Mad Duds, June 1987, W
'til Mad Do Us Part, Oct. 1987, W
The Spare Mad, Feb. 1988, W
The Mad Cooler, June 1988, W
Mad Blasts, Oct. 1988, W
Mad Jackpot, Feb 1989, W
Mad in the Box, Oct. 1989, W
Soaring Mad, Dec. 1989, W
The Weather Mad, Feb. 1990, W
The Aimless Mad, June, 1990, W
The Ages of Mad, Oct. 1990, W
See No...Hear No...Speak No...Mad, Feb. 1991, W
Swing Along With Mad, June 1991, W
The Porpoise-ful Mad, Oct. 1991, W
Mad Capades, Feb. 1992, W
Mad Takes the Cake, June 1992, W
Unstoppable Mad, Oct., 1992, W
The Spring Training Mad, Feb. 1993, W
Bristling Mad, June 1993, W

*It's a World, World, World,
World, Mad*

Polyunsaturated Mad

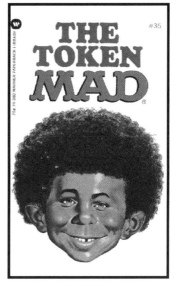

The Token Mad

A Mad Treasure Chest

The Qwerty Mad

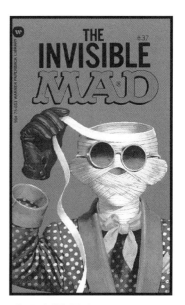

The Invisible Mad

SPECIALTY PAPERBACKS, by author:

SERGIO ARAGONÉS
Viva Mad!, July 1968, S, WPL
Mad About Mad, July 1970, S, W
Mad-ly Yours, June 1972, PL
In Mad We Trust, March 1974, WPL
Mad Marginals (5 1/8" x 7 3/4"), May 1974, WPL
Mad as the Devil, March 1975, WPL
Incurably Mad, April 1977, W
Shootin' Mad, Jan. 1979, W
Mad Marginals (4 1/4" x 7"), Dec. 1980, W
Mad as a Hatter, Jan. 1981, W
Mad Menagerie, April 1983, W
More Mad Marginals, April 1985, W
Mad Pantomines, Jan. 1987, W
More Mad Pantomines, Nov. 1988, W
Mad as Usual!, May 1990, W
Totally Mad, Aug. 1991, W
Next Mad Book, Aug. 1992, W

DAVE BERG
Looks at the U.S.A., Jan. 1964, S, W
Looks at People, Feb. 1966, S, WPL
Looks at Things, Nov. 1967, S, WPL
Looks at Modern Thinking, Nov. 1969, S, W
Looks at Our Sick World, Nov. 1971, S, W
Looks at Living, Nov. 1973, WPL
Looks Around, Nov. 1975, W
Takes a Loving Look, Nov. 1977, W
Looks, Listens, and Laughs, Nov. 1979, W
Looks at You, Jan. 1982, W
Looks at the Neighborhood, April 1984, W
Looks at Our Planet, April 1986, W
Looks at Today, July 1987, W

DICK DE BARTOLO
A Mad Look at Old Movies, Nov. 1966, S, WPL
The Return of a Mad Look at Old Movies, March 1970, S, W
Madvertising, July 1972, S, W
A Mad Look at TV, July 1974, WPL
A Mad Guide to Leisure Time, Sept. 1976, W
The Mad Guide to Self Improvement, March 1979, W
A Mad Guide to Fraud and Deception, March 1981, W
The Mad Book of Sex, Violence, and Home Cooking, May 1983, W
Mad Murders the Movies, July 1985, W
Mad Tales from the School of Hard Yocks, Nov. 1991, W (contains text from *Don Martin Comes on Strong*, redrawn by Harry North)

JERRY DE FUCCIO
Clod's Letters to Mad (5 1/4" x 8"), Dec. 1974, WPL
Clod's Letters to Mad (4 1/4" x 7"), July 1981, W

SERGIO ARAGONÉS

DAVE BERG

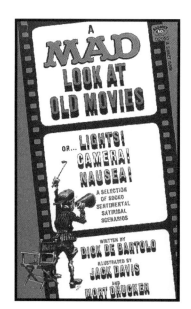

DICK DE BARTOLO

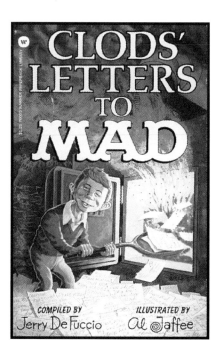

JERRY DE FUCCIO

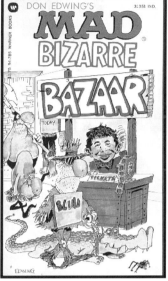

DON EDWING

STAN HART

DON EDWING
Mad Bizarre Bazaar, Nov. 1980, W
Mad Book of Almost Superheroes, April 1982, W
Mad Variations, Sept. 1984, W
Mad's Bizarre Biz, April 1987, W
Mad's Sheer Torture, May 1988, W
Mad Fantasy, Fables, and Other Foolishness, June 1989, W
Madventures of Almost Superheroes, April 1990, W
Mad Bizarre Blast, April 1991, W
Mad Disasters, April 1992, W
Mad's Creature Presentation, April 1993, W

STAN HART
The Mad Book of Revenge, May 1976, W
The Mad Guide to Careers, Sept. 1978, W
The Mad Survival Handbook, Sept. 1980, W
Mad's Fast Look at Fast Living, Nov. 1982, W
A Mad Guide to Parents, Teachers, and other Enemies, Aug. 1985, W

FRANK JACOBS
Mad for Better or Verse, Nov. 1968, S, W
Sing Along With Mad, Nov. 1970, S, W
Mad About Sports, Nov. 1972, WPL
Mad's Talking Stamps, June 1974, WPL
The Mad Turned-On Zoo (5 1/4" x 8"), Aug. 1974, WPL
The Mad Jumble Book, Feb. 1975, WPL
More Mad About Sports, Jan. 1977, W
Mad Around the World, Sept. 1979, W
Mad Goes Wild, April 1981, W (has material from *The Mad Turned-On Zoo*)
Get Stuffed with Mad, Oct. 1981, W
The Mad Jock Book, Jan. 1983, W
Mad Goes to Pieces, July 1984, W
Mad's Believe It or Nuts!, May 1986, W

AL JAFFEE
Spews Out Snappy Answers to Stupid Questions, Feb. 1968, S, W
The Mad Book of Magic and Other Dirty Tricks, Feb. 1970, S, W
Spews Out More Snappy Answers to Stupid Questions, Feb. 1972, S, W
Mad (Yeech!) Monstrosities, Feb. 1974, WPL
Clod's Letters to Mad (5 1/4" x 8"), Dec. 1974, WPL
Spews Out Still More Snappy Answers....., March 1976, W
Mad Inventions, March 1978, W
Good Lord! Not Another Book of Snappy Answers...., March 1980, W
Clod's Letters to Mad (4 1/4" x 7"), July 1981, W
Freaks Out, May 1982, W
Snappy Answers to Stupid Questions #5, Aug. 1984, W
Mad Brain Ticklers, Puzzlers, and Lousy Jokes, July 1986, W
Once Again...Spews Out More Snappy Answers.....#6, Nov. 1987, W
Sweats Out Another Book, Aug. 1988, W
All New Snappy Answers to Stupid Questions #7, Aug. 1989, W
Mad (yeech!) Rejects, Aug. 1990, W
Holy Cow! Not Another Mad Snappy Answers..., Dec. 1992, W

FRANK JACOBS

AL JAFFEE

CHAPTER FiFTEEN

TOM KOCH

History Gone Mad, Sept. 1977, W
The Mad Worry Book, Jan. 1980, W
The Mad Weirdo Watcher's Guide, July 1982, W
The Mad Self-Improvement Yearbook, May 1985, W

DON MARTIN

Steps Out, April 1962, S, W
Bounces Back, May 1963, S, W
Drops Thirteen Stories, July 1965, S, W
The Mad Adventures of Captain Klutz, Feb. 1967, S, WPL
Cooks Up More Tales, June 1969, S, W
Comes On Strong, July 1971, S, W
Carries On, July 1973, WPL
Steps Further Out, July 1975, WPL
Forges Ahead, August 1977, W
Digs Deeper, August 1979, W
Grinds Ahead, August 1981, W
Captain Klutz II, August 1983, W
Sails Ahead, Jan. 1986, W

NICK MEGLIN

Mad Stew, Jan. 1978, W
The Sound of Mad, May 1980, W
A Mad Look at the '50s, Jan. 1985, W
A Mad Look at the '60s, April 1989, W

PAUL PETER PORGES

The Mad How Not to Do It Book, May 1981, W
Mad Cheap Shots, Jan. 1984, W
Mad Lobsters and Other Abominable Housebroken Creatures, Nov. 1986, W

ANTONIO PROHIAS

The All New Mad Secret File on Spy vs Spy, Nov. 1965, S, WPL
Spy vs Spy Follow-Up File, April 1968, S, WPL
The Third Mad Dossier of Spy vs Spy, March 1972, PL
The Fourth Mad Declassified Papers on Spy vs Spy, Nov. 1974, WPL
The Fifth Mad Report on Spy vs Spy, Aug. 1978, W
The Sixth Mad Case Book on Spy vs Spy, Aug. 1982, W
The Updated Files, Dec. 1989, W (ghosted by Don Edwing and Bob Clarke)
Spy vs Spy The Updated Files #8, Aug. 1993, W (ghosted by Don Edwing and Bob Clarke)

LARRY SIEGEL

Mad's Cradle to Grave Primer, June 1973, WPL
The Mad Make Out Book, May 1979, W
Mad Clobbers the Classics, Sept. 1981, W
Mad's How to be a Successful Dog, Nov. 1984, W

LOU SILVERSTONE

Politically Mad, Jan. 1976, W
A Mad Look at the Future, May 1978, W
The Mad Book of Mysteries, Aug. 1980, W
The Mad Tell It Like It Is Book, Nov. 1983, W
The Mad Book of Horror Stories, Yecchy Creatures, and Other Neat Stuff, Aug. 1986, W

MISC. AUTHORS

The Mad Book of Word Power by Max Brandel, Feb. 1973, WPL
The Mad Pet Book by Paul Coker, Jr., July 1983, W
The Mad Book of Fears and Phobias by John Ficarra, Nov. 1985, W

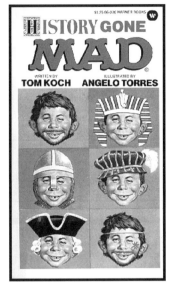

TOM KOCH

DON MARTIN

NICK MEGLIN

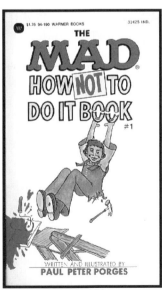

PAUL PETER PORGES

ANTONIO PROHIAS

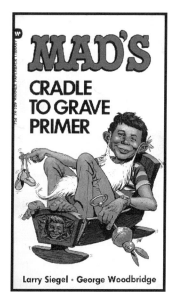

LARRY SIEGEL

LOU SILVERSTONE

JOHN FICARRA

CHAPTER FIFTEEN

Mad Big Books

With *The Completely Mad Don Martin* in June, 1974, Warner Paperback Library began a series of magazine size paperbacks that came to be known as "*Mad* Big Books." Although many of the titles are out of print, books in the series continue to appear. Some have been reprinted over the years with alternate covers, notably *The Completely Mad Don Martin* (two different covers), *Dave Berg's Mad Trash* (two covers), *Sergio Aragonés On Parade* (two covers), and *Mad's Vastly Overrated Al Jaffee* (three covers).

Mad Big Books, various: $3-$5 each, Sergio Aragonés $10

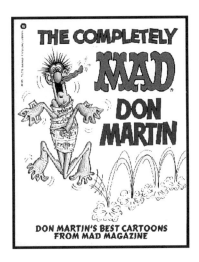
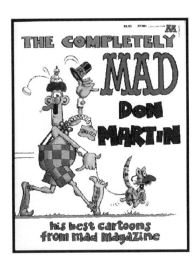

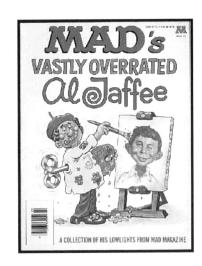

Magazine articles about *Mad*

Numerous magazine articles have been written about *Mad*, Gaines, and combinations thereof. While this list is not 100% complete, all major and most minor articles are believed to be accounted for.

Magazines with *Mad* articles, various: $1-$25 each, depending on age

Adweek, Jan. 23, 1989, "New Yorker Takes Cue from *Mad*" article
Atlantic Monthly, Sept. 1963, "A Case for *Mad*," first "highbrow" approval of *Mad* magazine
Bananas #1, 1975, Don Martin interview
Bestsellers (trade magazine), August 1963, photo of *Mad* Signet paperback display rack
Bestsellers (trade magazine), Feb. 1972, ad for *Mad* magazine
Boston, August 1979, "*Mad* Magazine's Alfred E. Neuman: A 400 Year Old Ancestor?"
Campus Life, Jan. 1974, "In Search of Alfred E. Neuman" article
Catholic Family Magazine, July 1965, "Who Reads *Mad*?" article
Cavalier, Sept. 1965, article about super hero comics with brief mention of *Mad*
Christian Century, Dec. 12, 1967, "The *Mad* Morality" article, later expanded to book length
Christian Century, Feb. 28, 1968, letter to editor about "The *Mad* Morality" article
Cleveland Magazine, Oct. 1990, article about local radio station, *Mad* mentioned
Club International, Nov. 1977, article featuring British *Mad* covers
Columbia Journalism Review, Jan./Feb. 1989, Alfred E. Neuman on cover
Congressional Record, Vol. 108, May 17, 1962, 10th ann. salute to *Mad* by Representative Benjamin Rosenthal
Connoisseur, The, July 1988, *Spy vs Spy* illustrations used
Consumer Reports, Nov. 1981, article about board games, "The *Mad* Magazine Game" mentioned
Coronet, May 1960, *Mad* article with art reproductions
Diner's Club Magazine, circa June 1962, *Mad* article reprint
Discover, March 1988, *Spy vs Spy* illustrations used on cover and interior
Dynamite #3, Spring 1974, "A Visit to the *Mad* house" cover and article
Dynamite #26, 1976, article on the origins of Alfred E. Neuman
Dynamite #47, 1978, article about *Mad* 's 25th anniversary (#10 on cover of some copies)
Eastern Review, March 1987, airline magazine, reprints *Manhattan, Inc.* (Aug. 1986) article
Editor and Publisher, June 4, 1988, Mort Drucker wins Reuben award
Editor and Publisher, June 24, 1989, article linking *Mad* and Thomas Nast
English Journal, Feb. 1970, "*Mad* Magazine in the Remedial English Class"
English Journal, March 1989, *Mad* in school article
Entertainment Weekly, Nov. 22, 1991, review of *Completely Mad*, "Blecch" parody shown
Entertainment Weekly, June 19, 1992, obit of Gaines with Al Jaffee portrait.
Esquire, Aug. 1964, "Bad" *Mad* parody
Esquire, Sept. 1990, AEN drawing in article about look-alikes
Esquire, June 1992, George Bush as Alfred E. Neuman on cover, painted by Richard Williams
Fact, Nov./Dec. 1965, "Don't Go Away *Mad*," *Mad* vs. John Birch society article
Famous Monsters of Filmland #2, 1958, short article with reprints from *Mad*
Folio:'s Publishing News, June 15, 1991, article on *Mad* with new Mort Drucker illustration
Forbes, June 15, 1987, *Mad* article, Gaines pictured
Game Players, Dec./Jan. 1989/1990, *Spy vs Spy* game review
Gauntlet #3, 1992, Bill Gaines interview
Gauntlet #4, 1992, William M. Gaines tribute by Steve Ringgenberg
Genesis 2, Summer 1987, "Beware of Imitations! The Jewish Radicalism of *Mad* Comics"
Heavy Metal, Feb. 1985, Jack Davis interview, *Mad* references
Hits Magazine Third Anniversary special, Aug. 1989, Alfred E. Neuman on cover
Hollywood Reporter, The, June 4, 1992, obituary of Bill Gaines
How, July-Aug. 1988, "Working *Mad*," article about Al Jaffee's "*Mad* Fold-in" techniques
Hustler, Feb. 1981, piece on Bill Gaines by Frank Jacobs
Hustler, July 1985, "*MADD*" parody cover
Image, The, vol. 2, #4 (British), 1973, *Mad* article
Journal of Communication, Winter 1984, "*Mad* Economics: An Analysis Of An Adless Magazine"
Kinagram (Kinney Corp. house organ) vol. 1, #2, July 1969, interview with AEN; Gaines pictured.
Kirkus Reviews, Oct. 1991, review of *Completely Mad* book
Kite Lines, Spring 1985, letter reporting pre-*Mad* "Me Worry?" face on a kite
Library Journal, Oct. 15, 1991, review of *Completely Mad* book
Life, March 11, 1966 ("Batman" cover), *The Mad Show* article and photos

Life, June 1986, AEN appears with other comics characters
Life, Sept. 1986, *Spy vs Spy* illustrations used
Life, August 1992, tribute to *Mad* by Art Spiegelman
Look, March 19, 1968, "The *Mad* Miracle" article
MAC Report (radio industry trade magazine), April 1, 1989, *Mad*/Alfred E. Neuman homage on cover
Manhattan, Inc., Aug. 1986, "*Mad* Infinitum" article, Gaines pictured
Merrill-Palmer Quarterly, July 1962, "Teenagers, Satire, and *Mad*," Charles Winick (Columbia U.)
Money, Oct. 1989, Alfred E. Neuman's picture (25¢ portrait, Mingo art) used in stock market article
Music Express #129, Oct. 1988, article about *Mad* and "Comic Book Confidential" film
National Geographic, July 1986, "Statue of Liberty" article featuring Bill and Anne Gaines collection
National Geographic, Sept. 1988, "Spoofing the Geographic," *Mad* reprint ("National Osographic")
National Observer, Oct. 10, 1969, feature article with photo of Gaines and staff
National Review, Oct. 9, 1987, Alfred E. Neuman on cover, Mort Drucker art
National Screw, Nov. 1976, "The *Mad, Mad* World of Bill Gaines" article
Network Computing (trade magazine), July 1991, *Spy vs Spy* drawing on cover, article (not Prohias)
New Republic, Jan. 29, 1966, *The Mad Show* review
New Republic, May 5, 1985, *Spy vs Spy* type illustrations accompany article
New Republic, July 17-24, 1989, film review of *Comics Confidential*, *Mad* discussed
New Republic, Feb. 10, 1992, *Completely Mad* book review
New York, Oct. 1, 1973, *Mad* article
New Yorker, The, Nov. 29, 1958, *Mad* described in article about teenagers
New Yorker, The, Jan. 22, 1966, review of *The Mad Show*
New Yorker, The, March 29, 1993, Kurtzman tribute by Art Spiegelman
Newsweek, August 31, 1959, *Mad* article "Crazy Like a Fox," Gaines and Feldstein pictured
Newsweek, April 9, 1962, "Who's *Mad*?" article, Gaines and Feldstein pictured
Newsweek, April 6, 1964, Irving Berlin/*Mad* lawsuit article "Sing Along with *Mad*"
Newsweek, Jan. 24, 1966, *The Mad Show* reviewed, Alfred E. Neuman pictured
Newsweek, Sept. 30, 1974, editorial cartoon with Alfred E. Neuman, from Louisville Courier-Journal
Newsweek, April 25, 1983, *Mad* sidebar in article about humor magazines, Gaines pictured
Newsweek, March 20, 1989, *Mad* article related to Warner/Time merger, Gaines pictured
Newsweek, Dec. 2, 1991, brief review of *Completely Mad* book
Newsweek, June 15, 1992, full page obituary of Bill Gaines, with color photo
Nintendo Power, Jan./Feb. 1989, *Spy vs Spy* game review
Oui, Feb. 1979, Gaines interview, Gaines portrait by Norman Mingo, done especially for article
Paris Match, June 13, 1959, French article about *Mad*
People, Aug. 28, 1989, reference to Alfred E. Neuman in review of Beastie Boy's album
People, Nov. 18, 1991, *Mad* #180 cover shown in review of *The American Magazine* book
People, Jan. 13, 1992, negative review of *Completely Mad* book with Don Martin cartoon reprint
Picture Week, August 27, 1955, six page article on *Mad* illustrated by Jack Davis and Bill Elder
Picture Week, Jan. 17, 1956, article on *Inside Mad* paperback, reprints "Slow Motion" (Davis)
Playboy, Dec. 1957, "The Little World of Harvey Kurtzman" article, reprints from early *Mad*
Player's Guide to Nintendo, Aug./Sept. 1989, *Spy vs Spy* game review
Players Strategy Guide, Dec. 1989/Jan. 1990, *Spy vs Spy* game review
Popular Science, March 1961, Alfred E. Neuman's face in computer print out
Publishers Weekly, Dec. 30, 1963, "When is Parody Plagiarism?" article about Berlin/*Mad* lawsuit
Publishers Weekly, Oct. 5, 1964, "Parody and Satire Deserve Substantial Freedom," *Mad* mentioned
Publishers Weekly, Jan 10, 1986, "Don't Get *Mad*, Get Even" article by Lyle Stuart
Publishers Weekly, Sept. 13, 1991, review of *Completely Mad* book
Read, April 1, 1966, "Read Goes *Mad*," Feldstein interview and *Mad* office photos
Reader's Digest, Feb. 1956, article about "cleaning up" comics, *Mad* called a "thriller"
Realist, The, #121, Autumn, 1992, AEN cover, article dedicated to Gaines by Paul Krassner
Rogue, Dec. 1965, Kurtzman interview, *Mad* references
Rolling Stone, July 10, 1980, Norman Mingo obituary
Rolling Stone, Oct. 18, 1990, article about *Mad* rock parodies
Rolling Stone, August 6, 1992, tribute to Bill Gaines with color photo
Saturday Evening Post, Dec. 12, 1963, major *Mad* article, classic photos of Gaines and staff
Saturday Evening Post, Jan. 25, 1964, letter from Harvey Kurtzman re: Dec. 12, 1963 article
Scene, Aug. 1958, *Mad* article
Scholastic Scope, April 2, 1973, "*Scope* Visits *Mad* Mag.," Alfred E. Neuman cover and *Mad* article
Scholastic Search, vol. 17, #8, May 1989, *Mad* #1 on cover
Screw, August 1, 1988, "Ill Gotten Gaines"
Seventy Three (amateur radio magazine), April 1967, Alfred E. Neuman face (with glasses) on cover
SH-BOOM, vol. 1, #3, March 1990, 1959 photo of Pat Boone at newsstand, *Mad* #49 on rack

From Newsdealer, Oct. 1958

From Esquire, Aug. 1964

Hits Special, 1989

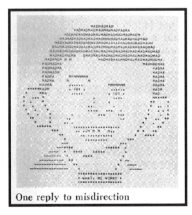

One reply to misdirection

From Popular Science, March 1961

From Hustler, July 1985

True West, August 1956

From Coronet, May 1960

From TV Guide, Oct. 26, 1968

From Oui, Feb. 1979

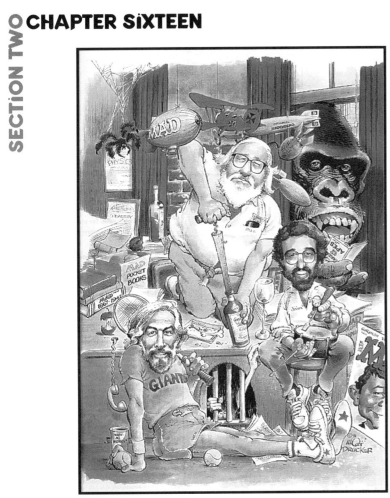

From Folio:'s Publishing News, June 15, 1991. Thirty-two copies of this page were signed by Gaines, Meglin and Ficarra; nineteen of these were matted and sent out to distributors and other related parties by Warner Publisher Services. The remaining prints were given away, and a few were sold to collectors at $100 apiece. Three thousand hand-numbered postcards bearing this image were also sent out for promotional purposes.

Newsweek—Bob Brower

Gaines, Neuman, and Feldstein: 'What, me worry?'

From Newsweek, Aug. 31, 1959

Scholastic Scope, April 2, 1973

Dynamite #47

Unused photo from Dec. 12, 1963, Saturday Evening Post article on Mad; the print was "customized" by Nick Meglin's dog Oscar.

From Newsdealer, Nov. 1959

From Bestsellers, Feb. 1972

From Newsdealer, April 1960

MAC Report, April 1, 1989

Maddiction

The reading primer ("Easy little steps for muddy little feet") is completely *Mad:* "My teacher is Miss Furd. I tell the school board Miss Furd is a Commie. Miss Furd is through in this town ... This is Bobby Smith. He is our playmate. Bobby sells reefers to the other children in school."

Through such zany mockery of the solemn, the pretentious and the inane, the bimonthly *Mad* is compiling a growth chart that is no laughing matter. For its sixth-anniversary number out last week, *Mad* printed 1,300,000 copies, a 100%

PUBLISHER GAINES
With mockery and money.

increase in a year. What is more, *Mad* is solidly in the black though it carries not a line of advertising, has spent only $350 on outright promotion. In fact, the essence of *Mad's* success is its nimble spoofing of promotions of all kinds. In its parodies of advertisements and travel stickers, vending machines and lovelorn columnists, *Mad* is a refreshingly impudent reaction against all the slick stock in trade of 20th century hucksterism, its hopped-up sensationalism, its visible and hidden persuaders.

For its anniversary issue, *Mad* conjures up magazines like *Caveman's Weekly* (sample article: "Is the Stone-Axe the Ultimate Weapon?") and the *Pilgrim's Home Journal* ("I Should've Kept My Big Mouth Shut," by John Alden), gives advice on how to play golf ("The grip should be about the same as one would use clutching a dead trout"), and quotes some woman-meets-native dialogue from the *National Osographic:* "Evelyn stepped forward and asked in Swahili, 'What I want to know, and I want you to give

me a straight answer to, is—I mean—I want to know if you really got cannibals up this way. I mean I heard the rumble. I know the story.'"

"What—Me Worry?" Most fascinating aspect of *Mad's* success is that its spoofs appeal mainly to teen-agers. They bombard *Mad's* tiny editorial offices just below Manhattan's Greenwich Village with some 400 fan letters a day, wear T shirts emblazoned with the face of *Mad's* grinning imp Alfred E. ("What—me worry?") Neuman, and treasure old issues like collector's items. *Mad*diction also has become a cult in some adult circles. Comics Ernie Kovacs, Bob and Ray, Henry Morgan and Orson Bean contribute frequently and willingly for next to nothing.

Publisher William M. Gaines, a hearty, hefty man of 250 lbs., launched *Mad* in 1952 as a sideline to the comic-book business he inherited from his father, M. (for Max) C. Gaines, who started the whole industry in the early 30s when he hit on the idea of selling reprinted newspaper comic sections for a dime. Using the standard comic formula—32 pages, newsprint, four colors, a 10¢ price tag—*Mad* was just holding its own when Gaines played a hunch in 1955, switched to semi-slick paper and higher quality black-and-white drawings, upped the price to 25¢ and promptly had a boffo success. The magazine now clears $43,000 an issue.

Mad's booming popularity astonishes Publisher Gaines. Says he: "All I can say to explain it is something glib like, 'Everyone is under a strain, and some sort of comic relief is a good thing.' If we knew exactly what we were doing right, we'd do more of it."

TIME, JULY 7, 1958

From Time, July 7, 1958

Newspaper articles about *Mad*

It would be an impossible task to track down every, or even most, of the *Mad*-related newspaper articles that have appeared over the years, so what follows is a list of the more interesting ones we have run across. Many of the stories went out over various wire services, and therefore the same article would appear in as many papers as picked up the story.

Newspaper articles about *Mad*: clippings 50¢ to $3, Sunday magazine sections $3-$20

Arizona Republic, Dec. 30, 1991, review of *Completely Mad*
Arkansas Gazette, Sept. 4, 1977, "*Mad* Magazine Latest Fad in Argentina" article
Arkansas Gazette, April 11, 1978, Al Feldstein interview with photo
Asbury Park Sunday Press, Jan. 16, 1972, Q & A with William M. Gaines
Sun (Baltimore, Md.), April 19, 1982, "It May Be *Mad* but There's a Method in It" article
Boston Globe, Feb. 3, 1988, "*Mad* Marches On" article
Boston Globe, Nov. 9, 1990, "What–Me Worry?" political cartoon
Boston Globe, Dec. 10, 1990, "300 issues, and Not a Worry" article
Boston Globe, Jan. 14, 1992, feature article on *Completely Mad* book
Chicago Sun Times, June 10, 1980, *Up the Academy* film review
Chicago Tribune Magazine, May 4, 1980, "*Mad* Marches On" article
Chicago Tribune, June 9, 1980, "Up the Academy" film review
Cleveland Plain Dealer, July 31, 1977, article on *Mad*'s 25th anniversary
Cleveland Plain Dealer, Nov. 5, 1989, "Drawing on Life," Sergio Aragonés featured
Cleveland Plain Dealer, Dec. 12, 1990, music article with one-line reference to AEN
Cleveland Plain Dealer, April 7, 1991, photo of Sergio Aragonés at North Coast Comic Con
Cleveland Plain Dealer, Jan. 4, 1992, article on *Mad* and *Completely Mad* (from Washington Post)
Cleveland Plain Dealer, Feb. 9, 1992, *Completely Mad* book review (from Cox News Service)
Cleveland Plain Dealer, June 6, 1992, obit and appreciation of Bill Gaines (reprinted from the *Baltimore Sun*)
Courier-Journal and Times, Jan. 23, 1972, same as SF Examiner article of same date, alternate headline
Courier-Journal (Louisville, KY), Dec. 29, 1978, AEN in editorial cartoon by Chuck Haynie
Daily News (Los Angeles), June 4, 1992, obituary of Bill Gaines
Dallas Morning News, April 4, 1982, *Mad*'s business woes article
Dallas Morning News, Sept, 19, 1987, "What, *Mad* 35?" article
Detroit News, Nov. 20, 1987, "Middle Aged *Mad*," 35th anniversary article
Fort Myers, Fla. News Press, Oct. 2, 1977, "After all these Years," *Mad*'s 25th anniversary
International Herald Tribune, Dec. 18, 1991, *Mad* article (from Washington Post, Dec. 18, 1991)
Long Beach Press Telegram, Feb. 3, 1988, "35 Years of *Mad*ness"
Los Angeles Times, May 10, 1980, Norman Mingo obituary
Los Angeles Times, Oct. 1, 1984, Alfred E. Neuman in editorial cartoon
Los Angeles Times, June 4, 1992, obituary of Bill Gaines
Los Angeles Times Book Review, Dec. 1, 1991, *Completely Mad* review, color *Mad* cover repros
Los Angeles Times/Calendar, July 25, 1982, "*Mad*'s Name is Far from Mud" article
Los Angeles Times TV Times, June 3-9, 1990, HBO "Crypt" featured, Gaines photo, *Mad* mentioned
Los Angeles Times View, Nov. 6, 1991, interview with Maria Reidelbach re: *Completely Mad*
Louisville Courier-Journal, Dec. 29, 1978, editorial cartoon with Alfred E. Neuman
Metro Times (Detroit), April 8-14, 1992, "The Legacy of Alfred E. Neuman" article
Miami Florida Herald, Nov. 25, 1989, "Middle Aged and Still *Mad*" article
Miami Herald Tropic, May 20, 1990, cover and article about Don Martin getting "screwed" by *Mad*
Miami Herald Tropic, Aug. 26, 1990, blistering reply from Gaines re: May 20th article
Miami Herald, June 6, 1982, "Drawing on a *Mad* Wit," Don Martin featured
New York Daily News, Feb. 7, 1967, "Mystery Lifts a Little," article on the origins of AEN
New York Daily News, June 9, 1980, *Up the Academy* film review
New York Daily News, Dec. 8, 1991, "Funny Stuff" (brief review of *Completely Mad* book)
New York Daily News, June 9, 1992, column on Don and Norma Martin's reactions to Gaines's death
New York Newsday, Nov. 11, 1986, "*Mad* Lampoons the Governor" article
New York Newsday, Dec. 17, 1991, article on *Mad*'s 40th anniversary
New York Post, June 10, 1980, *Up the Academy* film review
New York Times, March 24, 1964, article on Irving Berlin/*Mad* lawsuit
New York Times, June 10, 1964, article about *Mad* being purchased by National Periodical Publications
New York Times, Oct. 13, 1964, "Magazine's Right to Parody Lyrics Backed on Appeal" article
New York Times, Jan. 10, 1966, *The Mad Show* review
New York Times, June 7, 1980, review of *Up the Academy*
New York Times, June 12, 1990, Don Martin's cartoons advertise VH-1, *Mad* mentioned

New York Times, Feb. 10, 1991, article about *thirtysomething* TV show, reference to the *Mad* spoof
New York Times, Dec. 2, 1991, brief review of *Completely Mad* book
New York Times, June 4, 1992, obituary of Bill Gaines with photo
New York Times, June 10, 1992, full page tribute to Gaines from staff on back of first section
New York Times, Feb. 23, 1993, Harvey Kurtzman obit
NYT School Weekly, Jan. 22, 1979, Jimmy Carter with caption "What—Me Worry?"
New York Times Magazine, July 31, 1977, *Mad* article with new Norman Mingo art
New York Times Magazine, Jan. 25, 1981, article on childhood innocence, *Mad* discussed
New York Times Sunday Travel, July 11, 1971, Frank Jacobs article on the *Mad* trips
Ohio State Lantern, Feb. 6, 1970, "*Mad*-ness Has Its Method" article
Orlando Sentinel Florida Magazine, May 12, 1985, Don Martin cover and interview.
Palo Alto Peninsula Times Tribune, Sept. 26, 1983, "The *Mad Mad* World of *Mad*," Gaines Q & A
People of Peoria (*P.O.P.*), Fall 1991, "485 MADison Ave." article, writer from Peoria visits *Mad*
Philadelphia Enquirer, Dec. 23, 1987, 35th anniversary article
Pittsburgh Press, June 6, 1980, *Up the Academy* film review
Plattsburgh Press-Republican (Plattsburgh NY), Aug. 17, 1960, photo of Gaines and Joe Orlando in town for fishing trip. Gaines quoted on *Mad*.
San Diego Union, April 15, 1982, "Circulation Slide" article
San Francisco Examiner, June 4, 1992, appreciation of Bill Gaines with color photo, by staff writer Bob Stephens
San Francisco Chronicle Datebook, March 17, 1991, *Mad* art exhibit (Mark Cohen)
San Francisco Examiner and Chronicle, Jan. 23, 1972, "The Freaky World of AEN" article
San Jose Mercury News, Jan. 4, 1990, "*Mad*'s Still Crazy After all These (37) Years" article
San Jose Mercury News, Nov. 25, 1990, "What *Mad* Worry?" article
San Jose Mercury News, June 4, 1992, obituary of Bill Gaines with photo
Sun Newspapers, April 4, 1991, "Simply *Mad* About Cartooning," Sergio Aragonés appears at con
Sydney (Australia) Morning Herald, Aug. 16, 1982, full page AEN face,"If you don't advertise in newspapers, you're an idiot"
Topeka State Journal, Jan. 15, 1910, ad for dentist "Painless Romaine" with pre-*Mad* image of AEN
USA Today, Nov. 10, 1987, "Artist Goes Away *Mad*," article on Don Martin leaving *Mad*
USA Today, Nov. 16, 1987, 35th anniversary article
USA Today, March 7, 1989, Time-Warner merger article, *Mad* reference
USA Today, March 10, 1989, "Karma Bad for Merger?," Time-Warner merger, *Mad* reference
USA Today, June 4, 1992, obituary of Bill Gaines with color picture
USA Today, July 12, 1993, blurb on *Mad's* first "Big Question" survey
USA Weekend, Jan 6, 1989, Q & A about *Mad*, Gaines pictured
Washington (D.C.) Times, May 26, 1987, "*Mad* Mag. is Still Zany at 35" article
Washington Post, Dec 18, 1991, *Mad* article
Yale News, March 1, 1973, article and photos on *Mad* staff appearing at Yale (Feb. 28, 1973)

New York Times, July 11, 1971

Beasties for the Kiddies | Page 23

BOOK REVIEW

LOS ANGELES TIMES • SUNDAY, DECEMBER 1, 1991

MAD

"What--me worry?"

Children of MAD

COMPLETELY MAD
A History of the
Comic Book and Magazine
By Maria Reidelbach
(Little, Brown; $39.95; 208 pp.)

Reviewed by Randy Cohen

*LA Times Book Review,
Dec. 1, 1991*

QUESTION OF THE WEEK

FUNNY MAN: Bill Gaines claims 1 million Mad readers.

'Mad' still laughing

Q: How long has *Mad* magazine been around, and who is the original creator?
— Ben Van Dyke, Everett, Wash.

A: Bill Gaines, a former horror comics publisher, founded *Mad* in 1952. It's the USA's longest-running humor magazine.

But Gaines, president and publisher, credits the whole staff: seven mad-people (including Gaines' wife Anne) who create hilarity at Madison Avenue offices filled with gorilla likenesses and rubber toys. The atmosphere is "a little Marx Brothers," admits Gaines, who collects Statue of Liberty miniatures. He once flew the whole staff en masse to Haiti to get a subscriber to renew (he did).

Nowadays, the ad-free *Mad* is pursuing licensing deals, including a watch with smirking mascot Alfred E. Newman in a straitjacket. Newman originally was "used as an ad for a painless dentist in Topeka," says Gaines, 66, who fell for his "What, me worry?" look.

USA Weekend, Jan. 6, 1989

MAD

WE'LL CARRY ON WITH THE LAUGHTER, THE IRREVERENCE, THE MISCHIEF AND, OH YEAH, THE MAGAZINE, TOO.

WE'LL MISS YOU, BILL

LOVE,

"THE USUAL GANG OF IDIOTS"

*New York Times,
June 10, 1992*

THE NEW YORK TIMES, FRIDAY, JANUARY 10, 1975

The Face Is Familiar. Have We Met?

By Harvey Kurtzman

MOUNT VERNON, N. Y.—There's a question that nags wherever I go. Again and again I am asked, Where did Alfred Neuman come from? For those of you who didn't hear a bell ring at the mention of Alfred N., he is the face you see on the covers of Mad magazine. And for those of you who ring, let me put the eternal question to rest, once and for all.

The face first came to my attention when I was doing the comic book Mad for publisher William Gaines in the middle fifties—I think it was 1954. We were working with Ballantine paperback books on the first of a series of Mad reprint collections.

Since I was Mad's chief cook and bottle washer at the time, there wasn't a moment of my waking life that wasn't devoted to the search for more and more Mad material.

In this condition, and while passing the time of day in the office of an editor, Bernard Shir-Cliff, I noticed on the Ballantine Book bulletin board a postcard with this face. The card had some ad message—I don't recall what.

And the face itself was printed alongside in a space, maybe an inch by an inch and a half. The face was not unfamiliar. I associated it with the funny-picture postcards in Times Square penny arcades and tourist traps, this one with the caption "What, Me Worry?" under the bumpkin portrait—part leering wiseacre, part happy-go-lucky kid.

But what interested me about this Ballantine version was that of all the reproductions I'd remembered, this one looked like the authentic, original-source portrait—the real goods.

While everything I'd seen before was cartoon, this seemed to be a photograph of the *actual face!* So I pocketed the card and rushed back to the workshop where I inserted the "What, Me Worry?" face on and in subsequent issues of Mad magazine.

I was very fond of plastering Mad with inanities—items like Potrzebie, Melvin Cowznofski, Alfred E. Neuman. The readers apparently liked them. Potrzebie was a word clipped at random from a Polish-language newspaper. Melvin was borrowed from the old Ernie Kovacs Show, as Alfred E. was borrowed from Hollywood by way of the old, old Henry Morgan show.

Alfred Newman (the late) was in reality a movie-music man whose credits were legion on the silver screen.

Morgan would use the name for various innocuous characters that passed through his show, and I did in Mad, after Morgan's fashion. And even though the face was, and ever would be, to me, a What, Me Worry? kid, our fan mail insisted on calling him Melvin Cowznofski and Alfred E. Neuman.

As a matter of fact, in the ensuing fan enthusiasm over the face, we ourselves became curious as to its genealogy, and in our letters page we asked the readers for whatever source information they might have.

The answers were astonishing. The face dated back to the 19th century. It was supposed to have been used for selling patent medicine, shoes and soft drinks. The kid was depicted as a salesman, a cowboy, a doughboy, and was rendered in dozens of slight to grossly altered variations.

But the answer I have always liked to believe was that the face came from an old high school biology text—an example of a person who lacked iodine.

Whatever the truth might be, Mad adopted the face as its mascot, and we used it like a trade mark on all of our covers.

With the success of Mad, disputations arose. Readers laid copyright claim to the face, and eventually the issue went to court — not to just any court, but to the Supreme Court of the Land. In this lofty council, Mad won, once and for all, the right to use the face. The What, Me Worry? kid was permanently baptized Alfred E. Neuman by Albert Feldstein, the editor who came after me.

So that's the story, once and for all. Don't ask me any more.

Harvey Kurtzman produces, with Will Elder, the cartoon feature Little Annie Fanny in Playboy magazine.

Alfred Neuman © E.C. Publications 1975

New York Times, Jan. 10, 1975

Books with *Mad*-related features

Books with *Mad*-related features, various: average price $15-$20

A Casebook on Ken Kesey's One Flew Over the Cuckoo's Nest, edited by George J. Searles, University of New Mexico Press, 1992, reprints parody.

Album Cover Album, by Hipgnosis and Roger Dean, Dragon's World (England), 1977, reproduces unused AEN painting by Rick Griffin for group "Man"

Art of Humorous Illustration, The, by Nick Meglin, Watson-Guptill, 1973, various *Mad* artists featured

Art of Jack Davis, The, Stabur Press, 1987, AEN on cover

Aurora History and Price Guide, Bill Bruegman, Cap'n Penny Prods., 1992, Alfred E. Neuman model kit featured

Best of Ernie Bushmiller's Nancy, The, by Brian Walker, Comicana Books/Henry Holt, 1988, section on *Mad* "Nancy" parodies

Canvas Confidential by Sy Reit, Frank Jacobs and Kelly Freas, Dial Press, 1963 (all are *Mad* contributors)

Coast to Coast by Rod Dyer, Brad Benedict and David Lees, Abbeville Press, 1991, book on travel decals, shows "Like Man–Me Worry?" decal

Comic Book in America, The, by Mike Benton, Taylor Publishing, 1989, section and cover repro from *Mad* comics

Complete Book of Caricature, The, by Bob Staake, North Light Books, 1991, *Mad* mentioned and various artists covered

Crawford's Encyclopedia of Comic Books by Hubert H. Crawford, Jonathan David Publisher's, 1978, reprints from *Mad* but full of factual errors

Directory of Humor Magazines and Organizations in America (2nd ed.), 1989, *Mad* logo and pub. info

Draw 50 Famous Caricatures by Lee J. Ames and Mort Drucker, Doubleday, 1990 (Drucker is a long time *Mad* artist)

Draw 50 Famous Cartoons by Lee J. Ames, Doubleday, 1979, AEN on cover, how to draw AEN inside

Dvorak's Inside Track to the MAC, 1992, AEN on cover

Esquire's World of Humor, Esquire-Harper and Row, 1964, hardback, reprints "Bad" parody from *Esquire* August 1964

Familiar Faces: the Art of Mort Drucker, Stabur Press, 1988, reprints from *Mad*

From ARRGH to ZAP!, A Visual History of Comics by H. Kurtzman, Prentice Hall Press, 1991, EC and *Mad* reprints

Great Comic Book Artists, The by Ron Goulart, vol. 1, St. Martin's Press, 1986, bios and art repros of various *Mad* artists

Great Comic Book Artists, The by Ron Goulart, vol. 2, St. Martin's Press, 1989, bios and art repros of various *Mad* artists

Great Comics Game, The, Price/Stern/Sloan, 1966, quiz book, AEN pictured

Hey Look! by Harvey Kurtzman, Kitchen Sink Press, 1992, *Mad* #3 on back cover

Highly Unlikely Celebrity Cookbook, The, Frank Jacobs and Mort Drucker, New American Library, 1964 (both are *Mad* contributors)

History of Underground Comics, A by Mark James Estren, Straight Arrow Books, 1974, *Mad* info and Kurtzman interview

Humor and Cartoon Markets by Bob Staake, 1991, Gaines interview and *Mad* info

Hurried Child, The by David Elkind, 1990, *Mad* references

Illustrated Harvey Kurtzman Index, The by Glenn Bray, 1976, many reprints from *Mad*

International Book of Comics, The by Denis Gifford, Crescent Books, 1984, section on *Mad*, *Mad* #1 on cover

Jack Davis: Some of My Good Stuff!, Stabur Press, 1991, AEN on cover, *Mad* cover repro

JFK Coloring Book, The, Kanrom, Inc., 1962, Mort Drucker art

Kovacsland by Diana Rico, 1990, brief mention of Kurtzman, Gaines, and Kovacs's *Mad* work

Lakeside Gone Mad, 1989, Atlanta, Georgia high school yearbook with a *Mad* theme

Masters of Comic Book Art by P.R. Garriock, Images Graphiques, 1978, reprints from *Mad* comics

My Life as a Cartoonist by Harvey Kurtzman, 1988, reprints from early *Mad*

Overstreet Comic Book Price Guide #12, Avon Books, 1992, AEN cover and Norman Mingo feature article

Photo-Journal Guide to Comic Books, The, E. Gerber, 1990, color covers to *Mad* #1-28

Pop Sixties, The by Andrew J. Edelstein, World Almanac Publications, 1985, short section on *Mad*

Postcard Companion, The by Jack H. Smith, 1989, repro of pre-*Mad* "AEN and Sister" postcard

Pow! Zap! Wham! Comic Book Trivia Quiz, The, by Michael Uslan and Bruce Solomon, William Morrow and Co., 1977, *Mad* related questions

Ronald Reagan Coloring Book, The, Andrews and McMeel, 1988, Mort Drucker art

Smithsonian Book of Comic Book Comics, A, Smithsonian-Abrams, 1981, reprints from *Mad* comics

Sotheby's Comic Books and Comic Art Catalog, Sotheby's, 1991, shows *Mad* #1 cover rough and other art

Superman at Fifty!, Dennis Dooley and Gary Engle, eds., Octavia, 1987, quote by Gaines about Superman

Theatre World, vols. 22 and 23, 1965-66, 1966-67, *The Mad Show* info

This Fabulous Century: 1950-1960, Time-Life Books, 1970, color cover to *Mad* #1 reproduced

Toys of the Sixties, Bill Bruegman, Cap'n Penny Prods., 1991-'92, short section on *Mad* collectibles

Wolvertoons: The Art of Basil Wolverton by Dick Voll, Fantagraphics Books, 1989, reprints from *Mad* comics and magazine

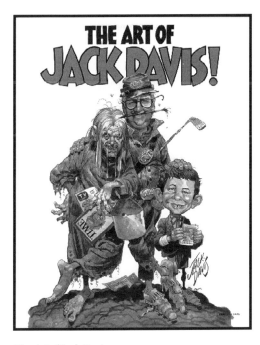

The Art of Jack Davis

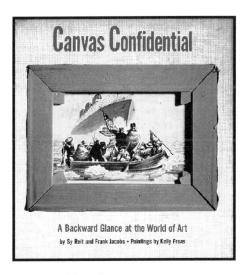

Canvas Confidential

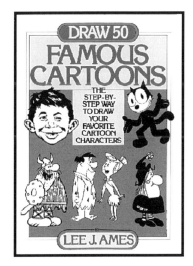

Draw 50 Famous Cartoons

Lakeside Gone Mad

Jack Davis: Some of My Good Stuff!

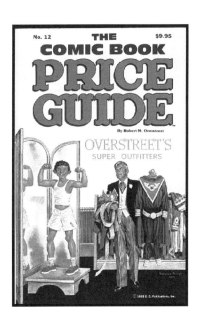

Overstreet Price Guide #12

Mad signed lithographs and prints

Stabur Graphics has issued a number of signed, limited lithographs and prints featuring art from *Mad* comics and *Mad* magazine. Color reproductions (17" x 24") of the covers to *Mad* #1, 2, 5, and 7 were issued in 1985. Limited to 500 copies each and signed by Harvey Kurtzman, Jack Davis, or Will Elder, the prints originally sold for $25. Unsigned posters on thinner paper were available for $5 each.

Lithos, *Mad* #1,2,5,7 (Stabur Graphics, 1985): signed lithos $30 each, posters $5 each

The Will Elder back cover to *Mad* #27 was issued as a signed, limited edition of 500 copies in 1985, priced at $25; the print is entitled "Visiting the Grandparents."

The Kelly Freas back cover to *Mad* #48 was issued in a signed, limited edition of 395 copies in 1988, priced at $75; the print is entitled "Presenting the Bill."

Litho, *Visiting the Grandparents* by Bill Elder (Stabur, 1985): $30

Litho, *Presenting the Bill* by Kelly Freas (Stabur, 1988): $75

CHAPTER SEVENTEEN

Two *Mad*-related lithographs have been issued by Stabur. The first to appear, "Voice for Children," was created by 69 artists and signed by 64 of them, including many past and present *Mad* artists; Alfred E. Neuman appears twice, as a green alien by Kelly Freas and as part of Jack Davis's contribution. Limited to 195 copies, the signed print was issued in 1986 and sold for $3,000 each. An unsigned poster was available for $4.00.

Litho, *Voice for Children*, has AEN cameos (Stabur, 1986): poster $4, signed print $3,000 retail

detail: Kelly Freas

detail: Jack Davis

The second *Mad*-related litho, "Cartoonist Constitution," was issued in 1987 and was created by 61 artists and signed by 59 of them. The print again features many past and present *Mad* artists; Alfred E. Neuman appears this time as Mort Drucker's contribution to the piece. The print was available in several editions: a signed limited edition of 195 prints at $2,000 each, an unsigned but numbered edition of 995 copies at $125 each, and as a poster at $4.00.

Litho, *Cartoonist Constitution*, has AEN cameo (Stabur, 1987): poster $4, signed print $2,000 retail

detail: Mort Drucker

Another Rainbow, known for producing high quality lithographs of Carl Barks's Donald Duck and Uncle Scrooge paintings, released in December, 1991, a limited edition lithograph of Harvey Kurtzman's original cover concept painting for *Mad* #1. The lithographs measure 10 1/2" x 10 1/2" and are signed and numbered by Kurtzman. Three states were offered: 100 "remarqued" signatures (with more elaborate doodles), 750 "regular" signatures, and five Progressive Proof sets (these came in a custom-made case). Prices varied with the lowness of the numbers; the "remarqued" lithos ran from $500 to $250, the "regular" edition from $450 to $195, and the five "Progressive Proof" sets were $950 each. Included with each were a certificate of authenticity and a 20-page booklet with biographies of *Mad* artists and writers by Maria Reidelbach (author of *Completely Mad*). This litho was originally made as a tip-in sheet for a planned signed, numbered edition of *Completely Mad* which never materialized.

Litho, *Mad* #1 concept painting: remarqued $250-$500

regular $195-$450

progressive proof set $950

CHAPTER EiGHTEEN

The Complete Mad Checklist

At the request of Bill Gaines, Fred von Bernewitz (compiler of *The Complete EC Checklist*) published three volumes of *The Complete Mad Checklist*, an exhaustive indexing and cross-referencing of *Mad* articles, artists, writers, reprint publications, et cetera. The first volume, covering *Mad* #24-66, was issued in September, 1961. Volume two, covering *Mad* #67-88, appeared in July, 1964. The third volume, covering issues #89-136 and which had to be split into two books due to size, appeared in July 1971. Volume one was $1.50, volume two was $1.00, and volume three was $3.50; all were mimeographed publications and were hand collated and stapled. After the third volume Fred found himself busy with his film editing career and could no longer work on the *Checklists* at the rate he was being paid, which was "about 5¢ an hour."

Complete Mad Checklist (Fred von Bernewitz): #1 $75, #2 $75, #3 (in two sections) $50-$75 for both

Dear E.C./Mad Fan:

I am sorry to inform you that there are no more copies left of:

✉ THE REVISED COMPLETE E. C. CHECKLIST ($1.50)

✉ THE COMPLETE MAD CHECKLIST ($1.50)

✉ THE COMPLETE MAD CHECKLIST NO. 2 ($1.00)

~~and that I am returning your money herewith.~~
I appreciate your inquiry but supplies are exhausted.

Fred von Bernewitz

Fred von Bernewitz form letter, late 1960s

Number 1

Number 2

Number 3 (two volumes)

Other *Mad* fanzines

The first fanzine devoted solely to *Mad* magazine was *Mad Freaks U.S.A.*, published by Ron Labbe. It lasted six issues, the final one appearing in 1981. The books measure 5 1/2" x 8 1/2".

Mad Freaks USA, six issues: $10 each

CHAPTER EiGHTEEN

Another fanzine, *MADzine*, ran thirteen issues between November, 1983, and March, 1985. Published by Don Cook of Ft. Myers, Florida, this 5 1/2" x 8 1/2" 'zine was cheaply produced and contained mostly reprints of various magazine articles about *Mad*. Some interesting items appeared.

MADzine, thirteen issues: $5-$10 each

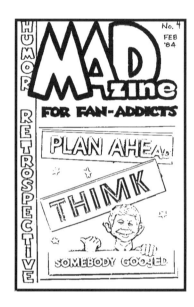

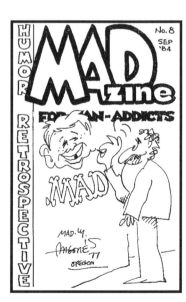

George Moonoogian contributed
this old E.C. Fan-Addict Club
membership card!

Sketch by Harvey Kurtzman

William M. Gaines

photo contributed
by Gunnar Stamper

Bob Barrett contributed
this MAD patch.

The Mad Panic, devoted to both *Mad* and EC's *Panic*, appeared in May, 1990. Production is via copier at the 5 1/2" x 8 1/2" size, but the computer typesetting makes it more readable than *MADzine*, for example. Twenty-seven issues have been published as of this writing. Errors with regard to copyright notices led Gaines to forbid any use of *Mad* material in *The Mad Panic*, but publisher Ed Norris (who was assisted on four issues by Michael Lerner) has continued publication nicely with an emphasis on text and non-*Mad* graphics.

The Mad Panic, #1 to present: $5 each

The

MAD

Panic

Volume: 1 Pint Number: 1   May 1990

Mad Marches On

New York - We begin with a fact to truly warm the hearts of the hundreds of thousands of groty little adolescents who regularly read Mad magazine: Its offices are as trashy as the humor mag itself. The walls are grimy, the furniture is mismatched and there's a pathetic artificial Christmas tree squatting atop a table in what passes for a lobby. Yecccech.

But there's more. Step into the inner sanctum of 66-year-old William Gaines, where Mad's portly publisher is surrounded by abject clutter. Notice that all the windows are covered and - this is in January, remember - that the air

(continued on page 6)

Number: 3   September 1990

The Freaky World of Alfred E. Neuman

New York - (AP) - Right away you know you're headed for the Mad Magazine offices because the elevator stops at the 13th floor.

Then you practically crash into a lifesized Alfred E. Neuman in lederhosen, following which:

● You hear a whirring sound from the stockroom which turns out to be an artist extracting fresh carrot juice.

● You come to a poster on a door - Karl Marx wearing glasses - behind which sits a living human of similar appearance who is mountainous, rumpled and bearded, and hair down to his shoulders, and you learn that he is millionaire publisher William Gaines.

(Continued on page 6)

Number: 5   January 1991

Still Mad After All These Years

Talk about your time warp: after 31 years, the "usual gang of idiots" who gave us "Spy Vs. Spy," back-cover fold-ins and those densely populated movie satires continue to confuse each other with, well, more of the same. Still running the show from his New York office decorated with toy zeppelins and stuffed gorillas, Mad publisher William M. Gaines, 61, manages to affect a vintage What-Me-Worry? tone even while discussing circulation figures, which show that single-copy sales have dropped nearly 50 percent, to an average of just over 1 million, in the last decade. "We're basically a kid's magazine," he notes with a shrug, "and there just aren't as many kids around as there used to be." It's not until their visitor alludes to an alleged humor boom that the staffers assume frozen smiles reminiscent of old Alfred E. Neuman himself.

Clearly, the warm regard that many of today's parodists express for Mad is not reciprocal. "I guess some   (continued on page 6)

NO. 11   JANUARY 1992

The MAD ___ ___ogo

Unless you are ___ ___ read a magazine/___ the ___ you have a braille ___ ___ logo for The MAD ___

Why change a good ___ that is simple. Why not!?

Besides, we've had the old ___ ___ now and the artist worked ___ ___his

Why are you trying to read ___ ___way real article. This was made ___ the ___his look more like a cover ___ Ma ___

○CHAPTER EiGHTEEN

Fanzines (and fan-oriented publications) with *Mad*-related articles

Fanzines with *Mad*-related articles, various: average price $4-$20

A Talk with H. Kurtzman (John Benson), 1966, *Mad* references
American Artist, April 1977, Jack Davis cover story by Nick Meglin
Antiqueweek, July 16, 1990, article on *Mad* collectibles
Antique Trader, May 5, 1993, inquiry letter re: pre-*Mad* "Me Worry?" picture
Antique Trader, Aug. 18, 1993, letters of reply to May 5, 1993 inquiry (replies from Jerry De Fuccio, Grant Geissman)
Antique Trader, Oct. 20, 1993, article on *Mad* artwork and collectibles
Baby Boomer Collectibles, Dec. 1993, article on *Mad* collectibles (with photos) by Michael Lerner
Cartoon News #13, Jan. 1976, Jack Davis interview
Cartoon News #17, June 1977, feature on Jack Davis magazine cover work
Cartoonist PROfiles #4, Nov. 1969, "*Mad* Magazine's Allan Jaffee" and "The Jack Davis Story"
Cartoonist PROfiles #5, Nov. 1969, "*Mad* Magazine's Dave Berg," interview with photos.
Cartoonist PROfiles #7, August 1970, Aragonés wraparound cover and feature on Aragonés
Cartoonist PROfiles #8, Nov. 1970, "*Mad* Magazine's A. Prohias," interview with photos.
Cartoonist PROfiles #10, June 1971, *Mad*-related cover (Woodbridge) and photos of a post-*Mad* trip party.
Cartoonist PROfiles #11, Sept. 1971, John Severin cartoon with AEN face, Don Martin cover roughs.
Cartoonist PROfiles #16, Dec. 1972, *Mad* artist Paul Coker featured, with illos
Cartoonist PROfiles #26, June 1975, Gaines cover by Mingo and feature on Norman Mingo
Cartoonist PROfiles #28, Dec. 1975, "*Mad* T-shirt profiles"
Cartoonist PROfiles #32, Dec. 1976, "*Mad* Christmas Cards," personal cards from *Mad* artists.
Cartoonist PROfiles #34, June 1977, "*Mad* Kong," feature on *Mad* artist Harry North
Cartoonist PROfiles #49, March 1981, tribute to artists and writers of *Mad*
Cartoonist PROfiles #52 & 53, Dec. 1981 and March 1982, Don Martin interview
Cartoonist PROfiles #61, March 1984, "Don Edwing, *Mad* 's Biz-artist"
Cartoonist PROfiles #68, Dec. 1985, article on *Mad* submissions policy by Nick Meglin
Cartoonist PROfiles #87, Dec. 1989, article on 1989 *Mad* trip
Collector's Showcase vol. 14 #2, Feb./March 1994, article on *Mad* collectibles (with photos) by Michael Lerner
Comic Book Marketplace #16, August 1992, Bill Gaines interview and tributes
Comic Crusader #10, 1970, "The *Mad* Men" article
Comic Reader #143, May 1977, Don Martin-inspired cover by J. Byrne
Comics Buyer's Guide #730, Nov. 13, 1987, "Don Martin leaves *Mad* " story and artwork
Comics Buyer's Guide #870, July 20, 1990, blurb about Chinese *Mad* publisher
Comics Buyer's Guide #875, Aug.24, 1990, review of T*he Mad Panic* fanzine
Comics Buyer's Guide #903, March 8, 1991, piece on *Mad* and Dick DeBartolo
Comics Buyer's Guide #971, June 26, 1992, Bill Gaines obit
Comics Buyer's Guide #972, July 3, 1992, "Remembering Bill Gaines" by Archie Goodwin, Denis Kitchen, Arnie Kogen, Joe Orlando, Bhob Stewart, and
   others
Comics Interview #12, June 1984, Jack Davis interview
Comics Journal #70, Jan. 1982, Wallace Wood memorial by Bhob Stewart
Comics Journal #128, April 1989, Sergio Aragonés featured
Comics Scene #16, Dec. 1990, H. Kurtzman interview, *Mad* mentioned
Comics Scene #21, Oct. 1991, feature on Bill Gaines (with photos), *Mad* covered
DC Super-Stars, vol. 2, #13, March 1977, Sergio Aragonés bio, *Mad* references
DISCoveries, April 1990, "*Mad* About the Dellwoods" letter and reply about *Mad* records
EC Fan Addict, The, #1, circa 1967, "It's a *Mad, Mad, Mad, Mad, Mad* " article by Bill Parente
EC Fan Addict, The, #2, 1968, "Masters of *Mad*ness" article by Bill Parente
Fanfare #1 (Bill Spicer), Spring 1977, AEN on cover, Al Feldstein interview
Gold and Silver, Overstreet's Comic Book Quarterly #3, 1994, brief piece on pre-*Mad* "Sure-I'm for Roosevelt" postcard
Graphic Story Magazine #14, Winter 1971, Basil Wolverton interview, *Mad* references
Honk! #1, Nov. 1986, Don Martin interview
Media Sight Magazine #3, Fall 1983, Gaines interview
Mediascene #16, Nov./Dec. 1975, "The *Mad* World of Jack Davis"
Model and Toy Collector #14, Spring 1990, article and photos on custom AEN statue by Kent Melton
Name of the Game, Jan. 1991, article about various *Mad* games
Overstreet's Advanced Collector #1, Summer 1993, article on *Mad* collectibles (with photos) by Michael Lerner, Harvey Kurtzman interview by Shel Dorf
Postcard Collector, August 1987, article on pre-*Mad* "Me Worry?" postcards
Seraphim (formerly *The EC Fan Addict*) #5, circa 1970, reprints "It's a *Mad* ,....*Mad* " from ECFA #1
Soda Net, July 1992, letters re: Cherry Sparkle and Happy Jack soda bottles
Spin Again #5, 1993, article on *Mad* collectibles (with photos) by Michael Lerner

Cartoonist PROfiles #26

Cartoonist PROfiles #7

A Talk With H. Kurtzman

Honk! #1

Fanfare #1

CHAPTER NiNETEEN

Mad Original Art Auctions (Russ Cochran)

In October 1986 Russ Cochran began a series of quarterly auctions to sell original art from *Mad*. The first six included the art from *Mad* comics (#1-23). Subsequent auctions (for a total of sixteen) offered art from *Mad* magazine. The first auction caused a stir when the cover to *Mad* #1 went to film director Steven Spielberg for $15,500. While none of the other pieces approached that figure in the auction's first six years, many of the painted covers to *Mad* went in the mid-to-high "four figure" range (the Jack Davis cover to *Mad* #27, for example, fetched $8,320, and the Norman Mingo "anniversary" cover to *Mad* #35 went for $6,500). The auction catalogs are worth collecting, as they reproduce *Mad* cover paintings (without logos or type) and contain a "prices realized" list from the previous auction. All pieces of art sold through Cochran's auctions have rubber-stamped copyright notices on the back.

Original Art Auctions (Russ Cochran): $3 each

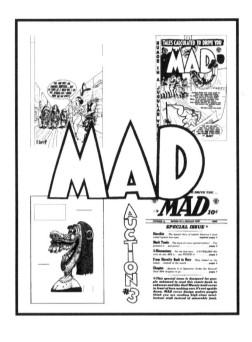

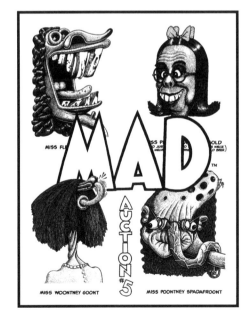

On December 18, 1992 Christie's auction house (in conjunction with Russ Cochran) presented "The Art of *Mad*." A total of 321 lots were offered, including sixty-seven cover paintings, spanning 1965-1992. Initial concern about "dumping" this much material in the market at one time proved unfounded, as prices reached all-time highs. Some examples: (prices include 10% buyer's premium) *Mad* #121 cover (Maharishi Alfred, Norman Mingo) $9,350; *Mad* #140 cover (General Patton Alfred, Norman Mingo) $9,900; *Mad* #148 cover (*Mad* paint, Norman Mingo) $8,800; *Mad* #106 back cover (Early One Morning in the Jungle, Frank Frazetta) $30,800; *Mad* #105 cover ('60s Batman, Norman Mingo) $10,450. The auction catalog itself is a collectible. Beautifully produced on slick paper, it pictures the art offered (in black and white and color) and contains brief biographies of *Mad* artists. The catalog retailed at $30 from Christie's.

The Art of Mad auction catalog: $30

Mad #58 back cover, Joe Orlando

Framed examples of *Mad* original art:

Mad #58 back cover, as printed

Mad #97 cover, Norman Mingo

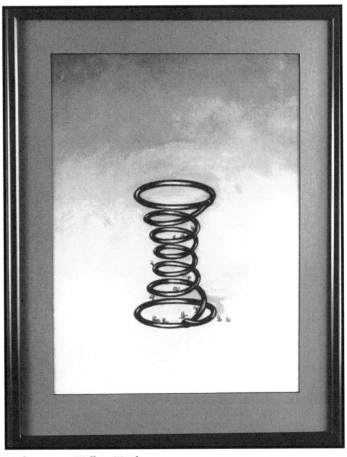

Mad #28 cover, Wallace Wood

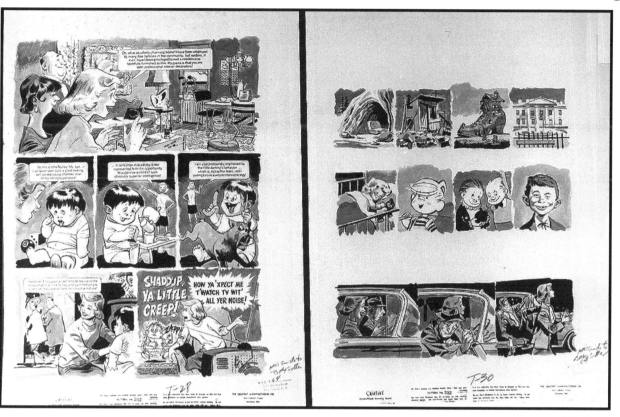

Bob Clarke

Bob Clarke (a la Charles Schultz)

Robert Grossman, paperback cover to Utterly Mad

CHAPTER NiNETEEN

Antonio Prohias

Wallace Wood

Caricature of artist/writer/editor Al Feldstein by Jack Davis, circa 1970s.

Other "one of a kind" items: roughs, etc.

Mad art can be found that has been released through less official channels than the Cochran auctions. This art is often in the form of artist's "roughs," the concept drawings used to get editorial approval of proposed work. Roughs can be quite attractive and often look nearly as good as the finished artwork, and it's interesting to compare them to the final printed versions. Usually these pieces came from the artists themselves, or from members of the staff; no stamped copyright notice appears on the back of these pieces. (Finished original art used in *Mad* can sometimes be found that did not come through official channels; with thousands of published pages extant, it is to be expected that some percentage of original art would get out.) Art from various "original" *Mad* paperbacks (books with all-new material) also turns up; Gaines did not archive this material.

Roughs of *Mad* paperback covers: price varies with artist, average $150-$450

Paperback pages: price varies with artist, average $100 per page

Jack Rickard

Don Martin

Jack Davis

Duck Edwing

Jack Rickard

The Art, Artists, and Artifacts of *Mad Magazine*, a sizeable exhibition of *Mad* original art (owned by Mark Cohen) was shown in San Francisco, California; Columbus, Ohio; Raleigh, North Carolina; Minneapolis, Minnesota; Seattle, Washington, and elsewhere, with the permission of Gaines. The show is scheduled to move to other cities. Promotional items have included T-shirts, posters, and a refrigerator magnet.

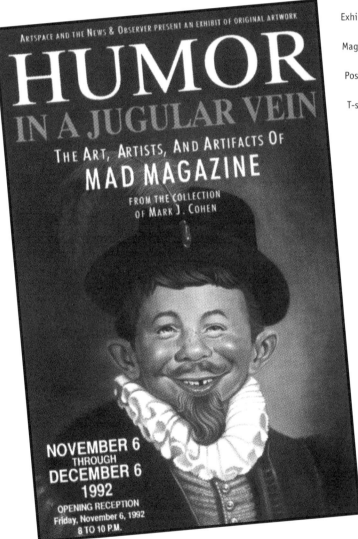

Exhibit catalogs, *Art, Artists, and Artifacts of Mad Magazine*: $5-$10

Magnet: $5

Posters: $10

T-shirts: $15-$25

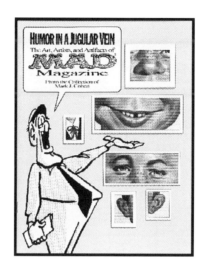

You are cordially invited to the
Opening Reception
Friday, January 24, 1992
6:00 pm - 8:00 pm

Meet These MAD
Artists in person

MORT DRUCKER
January 25 - 1 to 4 pm

AL JAFFEE
February 22 - 1 to 4 pm

SERGIO ARAGONES
February 22 - 1 to 4 pm

Sonoma County Museum
425 Seventh Street
Santa Rosa, California

"Bonus inserts" in the *Mad* annuals

Many classic bits of *Mad*-ness appeared as bonus items in the various *Mad* annuals; here is a complete checklist:

Annuals, Mad: see Overstreet Price Guide

The Worst From Mad

#1/*Mad* Record Labels (reprinted from *Mad* #32 back cover) and *Mad* Travel Stickers (reprinted from *Mad* #31 back cover)

#2/"Meet the Staff of *Mad*" flexi-record (later reprinted in *The Ridiculously Expensive Mad* hardback)

#3/"Alfred E. Neuman for President" Campaign poster (20" x 30," full color)

#4/Sunday Comic Section

#5/"She Got A Nose Job" flexi-record (track from *Mad Twists Rock 'n' Roll*)

#6/"She Lets Me Watch Her Mom and Pop Fight" flexi-record (track from *Fink Along With Mad*)

#7/*Mad* Protest Signs

#8/The "*Mad* Zeppelin" mobile

#9/"It's A Gas" flexi-record (track from *Fink Along With Mad*)

#10/*Mad* Bumper Sticker

#11/*Mad* Car Window Stickers

#12/"Get *Mad*" Picture Postcards

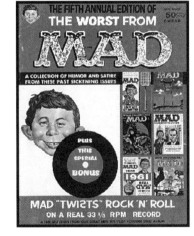

More Trash From Mad

#1/"Katchandhammer Kids" full color reprint from *Mad* #20

#2/*Mad* labels

#3/*Mad* Textbook Covers

#4/"Sing Along With *Mad*" lyric booklet. The booklet contains parody lyrics designed to be "sung to the tune of" various popular songs, and this resulted in a precedent-setting lawsuit filed by Irving Berlin and others claiming copyright infringement; the suit went all the way to the U.S. Supreme Court. Since no music was actually printed, *Mad* eventually won this case on the grounds that you can't copyright what is only in people's heads, or the *memory* of songs.

#5/*Mad* Window Stickers

#6/"TV Guise" booklet

#7/"Alfred E. Neuman for President" stamps

#8/"Pop art-Op art" full size Alfred E. Neuman poster

#9/*Mad* Mischief Stickers

#10/More *Mad* Mischief Stickers

#11/"Alfred E. Neuman for President" poster (14 1/2" x 20 1/4") and bumper sticker

#12/Pocket Medals

Mad Follies

#1/*Mad* Paperback Book Covers
#2/1965 *Mad* Calendar. Mort Drucker's art was colored by an uncredited Frank Frazetta, at the request of Nick Meglin
#3/*Mad* Mischief Stickers
#4/*Mad* Mobile
#5/*Mad* Stencils
#6/More *Mad* Mischief Stickers
#7/*Mad* "Nasty Cards"

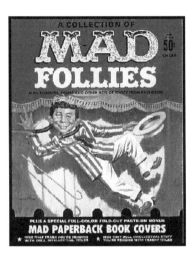
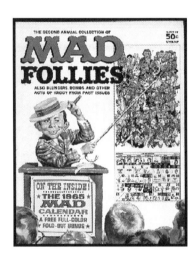

Mad Specials (called Super Specials from #11 on)

#1/*Mad* Voodoo Doll
#2/*Mad* "Wall-Nuts" portraits
#3/*Mad* Protest Stickers
#4/*Mad* Mini-posters
#5/"*Mad* Flag" poster
#6/*Mad* Mischief Stickers
#7/*Mad* Mini-posters
#8/"TV Guise" Fall Preview booklet
#9/"The Nostalgic *Mad*" #1 (comic book size reprints from *Mad* comics)
#10/Don Martin Nonsense Stickers
#11/"Gall In The Family" flexi-record (adaptation onto record of *Mad*'s "All in the Family" satire)
#12/"The Nostalgic *Mad*" #2
#13/*Mad* "Sickie-Stickers"
#14/Don Martin "Vital Message" and "Art Depreciation" posters
#15/"The Nostalgic *Mad*" #3
#16/"*Mad*-hesives" stickers
#17/Don Martin "Vital Message" and "Literary Heroes" posters
#18/"The Nostalgic *Mad*" #4
#19/"200 Year Old MADde" booklet
#20/Don Martin "Give 'Em Hell" Election Year Stickers
#21/"The Nostalgic *Mad*" #5
#22/*Mad* Awards
#23/Don Martin "Sound Effect" stickers

#24/"The Nostalgic *Mad* " #6
#25/Don Martin "Rock Music Posters"
#26/"Makin' Out" flexi-record
#27/*Mad* "Shock-Sticks" stickers
#28 (Fall 1979)/"The Nostalgic *Mad*" #7
#29 (Winter 1979)/*Mad* "Collectable Connectables" posters
#30 (Spring 1980)/note: contains no bonus
#31 (Summer 1980)/*Mad* Mystery Record "It's A Super Spectacular Day" (plays eight different endings depending which groove the needle
      falls into)
#32 (Fall 1980)/"The Nostalgic *Mad*" #8
#33 (Winter 1980)/"Alfred E. Neuman" stamps and stickers
#34 (Spring 1981)/note: contains no bonus
#35 (Summer 1981)/"Car and Home Window Stickers"
#36 (Fall 1981)/note: contains no bonus
#37 (Winter 1981)/*Mad* Map of the U.S.A. (Sergio Aragonés)
#38 (Spring 1982)/note: contains no bonus
#39 (Summer 1982)/The *Mad* Laugh Record ("A *Mad* Look at Graduation Day") note: has Alfred E. Neuman's face on the playing side
#40 (Fall 1982) through #48 (Fall 1984) contain no bonus material
#49 (Winter 1984)/*Mad* Wall Signs
#50 (Spring 1985)/note: contains no bonus
#51 (Summer 1985)/*Mad* Mini-Posters
#52 (Fall 1985) through #55 (Summer 1986) contain no bonus material
#56 (Fall 1986) Eight Full Color Posters
#57 (Winter 1986) through #70 (Spring 1990) contain no bonus material
#71 (Summer 1990)/*Mad*'s Dorky Door Hang-Ups
#72 (Fall 1990) through #75 (Summer 1991) contain no bonus material
#76 Collector's Series #1 (Fall 1991)/"*Mad* Mischief" and "New Kids Hate" stickers ("two color" printing) Every copy in the press run is
      numbered on the front cover
#77 (Winter 1991)/no bonus material
#78 (Jan. 1992)/no bonus material
#79 Collector's Series #2 (Feb. 1992)/"Vidiot Labels" (two color printing)
#80 (March 1992)/no bonus material
#81 (May 1992)/ no bonus material
#82 Collector's Series #3 (July 1992)/full color "Environ-mental" Post Cards
#83 (Sept. 1992)/no bonus material
#84 (Nov. 1992)/no bonus material

#85 Collector's Series #4 (Jan. 1993)/"Spy vs. Spy Planes"/Every copy in the press run is numbered on the front cover.

#86 (March 1993)/ no bonus material

#87 (May 1993)/ no bonus material

#88 Collector's Series #5 (July 1993)/"The *Mad* Maze"/Every copy in the press run is numbered on the front cover. Copies distributed to newsstands have the bonus bound-in, direct distribution copies have the bonus unbound and sealed in a poly bag

#89 (Sept. 1993)/no bonus in newsstand edition, direct distribution copies came sealed in a poly bag with a silver *Spy vs Spy* hologram

#90 (Nov. 1993)/no bonus material

#91 Collector's Series #6 (Jan. 1994)/"Flesh Funnies" tatoos/Every copy in the press run is numbered on the front cover.

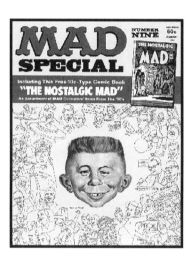

"One shot" issues:

Mad Disco

Released in 1980 at the tail end of the disco craze, *Mad Disco* contained a two-sided flexi-record of Mad disco originals by Dick DeBartolo and Norm Blagman (1963's "It's A Gas" was also trotted out) and 32 pages of disco-related *Mad* parodies. According to DeBartolo, *Mad Disco* was not a big seller as it seemed to be neither "fish nor fowl."

Mad Disco (1980): with record $5-$10

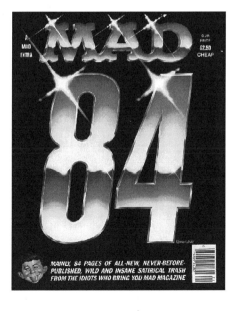

Mad '84

Mad '84 was an annual published in 1984; it features 84 pages of previously unpublished material, and contains no "bonus".

Mad '84: $2-$3

Mad imitations

As soon as the comic book *Mad* started showing a profit, imitators began appearing on the newsstands. Although there were at least 12 titles, none lasted beyond six or eight issues. Harvey Kurtzman managed to use the titles and logos of most of these imitators on page one of "Julius Caesar" in *Mad* #17; the story commenting on the imitators' lack of originality. EC issued its own "imitation" (really a companion title), *Panic*, in 1953. *Panic* was edited by Al Feldstein and contained work by Wallace Wood, Jack Davis, Bill Elder, and Joe Orlando.

Mad imitations, comic book, various: price varies, average $25-$30

Splash page from Julius Ceasar, Mad #17. Art by Wallace Wood.

Panic #1, 2, 4, and 12

By mid-1958 there were numerous imitations of *Mad* magazine, which is not surprising considering *Mad*'s circulation had swelled to a million copies per issue. Several of them had work by artists associated with *Mad*, including Bill Elder, Jack Davis and John Severin. These imitations were enough of a thorn that in issue #41 (Sept. 1958) *Mad* ran a feature called "How To Put Out An Imitation of *Mad*," which gave detailed directions on just how to copy *Mad*'s "formula."

Mad imitations, magazine, various: price varies, average $5-$35

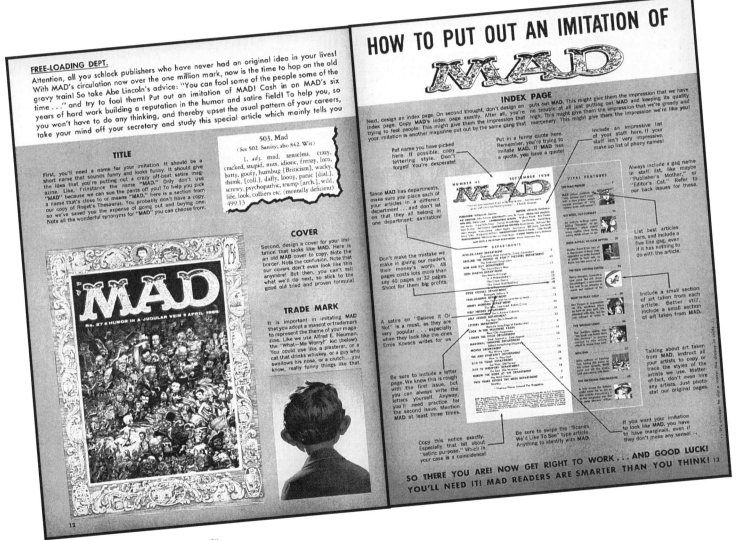

"How To Put Out An Imitation of Mad" from Mad #41, Sept. 1958.

○ CHAPTER TWENTY ONE

Alfred E. Neuman/*Mad*-related "cameos," and parodies of *Mad*:

Alfred E. Neuman "cameos," and parodies of Mad, various: price varies, average $5-$10 (notable exceptions: Superman Annual #3 $125 in mint, Trump #1 & 2: $65-$75)

Archie's MAD House #44, Dec. 1965, art swipes from "Superduperman" (*Mad* #4)

Barf! #1, May 1990, *Mad* parody

College Parodies, 1961, Ballantine paperback, has ad for the Ballantine *Mad* paperbacks

Cracked #99, March 1972, Alfred E. Neuman on cover

Cracked #107, Voodoo doll with Alfred E. Neuman shadow on cover

Cracked #142, July 1977, drawing of "Don't Get *Mad* get *Cracked*" T-shirt

Cracked #177, May 1981, Alfred E. Neuman on cover

Cracked #200, Dec. 1983, Alfred E. Neuman on cover

Cracked #202, March 1984, Alfred E. Neuman on cover

Cracked #250, Dec. 1989, *Mad*/Don Martin feud

Cracked #255, Aug. 1990, *Mad* mentioned in "put down"

Crazy vol. 4, #8, March 1959, (Charlton), "Bad," parodies of *Mad* features; Jack Davis art appears

Crazy #1 (Marvel magazine), Oct. 1973, *Mad* logo shown on cover, Kelly Freas art

Crazy #2, Feb. 1974, Alfred E. Neuman cameo in *Mad* office parody

Crazy #30, Oct. 1977, Alfred E. Neuman on cover

Crazy #34, Feb. 1978, drawing of Alfred E. Neuman on page 46

Crazy #61, April 1980, *Mad* reference on cover

Crazy Super Special #1, Summer 1975 , illustration of *Mad* magazines on cover

GRAD (Hallmark graduation card), 1987, *Mad*/Alfred E. Neuman parody

Harvard Lampoon, May 1991, poem "The Love Song of J. Alfred E. Neuman," Alfred E. Neuman pictured

Incurably Sick, 1962, paperback, Alfred E. Neuman on cover

Jerry Lewis #89 (DC), August 1965, Alfred appears as the "Wizard of Ooze"

John Wayne Adventure Comics #5, 1950, Kurtzman "Pot Shot Pete" with "Alfred *L*. Neuman"

Katy Keene Pin Up Parade #8, Fall 1959, "SMAD," a *Mad* parody

National Lampoon #11, Feb. 1971, partial Alfred E. Neuman face on page four, Norman Mingo art (unauthorized)

National Lampoon #17, August 1971, "What, My Lai?" cover by Kelly Freas; this cover was later sold as a poster without type or logos for $1.50

National Lampoon #19, Oct. 1971, the classic "*Mad* parody" (written by John Boni, Sean Kelly, and Henry Beard)

National Lampoon Comics #7, 1974, reprints "*Mad* parody" from *National Lampoon* #19

Not Brand Ecch #3, Oct. 1967, Alfred E. Neuman appears in "The Origin of Sore, Son of Schmodin" story

Not Brand Ecch #5, Dec. 1967, Alfred E. Neuman appears in "Thung vs Bulk"

Plop! #24 (DC), 1976, Gaines parody by Sergio Aragonés entitled "A Fate Worse Than Death"

Rockers #7 (Rip Off Press), 1989, Alfred E. Neuman on cover in "Sgt. Pepper"-type crowd scene

Scooter #9 (DC), late 1960s, mustached Alfred E. Neuman in one panel

Sick #6, 1961, Alfred E. Neuman on cover/Note: *Sick* was edited by comics veteran Joe Simon

Sick vol. 2, #8, August 1962, cover and humorous "open letter" on the "*Sick-Mad* war" containing references to *Mad*'s original Lafayette Street office and to Gaines and Feldstein.

Sick #56, Nov. 1967, Alfred E. Neuman on cover

Sick #68, June 1969, Alfred E. Neuman on cover

Sick Birthday #1, 1966, Alfred E. Neuman on cover

Superman #126, Jan. 1959, Superman appears as Alfred E. Neuman

Superman Annual #3, Summer 1961, "Goofy" Superman on cover

Thunderbunny #3, Oct. 1985, Alfred E. Neuman and Bill Gaines as Thunderbunnies on back cover

Trash #1, March 1978, Alfred E. Neuman on cover and *Mad* parody ("Mud")

Trump #1 (Harvey Kurtzman), Jan. 1957, "What–Me Worry" face in Bill Elder panorama

Trump #2 (Harvey Kurtzman), March 1957, "What-Me Worry" face on page 10, drawn by Al Jaffee

Wacko #1, 1981, Alfred E. Neuman on cover

Wimmen's Comix #17, 1992, Alfred E. Neuman in drag on cover

You Asked for It, Charlie Brown, paperback, 1973, Alfred E. Neuman pictured in strip

From PLOP! #24, Bill Gaines parody
by Sergio Aragonés.

Superman Annual #3; note
the face on the "Goofy"
Superman.

AN OPEN LETTER

DEAR READERS:

Of late, many of your letters have been attacking MAD for copying ideas in SICK or attacking SICK for being a carbon copy of MAD. We did not want a feud between the two magazines. Quite frankly, of the two leading humor publications in the field, we prefer MAD. MAD is more accurate than SICK, more poignant.

The thing that puzzles us is that we know all the guys up at MAD and they're stupider than we are. We mean, we're better looking, better educated (none of MAD's staff ever finished trade school), we're better dressers and we're nicer guys. We remember when MAD was published from the heart of the city's publication hub — the garment center down on Lafayette Street. We've watched it grow from an inane, formula-ridden, backward, pompous comic book into the magazine it is today.

Now they use better paper. SICK buys the paper that MAD trims off. We squeeze it back into pulp and stretch it to get three magazines out of one. Someone once said that the stuff that's left over is sold to CRACKED.

But getting back to high class magazines, we read MAD at all our editorial meetings when we're trying to come up with clever new ideas. Our writers hardly would touch a pen to paper without first asking themselves, "How would MAD do it?" Sure, we copy MAD, but who should we copy — McCalls? Field & Stream? The minutes of a Mafia meeting? Sure, MAD has better artists — they're better because they can draw. Our artists can only trace. Someone has to hold Leo Morey's hand when he traces.

Now, that we've made our stand, please don't send us any more letters asking why we aren't original, why we don't stop publishing, why we don't try a man's deodorant. We've had it up to our armpits with man's deodorants. We hope this will put a stop to all those nasty letters, particularly those from Bill Gaines and Al Feldstein.

—The Editors

"Open letter" from the August 1962 Sick

CHAPTER TWENTY TWO

Mad on TV

Mad has been featured numerous times on television, perhaps most notably on the Sept. 20, 1987, edition of *60 Minutes*, with interviews of Gaines and most of the staff by Morley Safer. A transcript of the show was available from Journal Graphics of New York for $3.00.

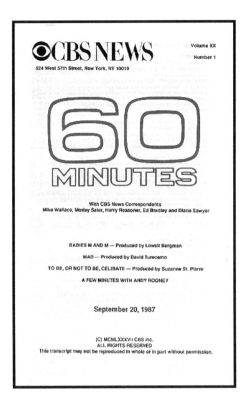

Other Television Appearances of Note:

30 Minutes, Dec. 9, 1978, CBS, segment on *Mad*

Another Evening with Fred Astaire, Nov. 4, 1959, NBC, Astaire dances to "That Face" wearing AEN mask

CNN/Headline News, Jan. 6, 1992, CNN, segment on *Mad*'s 40th anniversary

Ed Sullivan Show, The, Jan. 23, 1966, skits from *The Mad Show* with the original cast

Entertainment Tonight, Nov. 6, 1991, Syndicated, brief mention of *Completely Mad* book

Entertainment Tonight, Jan. 27, 1992, segment on *Mad*'s parody of the show from issue #310

Good Morning America, Nov. 7, 1991, ABC, Gaines and staff discuss *Completely Mad* book

Hard Copy, Feb. 22, 1990, Syndicated, segment on *Mad*

Headline News, July 21, 1990, CNN, Mort Drucker interview, *Mad* references

Into the Night with Rick Dees, May 9, 1991, segment with Nick Meglin about *Mad*

Later...with Bob Costas, April 2, 1991, NBC, half hour interview with Bill Gaines

Live with Regis and Kathy Lee, Dec. 6, 1991, ABC, Dick DeBartolo with *School of Hard Yocks* book

Nightly News (KABC, Los Angeles), Jan. 14, 1992, segment on *Mad*'s 40th anniversary

Real Story, The, April 1, 1991, CNBC, segment on *Mad*

Star Parade-Four for Tonight, Feb. 24, 1960, NBC, Tony Randall in sketches adapted from *Mad*

Steals and Deals, Jan. 6, 1992, CNBC, segment on Sotheby's auction and *Mad*'s 40th anniversary

Sundae in New York, 1984, AEN cameo in claymation film by Jimmy Picker

Sunday Today, Oct. 21, 1990, NBC, segment on *Mad*'s 300th issue

Take 30, Dec. 28, 1967, CBC, Canadian Broadcasting Corp. documentary on *Mad*

thirtysomething, 1991, Nick Meglin appears in "costume party" episode

To Tell the Truth, circa early 1960s, Gaines appears as a contestant

Mad and/or Alfred E. Neuman have reportedly also been seen on:

A Hard Day's Night, 1964 (The Beatles' first film), *Son of Mad* paperback appears in one scene

American Hot Wax, Mad #50 appears

Born on the Fourth of July, 1989, *Mad* #49 appears

Dirty Rotten Scoundrels, 1989, Steve Martin reads *Mad Special* #59

Ernie Kovacs: Between the Laughter, 1954

Get Smart, 1968

Goonies, 1985, kids reading issues #124, 208, and 227

Grease, 1978, *Mad* #1 shown in opening title

Hairspray, 1987, character reading *More Trash From Mad* #7

Happy Days, 1970s, "AEN for President" poster in Joanie's room

Leave It To Beaver, 1958

Life With Mikey, 1993, *Completely Mad* hardback appears

Matinee, 1993, an issue of *Mad* appears

Murphy Brown, most episodes show framed *Mad* covers in Murphy's office

Night of a Living Duck, 1987, Daffy Duck cartoon with Alfred E. Neuman cameo

Parker Lewis, air date 4/12/92, picture of Alfred E. Neuman appears

Rocky and Bullwinkle Show, The, 1962

Simpsons, The, 1992, *Mad* appears, along with *Cracked* and *Crazy*

Simpsons, The, 1993, Alfred E. Neuman face appears on tattoo

Simpsons, The, 1993, Bart reading *Mad* on season premiere

Wonder Years, 1989

Zazie (Louis Malle, circa 1960), *Mad* appears

Mad-related Videos

Comic Book Greats vol. 3: Sergio Aragonés, Stabur Home Video, 1991, *Mad* references

Comic Book Greats vol. 5: Kurtzman and Davis, Stabur Home Video, 1992, EC and *Mad* references

Mad TV Specials

ABC commissioned *The Mad Magazine TV Special* in the mid-1970s, but after it was completed they declined to air it. The animated film was produced by Focus Productions and used the art styles of George Woodbridge, Don Martin, Bob Clarke, Antonio Prohias, Jack Davis, Al Jaffee, and Mort Drucker to illustrate typical *Mad*-style features. Gaines was never sure why it wasn't aired, but heard a rumor that because one of the network's major advertisers was parodied the project was shelved.

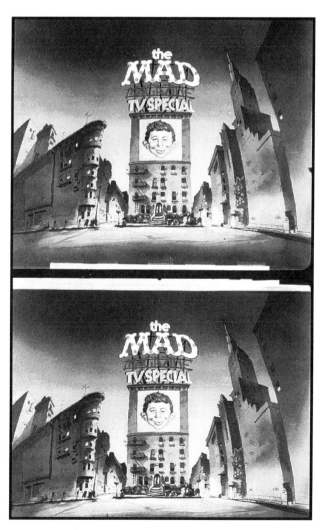

CHAPTER TWENTY TWO

Scenes from the un-aired ABC Mad Magazine TV Special

Scenes from the un-aired ABC Mad Magazine TV Special

CHAPTER TWENTY TWO

Another *Mad* special, *Goin' Mad*, produced in conjunction with Hanna-Barbera, was completed around 1990; an air date has not been announced.

Script, A World Gone Mad: $25

Early pre-production script outline for the Hanna-Barbera special Goin' Mad, dated April 14, 1988; the working title was The World Gone Mad.

Alfred E. Neuman statue and "Oscar" sculpted by Kent Melton to appear in *Goin' Mad*; extra statues were cast and spray painted gold to give as gifts to the *Mad* staff and *Goin' Mad* production people.

Alfred E. Neuman statue and "Oscar" (from Goin' Mad, sculpted by Kent Melton): no reported sales

CHAPTER TWENTY TWO

The Mad Minute radio shows

The Mad Minute radio show was begun as a
promotional device in 1985 by Dick DeBartolo,
who wrote and narrated each 60- second show.
(After about two years staffer Sara Fowler
joined on both the writing and narration.) The
shows were offered free to radio stations, and
at the show's peak it was heard on just under
100 outlets. Included were such sketches as the
"Two Hour School of Dentistry" and the "911
Public DIS-Service Message." The shows were
distributed on standard audio cassette with
spartan packaging: a *Mad Minute* logo sticker
with a stamped or hand-written show number,
enclosed in a clear plastic cassette box. New
shows were discontinued in June 1991, and the
"official" (and amusing) reason given was that
Bill Gaines found out he was actually *paying*
for *The Mad Minute* and pulled the plug. 57
cassette tapes were made, with each having 9
Mad Minute segments, so there were 513 *Mad
Minutes*.

The Mad Minute cassette tapes: no reported sales

Mad promo items

Numerous promotional items have been made over the years to promote *Mad* at trade
shows and elsewhere; many of them were the brainchildren of Dick DeBartolo:

Plastic "auto teller hold up" card:

"Auto teller hold up" card: $15

Mad window and logo
stickers:

Mad window sticker: $5-$10

Mad logo sticker: $5

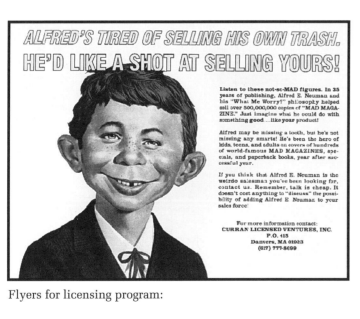

Flyers for licensing program:

Flyers for licensing program: no reported sales

Mad money and gift certificate:

Mad money: no reported sales

Gift certificate: no reported sales

3-D glasses:

3-D glasses, in envelope: no reported sales

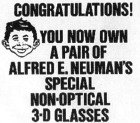

Calendar and note pads:

Calendar: $20

Note pads: full pad, $20

Mirrored-plastic logo sign, 8" x 26":

Sign, mirrored plastic, 8" x 26": $25-$50

Choking poster

Poster, choking: $15

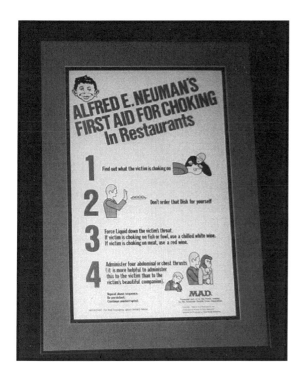

Balloon (yellow with red printing):

Balloon (yellow with red printing): $5

Mad Sport Caps

Sport caps, Mad, sold through office (1992): $15 each

CHAPTER TWENTY TWO

1988 Election subway poster (30" x 45"), Mort Drucker art

Poster, 1988 election (for subways, 30" x 45"), Mort Drucker art: $50-$75

For many years *Mad* cover artist Kelly Freas sent out these prints of Alfred E. Neuman to fans requesting autographs:

Picture of Alfred E. Neuman (black and white) by Kelly Freas, with autograph: $25

Kitchen Sink buttons with EC/*Mad* artists

Kitchen Sink Press released a series of pinback buttons called the "Famous Cartoonist Series" with self-portraits of each artist; there are six buttons of particular interest to EC and *Mad* fans: #7 (Sergio Aragonés), #17 (Will Elder), #19 (Kelly Freas), #28 (Harvey Kurtzman), #42 (John Severin), and #52 (Basil Wolverton).

Pinback buttons, Kitchen Sink, with EC/Mad artists: $1-$3 each

Mad Cover Trivia:

Mad #28

The cover of *Mad* #28 (July 1956) can be found with three different wordings in the banner on the lower right corner, due to distribution problems: "With enjoyable article on GUIDED MISSILES and how they can blow up earth," "With very useful INCOME TAX GUIDE: deductions, cheating, etc.," and "With very useful INCOME TAX GUIDE you could have used".

Mad #28, three cover versions: $100 in mint, value of each the same

Mad #122/recalled cover with Robert Kennedy

Printer's proofs to the cover of *Mad* #122 (dated Oct. 1968) showing various political candidates had just come in to the *Mad* office when Robert Kennedy was assassinated, and at the eleventh hour his image on the cover was replaced with Alfred E. Neuman's; almost none of these proofs ever got out of the office.

Mad #122/recalled cover slick with Robert Kennedy: $100

Unreleased version

Mad #123

Issue #123 (Dec. 1968) has the following phrase on the cover: "This copy of *Mad* is number _____ in a series of 2,148,000. Collect them all!". The issue can be be found with four different numbers in the blank: 1,111,784; 1,112,362; 1,189,168; and 1,376,485.

Mad #123, four cover versions: $6 in mint (value of each the same)

Mad #166 and letter of apology

Reaction to the "finger" cover of *Mad* #166 (April 1974) forced Gaines to send letters of apology to irate readers and retailers, signed by both Gaines and Feldstein. According to Nick Meglin, who thought up the gag as an office joke, the caption originally read "the number one magazine of good taste," but for some reason the other caption was used; the reaction would likely have been similar with either caption.

Letter of apology re: Mad #166 cover, signed by Gaines and Feldstein: no reported sales

Saudi Arabian "Hussein Asylum" Editions

Special editions of *Mad* #300 to #303 were created for shipment to troops serving in the Persian Gulf; these are exactly like the U.S. versions but have the image of "Alfred of Arabia" from the cover to *Mad* #86 in place of the UPC symbol. About 25,000 copies of each of these special issues were printed. The Overstreet Price Guide also lists *Mad Super Special* #76 as having a "Hussein Asylum" edition, but this may not exist.

"Hussein Asylum"/US Troops edition, Mad #300-303 and Special #76: $10 each

SECTION TWO

Other items of interest:

"*Mad* softball team" T-shirt

These T-shirts (with red overprinting on goldenrod colored shirts) were made for the "*Mad* Softball Team" circa 1978; only about 25 of the shirts were made as a special order.

T-shirt, "Mad softball team": no reported sales

"The *Mad* Cruise" T-shirt, September 1991

These shirts were made for travelers on the September 1991 *Mad* cruise from New York to Bermuda; only staffers and contributors that meet the minimum number of pages quota per year (and their significant others) are eligible for the *Mad* trips. About forty-six people went on this particular voyage.

T-shirt, "Mad Cruise," Sept. 1991: no reported sales

"*Mad* at Yale" poster:

This framed 13 1/2" x 20" poster was prepared to advertise the *Mad* staff's Feb. 28th, 1973 appearance at Yale University and is extremely rare. To commemorate the event the distributor's mark "IND" in the Mad logo was replaced with "YALE" on the cover of *Mad* #161.

Poster, "Mad at Yale," 1973: $100

Mad tote bag and personalized pen:

A *Mad* tote bag and personalized pen were given as gifts to the *Mad* staff, contributors, and friends for Christmas, 1992. The pen has a small full color image of Alfred E. Neuman at the top. Similar tote bags were made by DC/Warner for various promotional purposes.

Mad tote bag: no reported sales

Mad personalized pen: no reported sales

Mad-related records:

Anthrax, *State of Euphoria* (Island), 1988, Mort Drucker art on back cover, *Spy vs Spy* T-shirt shown
Beastie Boys, *Shadrach*, 1989, cassette maxi-single, lyrics mention Alfred E. Neuman
Firesign Theatre, *Everything You Know Is Wrong,* 1970s, William Stout art in the style of Bill Elder,
     sign on cafe reads "MA'S" in the *Mad* logo style.
Man, *Slow Motion* (United Artists), 1975, partial detail of Alfred E. Neuman-type face on cover. Artist
     Rick Griffin completed a full-facial view of an Alfred E. Neuman look-alike for this cover but
     at the last minute it was pulled and only the partial detail was used. Some full color proofs
     were made of the unused full cover, which were then signed by Griffin. Value of these
     signed proofs is about $400 each.
Motley Crue, *Don't Go Away Mad*, 1990, cassette single, Mort Drucker art, song title is a *Mad* tie-in
Ray Stevens, *Ahab the Arab*, 1962, lyrics mention reading *Mad*
Sick #2 (Amy Records LP), early 1960s, Alfred E. Neuman-type cameo on back cover

Records, Mad-related: various, average $3-$20

Recent or forthcoming Mad-related products:

Mad Pinball Machine

A full size arcade-style pinball machine based on *Mad* and Alfred E. Neuman had been announced but was cancelled. A few prototype models were completed.

Mad Candy

Berserk Candy Werks (Kraft Foods) released a line of *Mad* candy in Summer 1993. Samples of a Christmas version were made, but this was never marketed.

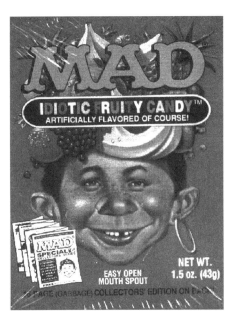

Mad Pinback Buttons

The Button Exchange released six *Mad* pinback buttons in 1993, each 1 3/4" in diameter. Plans for *Mad* keychains were abandoned.

Mad Products in Warner Brothers Studio Stores

As *Mad* is owned by Warner, plans are underway for products that are to be sold exclusively in the Warner Brothers Studio Stores. Items already offered include a high quality *Mad* denim jacket ($100) and companion sweatshirt ($52), a *Mad* watch ($55), *Mad* money clip ($12) and a *Mad* belt buckle ($26). A life-size full color plaster bust of Alfred E. Neuman with glass eyes and lifelike hair was issued in late 1993 for $2,500. An edition of 25 is stated on back, but at this writing only six had been completed. The bust was created by artist Gary Mirabelle (see front cover for a color depiction of the bust). A full figure Alfred E. Neuman statue done by Kent Melton (and modeled after the one he did for the unreleased Hanna-Barbera *Mad* special) was issued in 1994. The statue is among the nicest *Mad* collectibles ever released, and is priced at a modest $38. Other products have included puzzles, cocktail napkins, playing cards, and Dave Berg "Lighter Side of..." plaques, with more on the way.

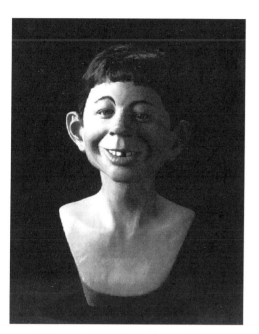

Life-size Alfred E. Neuman bust

Watch

Money clip

Belt and buckle

Alfred E. Neuman statue

Denim jacket

Sweatshirt

Even <u>more</u> recent Mad-related items:

Mad press kit

This *Mad* press kit was made for Warner Bros. Consumer Products to aid in the licensing of *Mad* products. The kit is in full color, with an embossed *Mad* logo. Inside the kit, a pocket holds specially created die-cut "*Mad* money" that opens to list all of the current licensees. This press kit was reportedly made at a cost of $15 per kit.

Mad press kit: no reported sales

Inside of Mad press kit

Mad/DC Online

DC Comics Online, available through America Online, has a *Mad* club section. Subscribers can access advance information, place messages, and download *Mad*-related pictures from any Macintosh or IBM-compatible computer. *Mad* artists, writers, and staffers frequent the message boards and participate in live chat rooms and online auditorium events as well.

Mad Valentine's Day mug

Special mugs were made as gifts for a *Mad* Valentine's Day Massacre party held for *Mad* and DC people. The party was given to help appease disappointed DC staffers who did not get invited to the 1993 *Mad* Christmas party. The mug gives February 9, 1994 as the date of the party, but (*Mad*ly enough) due to inclement weather the event was actually held several weeks after that. About 100 of the mugs were made.

Mad Valentine's Day mug: no reported sales

For Further Reference:

For information on high quality reprints of work by Harvey Kurtzman, Will Elder, and others contact:
Kitchen Sink Press
320 Riverside Drive
Northampton, MA 01060

1-800-365-SINK (7465)

For information on The Complete EC Library, EC Classics, Cochran/Gemstone EC comic books, and *Mad* and EC Original Art Auction catalogs contact:
Russ Cochran, Publisher
P.O. Box 469
West Plains, MO 65775

For information on *Mad* subscriptions, *Mad* Pin Collection, or recent back issues contact:
Mad Magazine
485 MADison Avenue
New York, NY 10022

For information on *Mad* and *Mad*-related signed lithographs and prints, contact:
Stabur Corporation
11904 Farmington Road
Livonia, MI 48150

For information on current collector's prices of *Mad* and EC Comics, refer to:
The Overstreet Comic Book Price Guide (Avon Books), at bookstores everywhere, or contact:
Overstreet Publications Inc.
780 Hunt Cliff Drive NW
Cleveland, Tennessee 37311

For information on current collector's prices of *Mad* and EC original art, refer to:
The Original Comic Art Price Guide by Jerry Weist (Avon Books), at bookstores everywhere, or contact:
Avon Books
1350 Avenue of the Americas
New York, NY 10019

For information on EC-related signed lithographs by Al Feldstein, Johnny Craig, Jack Kamen and others contact:
Phantomb Publishing Co.
Box 1313
2570 Ocean Avenue
San Francisco, California 94132

For a complete guide to all *Mad* and EC Collectibles, with descriptions, photos, anecdotes, pricing, and other information, refer to:
Collectibly Mad–The Mad and EC Collectibles Guide by Grant Geissman (Kitchen Sink Press), which is the book you're reading, you idio